P9-BAT-807

GOD'S GENTLE REBELS

GOD'S GENTLE REBELS
Great Saints of Christianity

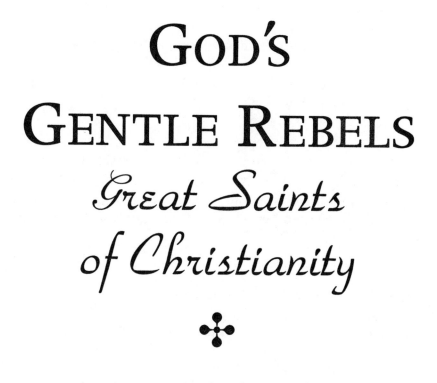

CHRISTIAN FELDMAN

Translated by Peter Heinegg

CROSSROAD • NEW YORK

1995

The Crossroad Publishing Company
370 Lexington Avenue, New York, NY 10017

Copyright © by Verlag Herder Freiburg im Breisgau 1984, 1994

Translation and abridgment copyright © 1995 by The Crossroad
Publishing Company

All rights reserved. No part of this book may be reproduced, stored
in a retrieval system, or transmitted, in any form or by any means,
electronic, mechanical, photocopying, recording, or otherwise,
without the written permission of The Crossroad Publishing
Company.

Printed in the United States of America

Library of Congress Cataloging-in-Publication Data
Feldman, Christian.
   [Gottes sanfte Rebellen. English]
   God's gentle rebels : great saints of Christianity / Christian Feldman :
translated by Peter Heinegg.
     p.   cm.
   ISBN 0–8245–1519–6 (pb)
   1. Christian saints—Biography. I. Title.
  BX4655.2F39   1995
282'.092'2—dc20
[B]   95–34629
                                              CIP

CONTENTS

INTRODUCTION

*A*t first people laughed at them. They declared them insane and even persecuted them. The altars, the statues, and the hymns came only later.

The saints! Today they seem to be pillars of the Church, models of solid obedience and iron discipline. But often enough their contemporaries saw them as rebels, agitators, and troublemakers.

This book has no intention of taking a few hopelessly antiquated figures from Church history and simply giving them a stylish new hairdo. That would be a dishonest maneuver. If there's one thing the saints deserve, it's truthfulness. What's at stake here is historical truth, and we owe them that much. It's an often astonishing, amazing truth, which lies hidden under the kitsch-filled legends.

Exotic heroes and heroines suddenly turn into companions. The plaster figures step down from their pedestals and stand revealed as human beings, torn and crushed by a thousand expectations, longings, anxieties, often weak and desperate. Otherworldly ideal images become our brothers and sisters, who found God in the world and who loved the earth. Human beings who had to fight for their faith the way we do, who experienced powerlessness, emptiness, and failure—though they never stopped yearning for the totally Other.

This yearning was the source of the saints' gentle rebellion. They refused to conform to an environment that was cold and aggressive, dominated by money, violence, and hypocrisy. God's gentle rebels turned the world upside down quite simply by living differently.

Living differently: like Francis of Assisi, who renounced weapons and the exercise of power, and who thought the division of society into masters and slaves, which everyone took for granted, was utterly ridiculous. His God was on the side of the little people, of the oppressed.

Living differently: like Elizabeth the princess, who began to understand that the misery of the poor was a shameful indictment of her own luxurious way of life.

Living differently: like Thomas More, who, facing a painful death, wouldn't knuckle under to the party line, who never wavered in insisting on his right to have his own opinion.

The gentle rebellion of the saints, the mild-mannered but radical change in their own sphere of living, can become a dangerous irritant to social norms. Taboos are broken, alternatives are lived—that's infectious. Seemingly private solutions develop an explosive power. Laughingly, almost playfully, these holy fools pull the rug out from under the powers that be.

For us balanced, compromised Christians—always intent on the golden mean, never going too far—all these symbol-laden lives raise a question for our conscience: Do *we* dare to live differently, to heed the Gospel, to get out of line, to let ourselves, if necessary, be declared insane?

Will we finally dare to be Christians?

GOD'S GENTLE REBELS

The Crazy Dropout

Francesco Bernardone—Francis of Assisi
(1182–1226)

You Have to Become a Fool in Order to Find Christ

> Let none be called "First."
> But all shall be named simply
> "Friars Minor."
>
> They must always
> remain faithful to Our Lady Poverty
> and love her.

*I*n the year 1211, the inhabitants of the Italian provincial city of Assisi were treated to an unusual spectacle: two seedy fellows in rags and tatters, wearing nothing but their underwear, climbed into a pulpit and launched into a fiery penitential sermon against luxury and unbelief. The horrified listeners recognized Ruffino and Francesco, the sons of respectable families, who had left the town some years before and had chosen to lead a dubious beggar's existence in the country.

Francesco—the fool. "*Un pazzo! Un pazzo!*" bawled the children chasing after him with sadistic joy: "An idiot! A nutcase!"

Francis—the crazy dropout, who all of a sudden threw overboard the finest opportunities and a secure life, to make his way through the villages in ragged clothes, fixing up decrepit churches.

Francis—the unassimilated, who no longer knew what was proper, the troublemaker, who offended everybody and voluntarily turned antisocial.

Francis—the gentle rebel, the irrational pacifist, the man turned childlike, who talked to flowers and fountains, who supplied bees with honey in the hard frosts of winter and carefully picked up the worms from the street. If there had been psychiatric clinics in the thirteenth century, he would surely have landed in one within weeks.

Because what sort of options does society have when somebody takes the Gospel literally? It can be stunned to discover what it lacks, and it can change—but that hurts. Or it can pronounce the troublesome foreign body crazy, which is a lot simpler.

The Church—the Catholic Church—has a third possibility for getting rid of all-too-radical Christians. It declares them saints—when they've long been dead. That makes it all the easier to explain why such a life was just not meant for the "normal" Christian and was certainly no alternative to the well-worn Church structures. And Francis made it easy for those who wanted to get rid of him this way to declare his message non-binding.

"The Lord told me that he wanted me to be a freshly baked fool in the world." He explained that to the learned Cardinal Ugolino, the later Pope Gregory IX, when the latter tried to convince him to adopt a correct rule for his still-unorganized order. But what if Francis's path is the only one that leads in a straight line to God? What if we all have to become fools like Francis, to find Jesus, who himself often struck his contemporaries as a fool?

"In the Name of God and Profit!"

The little town of Assisi in the hills of Umbria lies off the beaten track from the centers of world politics. But the merchants and canons, the artisans and day-laborers of Assisi sensed as much as the Florentines and Romans, as the men and women of Paris, Brussels, and Cologne, that they were living at a turning point in world history. With the twelfth century a whole epoch was coming to an end.

The certainty that the Church's world-picture once provided was beginning to crumble. Everywhere new schools and universities were cropping up. People were hungry for education, and no longer satisfied with the traditional answers. Horizons were broadening. In Europe an urban culture was taking shape, the cities were sprouting mightily and developing a booming trade across seas and continents. Along with landed property possession of money was becoming increasingly important. In the cities rich patricians were accumulating capital, founding manufacturing operations with branch offices all over, and artisans were busy: early capitalism was in the wings.

"In the name of God and profit!" a merchant named Francesco Datini from Prato, in Tuscany, proudly penned on the first page of his ledger—and presumably never even blushed. Banking families like the Buonsignori in Siena and the Pisani in Venice were seizing more and more power. And soon the Florentine banking houses of the Frescobaldi and Peruzzi would be financing the expensive policies of warlike popes.

A self-conscious bourgeoisie and moneyed class with airs of omnipotence were clawing away at the previously undisputed authority of Church and State. While a culture profoundly steeped in Christianity was blossoming as never before, and the pope in Rome was setting himself as a judge over emperors and kings, the Church's moral credibility was suffering losses on a broad front. Power-hungry bishops, plotting prelates, corrupt pastors, and demoralized monks were no longer met with pious veneration, but with furious songs of mockery. Critical questions about the Church's institutions were being raised not just by the people who slaved for starvation wages on the property owned by monasteries and cathedrals, but also by movements promoting voluntary poverty—and heresy. In the decades that followed, their members, thousands of often unassuming, peaceable Christians who longed for the simplicity of the primitive Church, would wind up being burned at the stake, whose flames were ignited by their power-conscious brothers in the faith. Around this time civil war and violence were also shaping the picture of a divided and torn Italy: the imperial (Ghibeline) and papal (Guelf) parties wrestled for control of the country. In the cities burghers fought nobles; and republican city-states, now come of age, revolted against high-handed lords of the castle.

The rich cloth dealer, Pietro Bernardone, in Assisi, was a classic example of the Italian burghers in this new age: a rising star from humble origins, according to the reports that have come down to us (which, to be sure, don't show much sympathy for him). He was a somewhat gruff, insensitive person, but enormously proud of his professional success, his flourishing business, his wares that were in such demand. He is said to have owned several houses in Assisi. Perhaps he himself produced some of the fabrics he sold, in one of the many mini-factories already mentioned or by homeworkers.

Upon returning from a business trip in 1182, Pietro Bernardone was extremely annoyed to learn that his wife, Donna Pica, an elegant Frenchwoman, had given the son born in his absence the name Giovanni. In his view the name Giovanni, Italian for John, was much too bland and simple-minded; it also smacked of the wilderness and renunciation. So he overturned her decision. His son was to be named Francesco, "the little Frenchman." The name had an air of worldly, metropolitan sophistication, of heroic, knightly deeds, and courtly gallantry.

Pietro's wish seems to have come true: Francesco grew up a typical spoiled little lord, arrogant and at the same time superficially sociable, the adored center of a noisy band of young people because he had the most money. He doesn't seem to have been especially handsome. His biographers depict him as short, slight, thin-legged. But he had a pleasant voice, easy-going manners, generosity—toward the poor too, even back then—and he was always in good spirits, especially when he sang the songs of the Provençal troubadours that his mother had taught him.

At the age of fourteen—such things happened more quickly in those days—Francesco Bernardone already belonged to the merchants guild, selected fabric at the markets, negotiated with clients at his father's place of business. Meanwhile he viewed the war with the competing, neighboring town of Perugia as a welcome adventure. He didn't much mind imprisonment in Perugia, where he spent a year waiting for the ransom to be sent from Assisi. But he had time to think things over.

When it comes to the turnabout in his life that occurred shortly after this, we have nothing but legends to go by. One such story reports that Francis wanted to join the army of the pope, so as to win fame as a warrior, and perhaps even a noble title. Then in a dream a voice asked him: "Who can give you a better gift, the Lord or the servant? Why are you leaving the Lord for the sake of a servant, and the rich man for a pauper?"

Here was the pope reduced to the rank of a poor servant, God as the only one whom it really pays to serve—we now hear for the first time a leading motif of Francis' life.

The twenty-three-year-old youth fell into a deep depression; "nothing could delight him," as one biographer puts it. He withdrew from his friends, went to a cave, and meditated on his former life. He dropped out—radically. He found new friends: beggars, lepers, people on the fringe of society. He ate with the lepers, washed the pus from their sores, and forced himself to kiss their hands. "And when I left them," he would later write in his Testament about this key experience, "I found that what had seemed bitter to me was transformed into sweetness." Sweetness, *dolcezza* is a word from the vocabulary of his beloved troubadours; it also means tenderness and gentleness.

Around that time Francis discovered close by Assisi the ruined church of San Damiano, where he liked to retreat and pray before a wonderfully beautiful crucifix. The cross, in the Roman-Byzantine style, bearing an extremely virile Christ, can still be seen today in the Basilica of St. Clare in Assisi. One day, the story goes, in front of this crucifix, the man who was seeking so passionately for a new content to his life clearly heard the voice of the crucified: "Francis, go and restore my house; it's falling apart, as you see."

> The sublimity of most high poverty
> has appointed you, my beloved brothers
> as heirs and kings
> of the kingdom of Heaven.
> It has made you poor in things
> and rich in power.

And in another abandoned little chapel, called the Portiuncula, Francis had a notable "Aha!" experience upon hearing the Gospel, when a priest happened to wander that way and celebrate the Eucharist: "And as you go proclaim the message, 'The kingdom of Heaven is upon you . . . ; You received without cost, give without charge. Take no gold, silver, or copper in your belts. No pack for the road, no second coat, no sandals, no stick. . . . '" (Matt. 10: 7–10).

Francis was thunderstruck. "That's what I want," he cried, "that's what I'm looking for, that's what I long to do from the bottom of my heart." And immediately, his biographer Thomas of Celano tells us, he threw away his shoes, put on the simple smock of the mountain shepherds, and exchanged his leather belt for a piece of rope—thus the habit of the Fransicans was born.

All these are skillfully dramatized snapshots, certainly not made up, but merely sidelights on a hard-fought struggle that lasted for years and that may have also had setbacks and phases of despair. Coping with a hitherto unknown loneliness meant fighting with a milieu that had no understanding for him, but was full of derision. It meant endless confrontations with his father, an authoritarian with the soul of a shopkeeper. In every way he possibly could, Pietro Bernardone tried to tame his son and heir, who had gone insane.

THE NAKED MAN IN THE MARKETPLACE

IT'S A FAMOUS SCENE: In the middle of the marketplace of Assisi young Bernardone sells his horse and goods from his father's warehouse. He gives the money to an old priest. The father, fearing for the reputation of his family and his business, is supposed to have gone straight out and had his son thrown in jail.

Let us keep his Word,
his life, his teaching, and his holy Gospel.
We all wish to love with our whole heart,
with our whole soul,
with our whole spirit,
with our whole strength and courage,
with all our senses,
with all our exhilaration,
with our whole mind,
with all our wishes and desires,
God the Lord.
We have promised him great things,
Great things have been promised us.
Let us cling to this,
Let us long for that.

In the same marketplace there was the memorable hearing before the bishop: Francis threw his clothes and all his finery at the feet of his father, who had accused him of squandering his fortune. "From now on," he declared to the speechless public, "I will freely say: Our father in heaven, and no longer: Father Pietro Bernardone. I want to go to heaven naked." Later on he would confess that this definitive break with the family was the hardest thing he ever did in his life.

From then on he traveled from village to village, restoring dilapidated chapels. To pay for the building materials he sang in the marketplace. A strange bird—the people laughed at him.

But some liked the way he talked about peace and the need for conversion. A businessman, the wealthy Bernardo of Quintavalle, sold his property and marched off with him. They were joined by a jurist, a young peasant, a knight, a canon, by the poet Guglielmo Divini, a giant of man named Brother Masseo, and the simple Brother "Juniper," as Francis tenderly called him. They lived together in a dormitory, or in barns and old chapels, and promised one another to follow the Gospel in all things.

"Those who came and adopted this life," Francis would say, looking back, "gave everything they had to the poor. They were content with a single cowl, patched inside and out, with a staff and underwear. We had no wish to have any more than that . . . We were uneducated and subject to everyone. I worked with my hands and I want to continue doing so, and I wish all the other brothers to do honest work. Whoever doesn't know how must learn . . . When we get no pay, let us take refuge at the table of the Lord and beg for alms from door to door."

The brothers didn't merely beg, as the legend has it. The Franciscan alternative to making money wasn't living at the expense of others—the medieval upper classes had been doing that long enough. The little community whose rule first consisted simply of the Gospel, fed itself with occasional jobs for farmers and in leper houses, telling anyone willing to listen how lovely it was to live depending on God alone.

Francis: "What are we servants of God other than strolling minstrels and players, who want to move the hearts of men and lift them to spiritual joy?"

That *is* the alternative. The dominant social strata of that time, knights, merchants, and prelates, surely lived well, but they didn't think of their activity as work. In any event there was no such thing as full employment, and decently paid work was rare. In this situation the brothers set up an unmistakable sign by throwing in their lot with day workers and beggars, who owned nothing but Christ, the poor Nazarene. They wanted to *be* poor—not simply to help the poor somehow or other, from a secure, condescending position.

Francis sent his friends out in pairs to preach: "Go, beloved, two by two into the world, and proclaim peace to men and women and penance for the forgiveness of sins." Their preaching was simple, close to everyday life, loving, not aggressive like the merciless, threatening sermons of some of the popular missionaries of the day, who terrified their listeners with extravagant descriptions of all the torments of Hell.

When several young girls left their bourgeois existence behind and joined their brothers, that led to the founding of a second community for women and to conflict with the public authorities. Francis wouldn't be budged. He trusted the persuasive power of the "other life," to which his communities had committed themselves:

> They are to love one another, as the Lord says: "This is my commandment, that you love one another as I have loved you." And they shall prove the love they have for one another with deeds. . . . And they shall be modest and show all meekness to everyone. And they shall not judge, they shall not condemn; and, as the Lord says, they shall not pay heed to the little sins of others, but ponder their own in the bitterness of their soul.

These typically Christian sins were nothing new to gentle Brother Francis, with his penetrating eye for everything human: "Many are zealous in prayer and worship. They fast a great deal and mortify their body. But if a single word upsets their self-centeredness, or if anything is taken away from them, that angers them and immediately makes them fly off the handle. They are not poor in spirit . . ."

There was to be no place for hypocrisy in these communities. Poverty was everything, because it left people free for the one thing that really mattered. For a long time Francis fought off having a canonical rule and fixed houses or even prayer books. A brother who was not satisfied with the simple repetitive prayers and the Our Father provoked Francis' displeasure: "When you have a prayer book, then you'll want to have a breviary. And when you have a breviary, you'll soon want to sit on a university chair. Then you'll say to your brother like a great prelate, 'Bring me the breviary!'"

It seems miraculous that this spontaneous, obscure community won such quick recognition from Rome. The story of the pope (Innocent III) who supposedly had a dream in which a ragged monk propped up the shaky Lateran Basilica probably belongs to the domain of legend. Another, more believable tradition has the pope saying to Francis: "Surely you will find a pair of swine, brother, to receive you into their stall. You can preach to them, and perhaps they will adopt your rule. In any case you resemble a pig more than a human being."

Rome's Most Arrogant Pope

INNOCENT III, THE NAME chosen by the noble Lothar of Segni as pope, was the greatest conceivable contrast to the ragged "Friars Minor" from Assisi in their mountain shepherds' clothes. With Innocent the medieval papacy reached its zenith. Born of an old aristocratic family, trained in Paris and Bologna to be an outstanding theologian and canon lawyer, he developed a self-consciousness unusual even for popes. The bishop of Rome, he used to say, was admittedly less than God, but more than a mere human being.

Innocent wrote to the Patriarch of Constantinople that the Lord had given to Peter and his successors not just the Church to rule, but the entire globe as well.

He discovered a more telling comparison to make his point: Just as God had placed two lights in the firmament, a greater to rule the day and a lesser to rule the night, so he had also instituted two ranks in the Church, a greater to guide souls and a lesser to rule bodies. "These two are papal authority and royal power. As the moon receives its light from the sun, but truthfully is inferior to it in magnitude and radiance, position and effect, so royal power receives the brightness of its dignity from papal authority . . ."

Innocent did not see himself merely as the "deputy of Christ," who in the final analysis could write off the emperor as an insignificant rival. His claim to leadership was a spiritual one, to which both emperors and kings were subject, insofar as they were Christians and members of the one Body of Christ. That didn't exclude the possibility of his acting as a political umpire if, say, a conflict between kings had to be mediated. Innocent played this role, too, with appropriate arrogance.

Meanwhile the chroniclers describe him as a deeply religious person and a gifted pastor. He got rid of the noble page boys and the golden drinking vessels in the Vatican. He drew up stricter moral criteria for the appointment of bishops, and at the first ecumenical council in the West—the Fourth Lateran Council—he set the reform of the clergy in motion.

Admittedly the same council also ordered the "yellow spot," the forerunner of the star, for all Jewish citizens, and legalized the beginnings of the Inquisition. At first Innocent fought the heretical poverty movement with relatively moderate laws. But when bishops and princes took their time in carrying them out, he mobilized the king of France to declare a holy war against the heretics. The Albigensian movement was drowned in a horrifying bloodbath. In the southern French town of Beziers alone, seven thousand people are said to have perished.

Innocent also campaigned enthusiastically for the notorious Crusade of 1203, which led not to victory over the Muslims, but (although the pope furiously condemned it) to the conquest and pillage of Christian Constantinople. The city had been a bothersome competitor for the lords of western commerce, and above all for the Venetian economy.

It was this man, cultivated, sophisticated, enamored with the dignity of his own throne, whom the little group of wandering preachers from Assisi now met face to face. Francis and his followers were hoping for an official confirmation of their Rule by the Church—a Rule that often spoke of absolute poverty, simplicity, and brotherliness. What was the papal court supposed to make of this simple-minded crew?

But Innocent III was not just conscious of power, he was also clever. Rome had hurled enough anathemas at preachers of poverty and radical Christian groups. It had sent Waldensians and Cathars to the stake. Could it afford to lose still more Christians who read the Gospel in a way that was surely naive but innocuous? And couldn't it take this movement, which was non-violent and truly devoted to the Holy See, and channel the energies that might one day prove dangerous to the powerful rulers of Church and State?

Or did the pope admit in embarrassment how close these artless believers were to the Lord from whom his office derived, to the rabbi from Galilee who had sought out poor fishermen as his companions and not the mighty in Jerusalem or Rome?

Jacques de Vitry, the eventual Latin patriarch of Jerusalem, had prophesied that Christ would save many souls through these poor people, "to the shame of the prelates, who like silent dogs cannot bark." At the papal audience, it was reported, the influential cardinal, John of Colonna, had weighed in with an illuminating argument for the Friars Minor: "This man merely wishes us to let him live according to the Gospel. Now if we tell him that this surpasses human strength, then we are declaring that it is impossible to follow the Gospel, and blaspheming Christ, the author of the Gospel."

Fortunately the Friars Minor went home with their papal recognition. They increased their preaching activity, appeared in Umbria, in Tuscany, and the Romagna, and in Marches of Ancona. When the pope called for a new crusade against the Muslims, the brothers countered with an authentically Franciscan alternative: they adopted the missionary idea as part of their program, a decidedly peaceful mission that aimed to convince by proclaiming the Gospel and living up to it.

Francis is even said to have had extremely fruitful discussions with the Sultan Melek-al-Kamil, a highly gifted ruler with a predilection for poor mystics and elaborate battle plans. But the Christian crusaders wouldn't go along with Francis's appeal to accept the armistice proposed by the Sultan.

Back home in Italy, he became a peacemaker in various local conflicts and civil wars. An old tradition claims that Francis was responsible for the "eternal treaty" of 1210 between the nobility and the people of Assisi, which decreed the emancipation of serfs, equality for the people from villages belonging to Assisi with the city residents, amnesty for exiles, and renunciation by the nobles of certain rights. In Bologna, Francis succeeded in ending the bloody, age-old hatred among aristocratic families.

Even when he lay critically ill, Francis intervened in a bitter feud that had broken out in his home town: the bishop had excommunicated the governor, who tried to starve out the clergy with an economic boycott. Francis sent two companions to the episcopal palace and delivered the following message: "Brother Francis has written a song in praise of God and for the edification of the neighbor, and asks you to listen to it in devotion." Then they sang a strophe of the famous "Canticle of the Sun":

Praise to you, my Lord,
 through those who forgive in the power of your love,
 and bear weakness and hardship.
 Happy are those who endure in peace.
 You, O Most High, will crown them.

Thereupon the governor, who was present, is said to have thrown himself at the feet of the bishop. The bishop embraced him and confessed: "My office should make me humble, but because I am violent-tempered by nature, you must be indulgent with me."

Only a few years before this, people had mocked the friars, who didn't look especially well-groomed in their shepherds' outfits, as "a sort of wild men of the woods." "The young girls fled trembling," we read in an early account, "simply upon seeing the friars from a distance, lest they be swept away by their madness." Francis was persecuted by his father with irreconcilable hatred; and on one cold winter day his younger brother shouted at him to go sell his sweat—then he wouldn't need to shiver and beg for alms.

But now in the eyes of many people Francis had already become his own legend. When he came into a town, according to the old biographers, the people rejoiced, and the children went out to meet him with fresh boughs. "He seemed to many to be like another Christ, who was given for the salvation of the world."

It is hardly imaginable that this adulation was especially pleasant to a man like Francis, especially since he would increasingly suffer grief the mistrust and bad conscience of highly placed clerics, above all curial officers. Counter-currents were rippling even in his own community.

The crowd of friends who once traveled around with no fixed plan had long since turned into a powerful movement, which counted its members in the thousands and longed for an organization with some kind of planning. There was a separate order for women, and a "Third Order" for married lay-people, who had committed themselves to a life of peace and reconciliation and renounced bearing arms. The state of absolute poverty that Francis demanded and the banishment of learning from the life of the Friars Minor were meeting with growing hostility.

Francis fought in vain against the trend toward a fixed organization, against the alignment of his community with the already existent orders. Fixed houses came into being, and in the final, papally approved version of his Rule, Francis had to accept dilutions of his original ideal. After years of struggle, he finally withdrew from the leadership of the Order.

This abdication from office has always been presented as humble obedience. But it wasn't that way. "I don't want you to mention any rule or any form of life except the one that was given me by the Lord," he protested before his gathered team, and angrily told his learned adversaries that he hoped God would destroy them through their own fabulous wisdom and knowledge. There was an embarrassed silence all around.

Brother Leo, who was one of his first and dearest companions, recalled Francis' bitter complaints about those brothers "who make my words empty" and who used their scholarly authority to break them down into permanently valid directives and outdated counsels. Marked by death, Francis rose up on his sick bed and gasped, "What sort of men are they who have ripped my Order out of my hands?"

That's not the voice of someone who has come to terms with everything in serene submission. Francis endured terrible anxieties about the future of his community. And the stigmata, the extraordinarily well-documented wounds of Jesus' crucifixion that he received toward the end of his life in the mountain solitude of La Verna, can also be interpreted as wounds that his own Church inflicted on him. Whenever the Church denies the poor and strives for possessions, power, domination, and security, it crucifies anew the one who wants to be its sole wealth and its unique security.

One may ask an entirely different question here: When the "different life" that had so spontaneously burst out in Assisi was forced into institutional structures, didn't that actually save this precious treasure for the future? Perhaps it was the "papal wisdom" that saved the Franciscan movement from shriveling into a "dry and second-rate sect," as Chesterton surmised.

Could a fixed order, a stricter set of regulations, have been a protection and not a chain? Could a milder, more flexible handling of the vow of poverty have been a sign of humane realism and not a betrayal of the founder?

Further developments suggest a rather skeptical answer to such questions. A hundred years later, Pope John XXII proclaimed that it was false to teach that Jesus and the apostles had had no possessions. The Franciscans themselves had long owned splendid churches and generously, furnished study houses, and soon the Order would be going into the lending business and charging 10 percent interest. In 1318 the first Friars Minor were burned at the stake, in Marseille. They had taken this business of radical poverty too literally. Exactly thirty years before that, Nicholas IV was the first Franciscan to ascend to the papal throne. He was a patron of the arts and founder of universities—and financially dependent on the noble Colonna family.

Francesco Bernardone, *io picciolino vostro fra Francecso*, as he called himself, "your little brother Francis," did not have to stand by watching: At the age of forty-four he had departed this life. In the final period he suffered from malaria, stomach and intestinal ulcers, anemia, dropsy, rheumatism, depression, and an extremely painful eye inflammation. The clueless doctors tormented him with red-hot irons on his temples and ears. When, not long ago, experts examined Francis's remains, they found clear signs of malnutrition.

As he wrote the famous "Canticle of the Sun"—perhaps the most light-hearted prayer known to the Christian world—he lay almost blind and racked with terrible pain in a wretched reed hut. When he got word from the doctor that he had only a few more months to live, Francis replied, "Welcome, brother death!" And he immediately added a final strophe to the "Canticle of the Sun":

> Praise be to you, my Lord,
> through our brother, bodily death.
> No one can escape him alive.
> Woe to those who die in mortal sin!
> Blessed are they whom he finds in your most holy will,
> the second death will do them no harm.

Altissimo, omnipotente, bon Signore,
highest, almighty, good Lord,
honor and all blessing . . .
Praise be to you, my Lord,
with all your creatures,
above all with my lord brother sun.
He brings us the day and light.
And he is beautiful and gleaming with great splendor,
a sign from you, O Most High.
Praise be to you, my Lord,
through sister moon and the stars:
You formed them in the heavens
brightly shining and precious and fair.
Praised be to you, my Lord,
through brother wind
and through air and clouds and clear sky
and all weather,
through which you maintain your creatures.
Praise be to you, my Lord,
for sister water.
She is most useful and humble and precious
and pure.
Praise be to you, my Lord,
through brother fire,
through whom you brighten the night.
And he is beautiful and gay and mighty and strong.
Praise be to you, my Lord,
through our sister, mother earth,
who nourishes and cares for us . . .

—From the "Canticle of the Sun"

In the last months of his life, Francis was cared for in the bishop's palace in Assisi. But when he felt the end was near, he had himself brought to the modest little convent of the Portiuncula, where he lay down naked on the cold ground. That was how he died on October 3, 1226.

Just two years later Pope Gregory IX came to Assisi to canonize Francis and lay the foundations for his splendid burial church. An opulent basilica, a cyclopean pile of towering walls and nested buildings, a church laid out like fortress—this was the final resting place of the malnourished wandering preacher, Francesco Bernardone.

The Gospel and Nothing Else

WHERE WAS THE ENERGY source for this equally wretched and electrifying life? How can we explain the mystery that a little clutch of vagrant popular missionaries and odd-job men could become one of the mightest religious communities in the history of the Church, an order that even today has 38,000 brothers, despite superannuation and a slump in vocations?

The Franciscan Rule supplies the answer. After some hard battles it was finally fixed in permanent forms, but even in its last official version it was little more than a commentary on the Gospel:

> This is the rule and the life of the brothers: To live in obedience, celibate and without property, to follow the teaching and the footsteps of our Lord Jesus Christ, who says: "If you would be perfect, go, sell what you possess and give to the poor, and you will have treasure in heaven; and come, follow me" (Matt. 19:21).

And further:

> All brothers are to strive to imitate the humility and poverty of our Lord Jesus Christ. And they should bear in mind that, as the Apostle says, we need nothing more from the whole world but food and clothing, and with that let us be content.

That was all. The Gospel and nothing more. God and nobody else. There were no extras, no special spirituality for the Franciscans. There was only the Gospel—but it had to be read radically, without reservations, without loopholes, without the golden mean. What shaped Francis' activity and that of his brothers was passion, not a clever balancing act, the same passion that stamped his experience of God, his relation to Jesus.

Some passages of his Rule read like the song of an enamored troubador: He wants to love God, "with total exhilaration, with total tenderness," with his whole heart and with all his strength. "He is the abundance of goodness, all good, the whole good, the truest and highest good, he alone is good. Tender and kind, gentle and loving . . . Nothing shall prevent us, nothing shall divide us, nothing shall separate us. Everywhere, in every place, at all hours, daily and incessantly, sincerely and humbly let us believe in the most high and most exalted eternal God, let us keep him in our hearts, love, honor and adore him. . . ."

One of his companions is supposed to have observed once how Francis lifted his hands to heaven all night long until dawn, continuously repeating only two words: *Iddio mio! Iddio mio!* "My God! My God!"

Mystical extravagance? Hardly. Religious neurotics are not such lively individuals, attuned to the world and their neighbor, as Francis was. There was nothing unpleasantly fanatical about him. We meet a smiling radical, who did not condemn the rich, foaming at the mouth with rage. He simply challenged the people to live differently—and thereby much more effectively pulled out the rug from beneath the feet of the powerful.

"Let none of you be led astray to anger or offence," he admonished his friends, "rather may each one by his gentleness move others to peace, to kindness, and compassion. To this we are called: to heal the wounded, to support the weak, to bring back those who have gone astray. Many who we think belong to the devil will yet be transformed some day into disciples of Christ!"

Of course, Francis also made mistakes and showed weaknesses, because saints are no angels, but human beings who have to strain and struggle. With religious deviants he was sometimes harsh and impatient to the point of tyranny. When the Friars Minor in Bologna built a house—an open affront to the vagabond lifestyle of the early days—it bothered him so much that he threw them all out, even the sick. He cursed the superior of the Bologna province, who defended erecting the house. Even when he was at death's door, he refused to be reconciled with him, saying: "I can't bless someone whom God has cursed, and so let him stay cursed!"

He categorically forbade the brothers to own books— he had great respect for theologians, and safely stored away every last piece of paper as though it were a treasure. Ultimately he was motivated by the thought that being well read and learned could all too easily seduce the brothers into arrogance and deflect their vision from the One who alone should be the way, the truth, and life for Christians.

"He scarcely or only seldom allowed himself the pleasure of cooked food," noted Thomas of Celano on Francis' ascetical self-discipline. "And when he did, he spoiled it with ashes or spoiled its flavor with cold water." He systematically ruined his body, "brother ass," by the way he lived.

He was really hardest on himself. Once when he was seriously sick he forgot his strict fasting for a moment and ate a few bites of chicken. Then to punish himself for this, he had a companion tie a rope around his neck and drag him through the streets. The brother had to shout to passers-by: "Look at him, the gourmet, who stuffed himself with chicken!" Thereupon, the citizens became "contrite of heart" and were encouraged to lead a better life. Or so his biographer observes. But he is evidently trying hard to give meaning to this weird behavior, and he's not very convincing.

Once when he had done wrong to Brother Bernard—though only in his thoughts—he threw himself down on the ground before him and ordered the horrified brother to put his foot on his throat and step over him three times, while reviling him as much as he could. "Just lie there, you scoundrel!," poor Brother Bernard had to say, "you fine son of Pietro Bernardone, where did you get your presumption, you utterly common creature?"

Of course, who knows how much the mercurial Francis made a game out of all this? And anyone who has seen the dramatic goings-on of today's group therapies will be inclined to see in such actions a sign of carefree vitality rather than of a sick brain. Despite his consistent harshness to himself, Brother Francis was also capable of boisterously enjoying the pastries that the noble lady Jacoba di Settesoli used to bring. He even once let her open the door to the little monastery of the Portiuncula, "Because the rule of cloister (forbidding entrance to women) doesn't hold for Brother Jacoba," he declared without further ado, transforming the lady into a "fellow brother."

Sometimes you have to twist the rules a bit to keep yourself from grim seriousness—as Francis did one night in Lent, when the brothers were awakened by loud moaning and groaning. One of the brothers complained, as he writhed in despair on his bed, of such terrible hunger pangs that he was definitely going to die. Francis smiled and made him something to eat, and then invited everyone to dine, so as not to shame the hungry brother. Afterwards he warned against exaggerated fasting and said that one stomach simply needed more food than another.

What amazes us about Francis's relation with God is its immediacy. Here everything is joy, enthusiasm, intimacy. There is no room for boring sanctimoniousness or highfaluting theory.

The same pattern marked the Franciscan community. Its purpose can be summarized in two sentences: In Jesus Christ, God comes palpably close to us men and women. Therefore we have to find Christ in everything—in people, in all living creatures, even in inanimate objects.

"He rejoiced in all works from the hands of the Lord, "Thomas of Celano recalled, "and whenever a lovely thing presented itself to his eye, he looked through it to the lifegiving ground of all things. He recognized in beautiful things the most beautiful One himself. All good things cried out to him: 'He who created us is the best!' He followed after the footprints of his Beloved and made all things into a ladder, with which to climb to his throne."

Thus Francis's faith is sensuous and oriented to the world. Otherwise the poor man from Assisi would hardly have become the inventor of the Christmas crèche. He kept staging games to explain what he was teaching.

One such "game" was the Christmas celebration of 1223, which Francis prepared in a cave near Greccio on the slopes of the Sabine mountains. "For I wanted to celebrate the memory of the child born in Bethlehem," he confided to a good friend. "I wanted to look on

> O Queen Wisdom!
> The Lord protect you
> through your holy sister,
> pure Simplicity.
> Holy Lady Poverty!
> The Lord protect you through your holy sister Humility.
> Holy Lady Love!
> The Lord protect you
> through your holy sister Obedience.
> You most high virtues,
> the Lord protect you all.
> From him you come forth,
> to him you return.

him with my bodily eyes, as palpably as I could, at the bitter need he had to suffer even as a little child, to look upon him as he was laid in a manger, with an ox and an ass alongside him, bedded down on the hay . . .''

When the holy night arrived, the people wended their way from the surrounding countryside, and the brothers from several Franciscan settlements came to the hidden cave, carrying candles and torches, "to illuminate that night, which with its shining stars brightened all days and years" (Thomas of Celano). A manger was prepared with hay, the ox and ass stood by, the singing voices resounded through the woods.

While a priest celebrated a solemn mass over the poor manger, Francis sang the Gospel and preached to the people standing there "about the birth of the poor king." He was visibly ecstatic and literally let the names "Jesus" and "Bethlehem" melt on his tongue, as the sources report: "Greccio became as it were a new Bethlehem. The night became as bright as day, and it was a delight to men and beasts . . . The child Jesus had been forgotten in many hearts. Then through his holy servant, Francis, he was reawakened unto them with his grace and impressed upon them in zealous memory."

This striving to make the stories of the Bible as vivid and concrete as possible also corresponded, of course, to a trend of the times. The returning crusaders had talked a great deal about

Palestine, and people felt closer to the places where Jesus had lived, where he had been born and crucified.

Before the cross Francis discovered that his existence wasn't to be that of a lonely hermit's in some hidden cell. Christ went out to people and died for them all. Hence Francis knew that he had been sent into the world. "The world is our monastery," his brothers would say later. That is why he founded his community and begged his companions to live the love that he himself had experienced.

"Happy the man who bears his neighbor with all his shortcomings as he wishes to be borne by him in his own weakness: . . . Happy the servant who loves and respects his brother just as much when he is far away as when he is close by, and says nothing behind his back that he could not also say to his face in love."

Property Isolates

To find Jesus and love people—that won't work when you cling to possessions, to your own power over things. That's why poverty was the alpha and omega of this community. Property isolates, that was Francis' basic experience. But he wanted to open himself to people. False security got in the way of devotion to God. He wanted to be completely free for his beloved Lord.

One day the mother of two of the brothers came to him and told him a story that may have been true or false: She was hard up and begged for alms. But the community had nothing except a New Testament.

One has to realize how precious such an object was at a time long before the invention of printing. In the scriptoria of monasteries it took a whole year to transcribe one copy of Holy Scripture. If he spent his entire year's salary, a university professor could afford just ten books (each one thinner than the Bible).

Yet Francis said to one of the brothers, in his casual fashion: "Give our mother the New Testament. She is to sell it for the sake of her need, for the book tells us to come to the aid of the poor. I believe it pleases God more when we give it away than when we read in it."

The Friars Minor were to be a radically poor community. It wasn't just the founder's will that no individual should own things, the community had to be poor as well. "When the brothers set out through the world," it says in the first unofficial version of the Rule, "they should take nothing with them on the way, carry no begging sack, no purse for supplies, no money, no staff." That's a verbatim quotation from the Gospel of Luke [not really—trans.]. In the definitive version of the Rule this sentence disappeared.

In the above-mentioned discussion about owning books Francis is supposed to have sharply criticized the brothers: " You want people to consider you followers of the Gospel, but in reality you are the same keepers of the purse as Judas!"

The brothers weren't supposed to own houses or stockpiles of things or gear for journeys, and certainly not a mount—Francis didn't want to preach the gospel of the poor Jesus from horseback, as was the fashion in the thirteenth century.

But the prohibition against money proved to have the most serious consequences, especially in the epoch of an increasingly powerful money economy. While Italian firms were setting up branch offices and warehouses all over the West, from Flanders to Greece and beyond in the Islamic countries and Asia, while the jingling coins piled up in offices and banks, and the gold scale became a part of every merchant's luggage, Francis placed the new idol of his age on the same level as dung.

This is one of the crudest stories told from the earliest years of the Friars Minor: A visitor to the church left a coin in front of the crucifix at the Portiuncula, a well-intentioned offering, which a brother deposited in the window niche. Francis immediately staged one of his little didactic scenes. The careless brother, who had touched the despised money with his hand, was told to pick it up from the windowsill with his mouth, take it out of the cloistered area (still holding it in his mouth), and drop it on a heap of donkey manure.

Thus the poor Christian from Assisi degraded capital—a sacrilege that solid churchmen and responsible secular Christians even today probably find hardest of all to forgive." From gold or coins," Francis's rule states, "we are allowed to have no greater profit than from stones. The devil is seeking to blind all those who long for such things and who take them to be more valuable than stones."

The brothers were to accept eggs, bread, and milk—but nothing else—as wages or alms. Nor were they allowed to wear expensive clothes, which, however, mustn't lead to the puritanical arrogance of the chosen. Francis said: "I warn and admonish them, not to despise and condemn those people who wear soft and colorful clothes, and indulge in choice food and drink. Rather each one should condemn and despise himself." For God had the power even to make the spendthrifts righteous.

It was supposed to be a poor community sharing the life of beggars and outcasts. Francis and his brothers chose poverty, not primarily out of protest, but because they wanted to be stripped of everything and follow the Crucified who called nothing his own. Poverty was a way of imitating Christ. Poverty was a prerequisite for freedom. The brothers were not to be ashamed of it, "because the Lord made himself poor in this world for our sake" (Francis).

But they also knew that possessions dehumanize and corrupt. "Why didn't they want to have any property at all?" asked the bishop of Assisi in suprise, and got the convincing reply," My lord, if we had property, we would also need weapons to defend ourselves. Property leads to disputes and quarrels, from which the love of God and our fellows so often suffers. That is why we wish to have no property in this world."

But this means that any naive talk about the purely spiritual, inward poverty of the Friars Minor conceals the explosive power of this symbolic existence and smooths over its political content. Poverty, as St. Francis lived it, automatically passes judgment on luxury that benefits the few at the cost of the many. Naturally Francis was biased. As a matter of course, he sided with the little people and the subjugated, saying in effect to the world: See, here is my poor God.

And because power means unfreedom, just as possessions do, Francis wanted a fraternal community without a hierarchy: "Wherever the brothers are and meet, they should deal with one another as lodgers in the same house. Everyone should confidently make known his needs to the other . . ."

"Likewise no brother should exercise power or domination, above all not over the brothers"—This unequivocal wording is to be found only in the first, unconfirmed Rule. Francis is also said to have issued a threat: "Woe to anyone who, after being put in charge by the others, will not voluntarily step down!" The exercise of authority, something that Francis ultimately couldn't avoid, was supposed to strengthen the brothers, not regiment them. Even according to the more accommodating, papally approved Rule there was to be no Prior (i.e., "first man"), but only a Minister, which means "servant." And the minister had an "imperative mandate," and was supervised from below:

> All brothers who are subordinate to the ministers and servants are to observe the actions of the ministers and servants carefully and reasonably. If they notice that one of them is walking in the flesh and not in the spirit, as befits our life, and if he does not improve after the third admonition, they should inform the minister and servant of the whole community at the Pentecost Chapter and not let themselves be held back by any protests he makes.

And if the remaining provincial ministers were convinced that the man was harming the welfare of the community, he could be voted out.

As these regulations for the supervision of the ministers show, Francis was leading no revolution *against* the Church but *in* the Church. The brothers' free charisma had to be integrated into the Church, and a promise of obedience bound the Franciscans to the pope.

Francis demanded respect for the clergy from the brothers:

> Happy is the servant who has trust in the clerics who truly live according to the form of the holy Roman church. Woe to those who despise them. For even though they be sinners, no one is entitled to pass judgment on them. The Lord alone reserves the right to judge them.

But he could also say quite commandingly: "We are sent to help the clergy for the salvation of souls, so that we may step in where they fail." Souls could be rescued better in a peaceful way than by conflict with the clergy. Francis: " If you are the sons of peace, you will win over the clergy and the people for the Lord. That pleases him better than if you only win the people, but anger the clergy. Therefore cover up their mistakes, compensate for their manifold faults. And having done that, then you will really be humble."

What he means is as clear as day: The clergy needs to undergo conversion. But that shouldn't seduce the Friars Minor into arrogance. We are all sinners.

A World Comes Apart at the Seams

No, Francis didn't make a bourgeois revolution, nor did he organize the starving underclass. But while he fought against all smug foregone conclusions and made foolishness the way of the Gospel, a new generation grew up with him, poor and self-aware, knowing God was on their side. For the sign of God is not splendor and glory and success in the world, but the unprotected, open heart of the poor. In the face of such a life, the division of the world into masters and slaves can only be called ridiculous.

And the powerful sensed just how dangerous these shabby tramps might yet be to them. "The brothers of St. Francis have risen up with power against us!" presciently complained the Hohenstauffen Emperor Frederick II, who was dreaming of a new edition of the Roman Empire.

Village mayors in Italy attacked the prohibition against bearing arms and the pacifist oath that Francis had imposed on the lay-people in the Third Order, which seems to have thrown the draft and military service into confusion.

Francis also didn't shy away from snubbing princes of the Church, such as Cardinal Ugolino, the Protector of his order. At one banquet arranged by Ugolino he showed up with his begging bag, sat down next to the Cardinal and then serenely distributed the food he had begged to the embarrassed noble guests. When the cardinal upbraided him, Francis supposedly told him that he felt more comfortable surrounded by his companions and eating stale barley bread than seated at such an aristocratic table.

Even in the papal court he once preached fearlessly about the arrogance of the prelates and their bad example, forgetting his carefully rehearsed speech. His burning zeal "shook the mountains," notes the chronicler, alluding to the hard character of the curial cardinals, and many of them became "contrite in their hearts."

The contrition, however, didn't last long. A hundred years later Pope John XXII put the all-too-radical Franciscans in their place and sent some of them to be burnt at the stake. The papal bull accompanying the condemnations announced that, "Poverty is a great thing, but greater still is blameless conduct, and the greatest good of all is perfect obedience."

Francis had never wanted to start a conflict in the Church. The task of the Friars Minor was supposed to be peacemaking—in society but also with nature. Francis knew that all creatures and all things in the world belong together and are dependent on one another. For this reason his order was the first "green" movement in western history. The fact that he called animals "brother" and "sister," that he ran through the woods and hugged the trees, was no childish quirk, but matched his will to live in harmony with all of creation.

The idea of seeing images of God in living creatures was not a new one, and it fit the medieval attitude. But we find in Francis no trace of the fear which that age still widely displayed toward unexplored, menacing nature. "With unheard-of devotion and love he embraced all things," writes Thomas of Celano. In him, Celano says, the kindness began to shine that one day would be all in all in God's new world.

"It was like the coming of spring to the world," says the ancient *Legend of the Three Companions*, looking back on Francis's life. Today, eight hundred years after his death, the poor man from Assisi is part of the Church's past that we have yet to come to terms with. He remains a nail in our conscience, an uncomfortable recollection of the Gospel, and a question: What do we want to make of it?

There's not much good in relishing the story of how within a short time the gentle rebellion of St. Francis was transformed into a new variation on the old order, of how the radical alternative was replaced by a flexible compromise. Of how the Franciscans, for example, became dependent on their financial backers, who took in contributions for them and managed the order's accounts, thus sparing it the necessity of (formally) breaking the vow of poverty.

But, as we said, there's not much good in that. Francis remains a challenge for us moderns, and looking back into history mustn't become an excuse for dodging our current responsibilities.

The most urgent of these is finally to make the poor Church a reality. That issue is just as vital and just as unresolved today as it was in the lifetime of St. Francis, who is credited with writing the hymn to "Lady Poverty":

> We throw ourselves at your feet and humbly beg you: Deign to be with us. Be for us the path to the king of glory, as you were the path for him. Thus make peace with us, and we will be saved—so that he who has redeemed us through you may accept us through you.

Perhaps the brave Franciscan missionaries in Brazil can pray that way, those friars who share the fate of the campesinos, the poor rural workers, who go hungry, and are persecuted by the powerful. Enlightened western Christians who have begun tithing for those who lack even the most basic necessities can pray that way with some hesitation. But what about the rest of us, who are much more concerned with our mutual funds and bank accounts and furniture than with the kingdom of God, and who talk our way out of it by claiming that the pope relies on his stocks too.

Francis can help us to learn again that the only Church of Christ is a poor Church. To learn that the Gospel can't be followed and realized anywhere near "normal" life, but must mold and change our whole lifestyle. Otherwise it's just talk.

But we also have to learn from Francis that a poor Church can't come into being through fine declarations of intent and a new choice of words: It presupposes a different structure. Both our private lives and the institution have to change.

Meanwhile some modest and self-critical voices saying such things can be heard even from the Franciscan order. In 1982 the Missionary Congress in Matili recalled the founder's wish "that his brothers remain on the level of the people and not to strive for higher positions. We have a special responsibility to meet in the Church, namely to be a living community of brothers and sisters, who are with one another on the way and thus represent the kindness of God for all people. For that reason we wish to seek the base and to live not just *for* the people but *with* the people."

When Franciscans live that way, they take the wind out of the sails of the well-known spiritual writer, Carlo Carretto, who pictures St. Francis himself preaching to his modern-day brothers like this:

> These basilicas are quite wonderful! You have been efficient . . . You play with poverty and cheat in the process . . . you live in a strange, contradictory, ambiguous time. The richer you are, the more you talk about poverty. The more bourgeois you are, the more you "play" poor Church. The more you talk about community, the more isolated and cut off you live. There's always an ocean between saying and doing, but how true that is of you! It's the ocean of your prattle, which you're still drowning in . . . It's terrible how hard, sharp, and radical you are—too bad this radicality is aimed only at the "others," and not against yourself.

We could learn from Francis to get away from just this sort of thing. We could rediscover the Gospel as something personal meant for us, we could find in Jesus Christ the center for our life. We could learn to live a redeemed existence, freed from trivialities. This would be an ascetical kind of consumption that has its roots in a new appreciation of things, a believing relationship with the environment that is more than fashionable enthusiasm for nature, an attitude that would undoubtedly have an effect on everything, including the world of politics.

"Try to imagine that we are all brothers," Carlo Carretto encourages us. An overwhelming offer. Francis's project—if only we were to adopt it—would spare us the nuclear apocalypse. This is always how it is: God proposes peace. Why not try it?

THE CHARMING MYSTIC

CATHERINE OF SIENA

(1347–1380)

A Dyer's Daughter Shows Popes and Princes What Courage Is

Sono sangue e fuoco—I am blood and fire.
Don't be satisfied with a little, God expects great things!

*J*ust imagine this today: A young woman, deeply committed but still wet behind the ears, is asked by a television news reporter about her relations with the Church. She begins cursing the incompetent clergy like a woman possessed:

They're miserly, greedy, stingy! They blather away in unbridled vanity, and are only after the good life. Oh, their wretched life! What Christ won on the wood of the cross, they waste with whores. You temples of the devil! The clerics are blades of straw, not pillars of the Church. They pour out a stench that befouls the whole world.

Most likely the editor in the television studio would listen to the first few words and then switch off the microphone in horror.

Just imagine this today: This same young woman, without any formal education and, in fact, with a thoroughly uncouth manner of speaking, bombards the pope in the Vatican with furious letters and barks at him to finally reform the Church, now gone to rack and ruin:

> Don't be a fearful baby, be a man. God orders you to deal strictly with the excess of depravity of all those who gorge themselves in the garden of the holy Church. Rip out the evil-smelling flowers, I mean the bad shepherds and administrators who are poisoning this garden. Bishops should seek God instead of living like pigs.

Any monsignor sorting through the pope's mail would let the shameless letters discreetly disappear.

Thirdly, just imagine the stubborn young woman—with an untamable hunger for justice but politically simple-minded—writing her letters now to the presidents, junta chiefs, and generalissimos all over the world. In all earnest she would admonish these men of power: "Repent! Think of death and its uncertainty. Be a father to the poor, as the steward of what God has entrusted to you. Don't you consider what great responsibility for evil falls upon you when you refuse to do what lies in your power? What a devilish botch in the eyes of God is this war between brothers. Cut out these stupidities!"

These naive gushes would likewise be dismissed by some zealous, head-shaking secretary in the anterooms of power. At most the young woman protestor would receive one of those inconsequential, preprinted replies signed by an assistant cabinet secretary: ". . . The president cordially thanks you for the expression of your opinion. Unfortunately the president is unable to respond personally to all his correspondents . . ."

No one would take such letters seriously.

But our little mental experiment is no fairy tale. The young woman who appealed so furiously to the conscience of the powers that be actually did live, more than six hundred years ago, in

Tuscany. Her barrage of abuse aimed at the clergy may be found in a mystical "Conversation with God," which was later one of the favorite readings of the Middle Ages. The stern calls for church reform were aimed at Pope Gregory XI. And the just-quoted appeal for peace landed on the desk of the king of France.

And meanwhile the most stunning thing of all: Catherine of Siena's letters, as impolite as they were long-winded, were carefully read at the papal Curia and the courts of princes. They got answers, and they led to invitations.

In her correspondence with Rome, Catherine didn't just formulate her concerns and questions. She boxed the Holy Father's ears with complaints and reproaches, and delivered veritable declarations of war against prelates and cardinals. Catherine was suspected and attacked, but no one sued her for libel. Eighty years after her death, she was canonized by a successor of the pope whom she had characterized as a "fearful baby."

We always think that the Christian Middle Ages were intolerant and unenlightened, stamped by bronze structures of power and subordination, but they can't have been as bad as all that.

THE STRUGGLE WITH MAMA

THE FONTEBRANDA DISTRICT was not necessarily one of the high class residential districts of Siena. Catherine was born here in 1347, the twenty-fourth child of a family of wool-dyers, the Benincasas. Her mother, Monna Lapa, was a classic Tuscan mamma, loud, vehement, domineering, hot-tempered, rooted to the soil, realistic. According to the sources, her father, Master Jacopo, seems to have been quiet and sensitive, a patient man who stayed in the background and looked upon the pious escapades of his daughter, who took after no one in the family, with more respect than did his resolute wife. Catherine grew up in simple, but not wretched, conditions. Neighbors and relatives gave the spirited child the nickname "little gaiety."

We get the first insight into the conflict-ridden family life of the Benincasas from Catherine's vision of Christ, which is somewhat too awfully reminiscent of typical saints legends: Jesus Christ is supposed to have appeared to her above the roof of her parish church sitting on a throne, in priestly vestments, with the papal tiara on his head, smiling and giving his blessing.

It is certainly true that early on the girl discovered another reality behind her little world of workshop smells, kitchen chores, and backyard games. It's true that in the following period there were exhausting struggles between the unruly, obstinate Catherine and her rather authoritarian mother, and that the main problem was the conflict between radical religious ways of life and so-called healthy common sense.

Early on, "little gaiety" waxed enthusiastic over the Egyptian Fathers of the Desert and their harsh penitential life. One day she stuck a loaf of bread under her arm and marched through the city gate to search for the desert. But she quickly got bored in the rocky cave where she had set up her living quarters. Her childish dream of following the model of a legendary woman saint and sneaking into a monastery in men's clothing seems no less adventurous. The virgin in the legend, at any rate, supposedly pulled off her deception for thirty years.

In her mature years Catherine swung back and forth between a Christianity full of *joie de vivre*, which didn't exclude harmless flirtations, and a totally negative, almost suicidal asceticism. Even her biographer and confessor, Fra Raimundo of Capua, mentions that under the influence of her married favorite sister, Bonaventura, Catherine began to "devote a great deal of care to her outer appearance." And yet Raimundo wrote his account in order to promote her canonization so, naturally, he accented the sort of things that would help it.

Nevertheless there is no doubt that Mona Lapa wanted a son-in-law for her daughter, who was not only quite pretty but also strikingly clever. She wanted a man who would boost the Benincasas' social status. And Catherine actually enjoyed getting dressed up in fashionable clothes. This must have happened relatively early because back then girls reached marriagable age at twelve.

But according to Raimundo, things never got so far "that Catherine cared very much for a man or for men in general." Given the proverbially rather loose ways of the Sienese in the fourteenth century, this was doubtless something of an achievement. By way of explanation, Raimundo adds that Catherine had already become "the bride of a far greater spouse."

We have no way of knowing whether she really, as Raimundo claims, promised to live a virginal, celibate life at the age of seven, and never wavered afterwards in her decision. At this age little girls are sometimes also absolutely convinced that they will marry a prince and live in a castle, and nobody nails them so relentlessly to the childhood dreams as some miracle-addicted lives of saints do.

At any rate, when her beloved Bonaventura, young and blooming, suddenly died in childbirth, Catherine seems to have made a momentous about-face. "She devoted her time to penance and meditation," notes Fra Raimundo, "and avoided meeting men." Indeed, so as finally to get some rest from her family's marriage plans and programs for her future, without a moment's hesitation, she cut off her splendid blond locks (blond hair was a specially valuable asset for attractive, young Italian women) and hid her shaven head in a kerchief, in utter defiance of fashion.

The family war now broke out into the open, and Raimundo describes it with dramatic flair. "You insolent rascal," they cursed her right in public, "Do you think you don't have to obey us anymore? Just wait, your hair will grow back, like it or not. Even if it kills you, you're going to get married. We'll give you no peace until you give in."

But all the power plays only made Catherine more headstrong. They took her own small room away from her, and put her to work as the kitchen maid, but they failed to break her resistance. Finally the family seems to have given in, grinding their teeth—probably under pressure from the father, of whom Raimundo reports that he participated least in the "violent action" against his rebellious daughter.

We may assume that Jacopo soon regretted his tolerance. Catherine, an admittedly strong but very young girl, had got it into her head to exhaust the whole arsenal of medieval penitential exercises. "Let reason keep sensuality in bounds" is how she later explained her motives: complete subordination of bodily needs under the control of "Mistress Reason."

To us today, however, the way Catherine imitated her idols, the early Christian Desert Fathers, doesn't seem especially rational. She drank nothing but water, she reduced her bill of fare to raw vegetables (she found the mere smell of meat unbearable), rigged up a bed of boards, wore sweaty woollen undergarments when it was hot, and got herself an iron penitential chain that chafed and bloodied her skin. She experimented with fifteen minutes of sleep a day. Three times a day she whipped herself with her chain, "once for herself, once for the living, once for the dead," reports Fra Raimundo and recalls he often said back then, "It's a miracle she's alive at all."

She probably got the strength for all this from the incredibly close relationship that binds a mystic to God. And she got it from the happiness of being able to break the fetters of all the things we take for granted, and of getting a look at the world that after our death will be our home. Raimundo notes that the conversations with friends about God had really "refreshed" her.

Catherine later spoke very self-critically of this sort of war against her own body. "Perfection," she said, "does not consist in chastising or mortifying one's body, but in destroying perverse self-will." Penitential exercises shouldn't be an end in themselves, but only a means to overcome egoism, for "only the power of love matters." What sense does it make to carry out works of penance and to imagine oneself great and filled with God, and not to notice at all the hidden conceit in this?

No, acts of penance are merely an instrument, to be used at the right time and in the right place. Catherine writes:

> If the body resists the spirit with too much vigor, grasp the rod, fasting, the knotty penitential girdle, and long vigils; and lay enough weight on the body so that it gets softened up. But if it has become weak and sickly, then the rule of discrimination would not have us go about it this way. Then you should not only stop fasting, but eat meat. If once a day is not enough, then have it four times a day.

Saints, too, can always learn something. It's even one of their characteristic features. Saints are the least stubborn, self-satisfied people in existence.

But at first the girl from Siena got harder and harder on herself, till she went too far. For three years, Catherine is supposed not to have spoken with her family members and locked herself up in her room—a monastic cell inside the house of the extended Benincasa family. She noticed only the poor and gave generously to them (with her father's consent).

With her usual doggedness she managed to gain acceptance (presumably at the age of fifteen or sixteen) to the lay order of St. Dominic, a community of older widows who were called *mantellate* after the capes they wore. Respected ladies above all suspicion, they lived withdrawn in their houses, and got together for prayer and charity. At first they fought tooth and nail against the unusual young recruit, who would only make people talk about them. When Catherine didn't give in and kept sending her equally reluctant mother to the Mantellates, two older sisters were assigned to check whether the young girl wasn't too attractive for their group. Fortunately, Catherine was just then afflicted by a skin disease with conspicuous pustules.

So now she was allowed to put on the black cape of St. Dominic. In Siena, the girl who seemed to be in something of a daze, who went to communion every day (extremely unusual at the time) was often overcome by ecstatic flights in church. Soon she was known all over town. Was she an overexcited teenager who wanted to be seen in a special light? Or, worse yet, was she pretending to be particularly blessed so as to curry favor with the dreamy young monks? In any event she *was* continuously seen together with clerics or the sons of the city nobility.

Malicious gossip began to haunt her. Even a woman leper, whom Catherine supplied with food and clean underwear every day, bickered and sneered: "Here she comes, finally, the queen of Fontebranda. All day long she stands around in the Dominican church. You might think she just can't get enough of these monks."

Catherine reacted by doubling her efforts on behalf of the embittered old woman.

Yet the hostilities took on much more dangerous forms. She was denied communion. They threw the supposed fake ecstatic out of the church and stamped on her outside on the pavement when she refused to wake up from her raptures. When people claimed she had had intercourse with young noblemen, she had to undergo a painfully embarrassing procedure to prove her intact virginity before the prioress of the Mantellates.

"GO AMONG PEOPLE!"

HER VISIONS AND MYSTICAL experience are said to have accumulated at that time. But she was also suffering from severe depression. Her hard life seemed meaningless to her, and she was haunted by extremely realistic erotic fantasies. Meantime, she believed that God was far away, and when the Crucified appeared again to her one day, covered with blood and in sparkling light, she asked him with a mild reproach: "My Lord, where were you, when my whole life was full of these horrors?"

"I was in your heart!" Christ answered.

Later she saw the Lord again in a heavenly light, as he took her heart out of her breast and put his own heart in its place. She likewise clothed the stormy inner process of those seemingly so tranquil years in the image of a vision: Christ had commanded her to leave her cell again and go among people. At first she thought her heart was going to break. It had been her temptation to look upon people only as factors disrupting her relationship with God.

Yet Christ spoke to her: "You shouldn't be useful only to yourself, but to others as well; and for that too I give you my grace. But I don't want to send you away from me. On the contrary, love for people will bind you still more closely to me."

Catherine had understood: One is never a Christian only for oneself. Those who encapsulate themselves so they can surrender pious sensations ("becoming a self," "finding your identity" we would call it today) love their own peace and quiet, but not God.

Catherine accepted the new turnabout in her life, and went to work with a true burning zeal. At home she helped out sick serving maids, hurried into the hospitals, looked after a prostitute. "Right and left her hands poured out love" (Raimundo). She didn't wait for relief organizations (which didn't exist in her day anyhow). At that time, linking contemplative monastic life with social activity was a new idea.

Then something even more astonishing happened: The Mantellatas, mature matrons who could have been Catherine's grandmothers, increasingly recognized her as a leading figure. By the time she was around twenty, Catherine had also gathered around herself a *famiglia*, a varied group of well-placed ladies, counsellors, monks, artists, and bankers, all of whom were fascinated by this not-particularly-cultivated girl. They addressed her a little enthusiastically as "sweet mother." People called them *Caterinati*, partly in amusement, partly in admiration.

In 1374, Catherine Benincasa was present at the General Chapter of the Dominican Order in Florence. It's not certain whether she had to submit to a strict test of her orthodoxy, as some think. In any event the Dominicans made the twenty-seven-year-old the official leader of the *famiglia* in Siena—perhaps so as to keep a sharper eye on her other activities. For she was assigned her own spiritual guide, the already mentioned Raimundo of Capua, a good theologian who later became a papal nuncio and general of the Dominican order, which he reformed. The two of them were bound by a cordial friendship, and they both learned from each other. They also sometimes jokingly told off and encouraged one another. When the plague swept over Siena in the same year, they both stood in the front line of the helpers.

"What good would it do me," Catherine wrote in her *Dialogue on Divine Providence*, "if I saw myself in possession of everlasting life, but your people were dying?" She wanted to be in the thick of things, wherever people were on the line, wherever their dignity and life were threatened. For that reason she now began her so-called political commitment, which represented only a practical application of her deepest religious convictions.

The city state of Siena was shaken in the fourteenth century by family feuds and civil wars. People loyal to the emperor fought against supporters of the pope, patricians against little tradesmen, nobles against artisans. At every moment new disputes were breaking out, the weapons were bared, and some unforgivable insult or other was forever having to be publicly avenged. In their ongoing war over trifles, the noble families of the Tolomei and the Salimbeni, the Malavolti, Piccolimini, and Saracini behaved like pugnacious schoolboys—except that blood flowed in torrents, and countless families were plunged into misfortune. And all this for the sake of the honor of their proud name, of offended vanity or simply because some fellow from a noble house had heard too many knightly stories and absolutely had to have an adventure.

Present-day tourists to Tuscany can still sense something of this remarkably explosive atmosphere at the traditional *Palio*, a horse race on the town square of Siena. The racers ride bareback, wildly, with grim determination, as if their lives were at stake. On the eve of the Palio the old neighborhoods meet for an outdoor banquet, and the victorious part of the city leads its horse in a nightly festive parade into the districts of its rivals, singing mocking songs and reliving centuries-old passions.

But Siena was also home to the rich merchant, Giovanni Colombini. Around 1345, he distributed all his possessions among the have-nots. In that strange time of extreme opposites there was the nobleman Ambrogio Sansedoni, who became a preaching monk; and there was Giovanni Tolomei, who dropped out of a no-less-famous family with all its opportuniites and founded the monastery of Monte Oliveto in the mountain wilderness of Monte Ancona.

Into this impulsive, electrifying world of hotheads, violent criminals, and people possessed by God, Catherine threw herself headlong. She lived the watchword of the time, "All or nothing," with the utmost passion. And the unexpected happened: little village mayors, city parliaments, lords of castles, the noble houses of Tuscany, indeed diplomats and tyrants, found their attention captured by a young woman with inexplicable charisma; and they brought her in as umpire and peacemaker.

To be sure, they were also trying to use her as a pawn in their political calculations. There was, for example, the tyrant of Milan, Bernabò Visconti, who had everyone guilty of causing the slightest damage to his woods tortured and hanged, who only loved his 5,000 hunting dogs. When papal embassadors brought him a letter of excommunication, he forced them to eat the parchment it was written on. This Visconti flattered her. He wanted to win her over as a propagandist for his claims to power, and so he lured her with attacks on the worldly papal church. Catherine wrote back chillingly that God needed no criminal judges for his servants. "Keep the peace in your own cities! . . . What you need, father, is love."

There had long been talk among both the rulers and the exploited, among the nobles and the rabble, that what they had here was a living, breathing saint. Catherine had become a sign, in which people—above and beyond any superstitious sensationalism—could see, to their happiness and relief, what God must be like.

Where did the magic of her pesonality lie? Where did this exhausted, sickly creature get her truly enchanting radiance, which not even bloodthirsty *condottieri*, ruthless dictators, and the "most irritable pope in all of church history," as Urban VI has recently been called, could escape?

It's amazing, it's incomprehensible how the handsome playboys of the Sienese aristocracy hung from Catherine's lips and suddenly no longer needed to score any erotic successes. And all this simply because a pale, unworldly half-nun, from the rather shabby Fontebranda district, had had a serious talk with them.

Unbelievable stories have been handed down about the self-confident mockers whose lives Catherine turned completely upside down with a single encounter. The rich Francesco di Messer Vanni Malavolti, twenty-five years old, married to a pretty, intelligent woman, but an incurable skirt-chaser, confessed that he had suddenly begun to quake with fear when Caterina looked him in the eye. From then on he took pains to live differently.

Then there was Doctor Gabrielle da Volterra, a Franciscan who admittedly knew a lot about theology, but little about the spirit of his order (his monastic cell consisted of three fantastically decorated rooms, with a silk bed and an expensive library). *Il Dottore* came with the intention of unmasking the ignorant girl as a fraud with a barrage of scholarly arguments. By the end of his discussion he was shamefacedly handing over the key to his apartment to one of Catherine's companions and asking him to give away all his deluxe furniture.

Ser Cristofano di Gano Guidini, politician, writer, and lawyer, came full of mistrust—and later translated Catherine's *Dialogo* into Latin.

She had an almost uncanny charisma.

To understand such effects, we must, of course, free ourselves from the idea of a sanctimonious ascetic, who with bittersweet amiability and a pointed tongue goes about her work of conversion among the great sinners, who regrettably surround her and—still more regrettably—are by no means grateful for her moral sermons.

On the contrary, the reports we have of Catherine betray an inimitable charm. Instead of running around like an ambulatory prosecutor, she must have had a broad smile on her lips for everyone; she must have radiated a great deal of warmth.

"In her presence," even afterwards, Fra Raimundo was astonished to recall, "one felt a powerful stimulus to the good and such an unrestrained joy in God that every trace of sadness left the heart." Young Stefano di Corrado Maconi, who at first rejected her as most others did, and who then became one of her closest friends, recalls his first meeting with Catherine: she had smiled at him, "as if seeing once more a brother who had long been away."

At some point in the history of Christianity somebody committed an unforgivable sin. This unfortunate person set up the ghastly, terrible error that charm is something "worldly" and that pious gloom and rigid-frigid manners were part of being a Christian. We still suffer today from the consequences of this mistake.

In any case people got the idea from the young woman from Siena that when she admonished them, it was out of genuine concern. "Your soul is dying of hunger," she wrote to the above-mentioned Francesco Malavolti in a tender tone, when, after "backsliding," he no longer came near her. "Do come, dear boy."

I would like to see you stretched out on the beloved cross of the Lord . . . Let us make of the cross our couch.

But it would be in vain to wish to dine at the Father's table without caring for souls with the Son, and overlooking the food on the Son's table, namely souls. And that can't be had without suffering . . .

Therefore we, as the serving maids who have been redeemed with his blood, must not sleep, if we wish to be his true brides. We must give up sluggish sleepiness and walk on the path that is the crucified Christ.

Christ, the Crucified one, is the source at which the soul slakes its thirst. Here it receives the loving desire that must embrace all of creation to the honor of God and the salvation of souls. If you do that, your words and actions will be like glowing logs that ignite fires wherever one throws them. They can't keep for themselves the glow they bear within. That is what happens to the soul that enters the fiery oven of God's love: It will spread afar the spark that it received in the fire.

—CATHERINE IN LETTERS TO HER CIRCLE OF FRIENDS

She didn't need a crowd of sinners around her to applaud her inspiring performance, nor did she want to soak up the limelight as a mediator between God and the world. She explicitly thanked people for criticism, and once she eloquently noted that no creature can ever surrender to idle fame.

"O goodhearted love," she confessed in a prayer a year before she died, "in all my lifetime I have never loved you." And she meant it very seriously when she chided other people using the formula "we sinners." When she called anyone's attention to a mistake, she was careful to add immediately, "like me." Instead of personally reproaching anyone with such a failing, it was better to speak of it generally and tactfully.

And one should certainly avoid setting oneself up as a judge over one's fellows or making oneself the standard and then criticizing others for going their own way. On the contrary, people who have overcome their own egoism, Catherine said, "rejoice over every kind of person they meet. Variety pleases them better than the uniformity of the sort of people who would all go the same way. And God's greatness is much more readily visible this way."

True saints never make themselves the norm. They don't demand to be "followed," like some authoritarian father, who sets his children the hideous goal, "Kindly become like me."

The knowledge that *all* of us are little before God removed any false respect that Catherine, the dyer's daughter, might have felt for authorities, rulers, and earthly demigods. Her healty sense of self could, to be sure, occasionally veer into arrogance. "I'd like to see you show some manly spirit," she barked at Pope Gregory XI, in one of her typical letters:

> free from fear and selfishness and free from the carnal love of kindred. For in the sight of God it's clear to me that nothing is a greater obstacle to your holy intentions and therefore to God's honor, the growth and reform of the Church. Hence my soul longs for the day when God in his mercy takes away your evil inclinations and your lukewarmness and makes you a new man . . .

She had the habit of cunningly prefacing such letters with the humble greeting, "the unworthy, wretched daughter Catherine" recommends herself to the Holy Father in the blood of Jesus.

Io voglio, "I want," is how all her writings begin. She could be infinitely stubborn, pushy, insensitive, and at times, by our standards, quite shameless. *Sono sangue e fuoco*, "I am blood and fire," was how the unruly daughter of the tyrannical Monna Lapa described herself. Her temperament often comes through in letters, and when that happens the prophetess of patient love curses and swears.

POETRY AND ARGUMENTS

BUT OH THOSE LETTERS! Catherine had grown up apart from bourgeois Italian culture, and she had had a hard time learning to read. She may have understood some Latin, but she most certainly did not know how to write. Yet this altogether uneducated girl has left us 380 astonishing letters with a highly individual style and a logical, well-argued structure. In no way do they bristle with the emotional excess that women, according to male dogma, display in their thinking. They are written in the vivid, poetic Tuscan of the fourteenth century (which has changed little to this day); and they are full of lyrical images.

The world, she writes, has "long been deathly sick and badly wounded, but the doctors prescribe only spoiled medicines." She compares the Church to a wine cellar, in which the blood of Christ is stored away. And speaking of the discomforts bound up with good intentions, she writes: "How foolish it would be to renounce the rose because you fear the thorns." We also sometimes find mischievous passages like the greeting, "Alessa, the lazy one, would like to wrap herself up in this letter, to be able to get to you."

Back then, when there were no telephones or word processors, a letter was something rare and precious. People read them out loud to one another, over and over. They thought about them all day long, guarded them like a treasure. However, these treasures were produced very quickly. Catherine is said to have dictated the letters without long pauses to think, in an ecstatic state. Sometimes she dictated several letters to different addresses to two or three secretaries without getting mixed up.

The letters were sent to kings and shoemakers, painters, nobles, nuns, and prostitutes. They all began *Al nome di Gesù Cristo crocifisso e di Maria dolce*, "In the name of Jesus Christ crucified and sweet Mary," and always ended with the same pointed phrases: *Non dico più. Permanete nella santa e dolce dilectione di Dio. Gesù dolce. Gesù amore.* "I say no more. Remain in the holy and tender love of God. Dear Jesus, Jesus love."

She unleashed the first avalanche of letters in 1375 during a stay in Pisa. A conversation with the legate of the Queen of Cyprus had sparked her dreamy passion for the crusades; and now she wrote hastily, stormily, aggressively to God and the world, to mobilize people for the *santo passagio*, the "holy crossing."

She appealed to the king of France to drop his quarrel with England and to set forth against the Muslims instead. Pope Gregory XI was rudely requested "not to go on sleeping," but to unfurl the banner of the cross. She wrote to the Duke of Anjou and the Queen of Hungary, to the city governments of Florence and Lucca, to princes and cardinals.

Her enthusiasm for the Crusades seduced her into altogether naive ideas. Of all people she asked the *mafiosi* of the Middle Ages, the bloodthirsty *condottieri*, who sold their armies to whoever could afford them, to show themselves "true sons and soldiers of Jesus Christ" and to sacrifice their lives in the service of Jesus as reparation for their atrocities—thus Catherina wrote in a friendly letter to the *condottieri* John Hawkwood: "If battles and war seem so entertaining to you," she says both sarcastically and sympathetically, "then please don't do this anymore among Christians—that would be an insult to God—but go to the unbelievers."

She encouraged Queen Joanna of Naples, who had sent several husbands packing and was known everywhere as "the great whore," to take advantage of the "splendid moment" of the Crusade. She invited nuns to a merry martyrdom. They should go on pilgrimage to the Holy Land and let themselves be butchered there: "Let us storm ahead as a unified brigade . . . let us set off to the Holy Sepulcher to sacrifice our lives there!"

Bound up with this are remarkable plans for fraternizing with the Muslims, who have been redeemed through Christ's blood, "just as we have." Together with the Christians they were somehow to form a new people of God—though only after their subjection by the Crusaders, of course. Criticizing imperialism and commerce, which from the first used the sublime ideal of the Crusades to mask their very earthly interests, was as foreign to Catherine as it was to most of her contemporaries.

In any case, the old mystical enthusiasm for Jerusalem had been extinguished for decades. People had largely sobered up. The laconic statement of a famous hermit from the Appenines is characteristic: "If you possess Christ in the eucharist, why then should you leave him to look at a stone?" (meaning the Holy Sepulcher).

Besides, Italy was incurably torn apart. Europe was much too estranged for a great unifying idea like Catherine's dream of a

First they should root out the stinking flowers in the garden of the holy Church, whose guardians they are. They are full of trash and lechery and bloated with pride. I mean the bad shepherds and administrators, who pollute this garden and let it molder and rot. For God's sake use your power, rip these flowers up and throw them out so that they have nothing more to rule. They should know themselves and learn to rule in a holy and good life. Plant fragrant flowers, shepherds and regents, who are true servants of the Crucified, who have only the honor of God and the salvation of souls in view, and are true fathers of the poor.

O pain! How shameful to see those who should be a model of voluntary poverty, who should distribute the Church's goods to the poor, luxuriating in honors, pomp, and worldly vanities. What they are doing is a thousand times worse than if they were men of the world. Indeed many lay people put these prelates to shame with their good and holy life.

—CATHERINE TO POPE GREGORY XI

Crusade to have any chance at all. The princes of the church and leading politicians, for the most part, answered politely but evasively. The pope dreamed her dream with all his heart, but his voice was too weak to be heard in Christendom. It came all the way from Avignon to Italy, where people saw the succesor of Peter as nothing more than a straw man for the king of France. Such a disappointing figure certainly couldn't kindle storms of enthusiasm for the holy ride to the East.

In those years, Avignon, once a little fishing town on the Rhone, became the crucial point for the stubborn Italian woman. Avignon was the test—which she brilliantly passed—of her love for Christ and the Church. But at the same time, it was the obstacle on which she ultimately came to grief.

For three quarters of a century the popes had been residing there in Provençe. They had built Avignon into a fortress which combined the atmosphere of a Gothic cathedral with the cultivated depravity of a pleasure dome. Nobles, musicians, court poets, chamberlains, and tailors teemed around the papal throne. Cardinals and bishops competed to see who could run the most elegant court. A single cardinal maintained five stables for his thirty-nine horses. The beautiful countess of Turenne quite openly bought and sold church offices. And Petrarch, who was himself an office-seeker, called Avignon a "school of madness," a "Babylon" full of "old men crazy for Venus" and "highpriestly hedonism." "Instead of the Apostles, who went barefoot," Petrarch writes that, "nowadays we see cardinals on horses, which are covered with gold and champ on gold bits and which shortly will be shoed with gold, unless God reins in their shameless wealth."

To pay for all this, the papal state needed fabulous sums of money. When John XXII died 18 million gold florins were found in the papal coffers, not counting the silver and precious stones. But as a rule gigantic deficits prevailed, which they tried to cover with the sale of benefices and the levying of ever new taxes from all of Christendom. Even ordination had to be paid for dearly. "Whenever I entered the chambers of the pope's court clergy," noted an infuriated Spanish prelate, "I found money brokers and clergy busied with the counting and weighing of the florins lying there in piles . . . Wolves have the Church in their power."

Of course there was more than just immorality and extravagance in Avignon. The seven French popes who held their courts there must also have been, with one exception, honorable men of good will, unassuming, and not all that weak. Clement V saved from the Inquisition the physician Arnold of Villanova, who had openly criticized the Church. Clement VI organized relief actions for the victims of the plague, provided asylum for Jewish refugees, who were repeatedly suspected of having caused the epidemic, and excommunicated their persecutors. Innocent VI sent a great part of the papal household back home and had the feared *condottiere* Hawkwood imprisoned by a no-less-warlike archbishop.

But such sympathetic traits don't change the fact that the papacy in Avignon was completely subservient to the diplomatic interests of France and was increasingly alienating itself from the other countries of Europe, above all Italy. Of the 134 cardinals appointed in this period, 113 were French. Boccaccio, Petrarch, and similar critics who called the pope back to the Roman heart of the Church, were under no illusion that morals would be any purer in Rome. But they wanted a pope more independent of political intrigues in a less wealthy environment.

Above all, the French legates, whom the pope had appointed in the Papal States (which still occupied a large part of central Italy), had to embitter Italian patriots. Many of the French behaved like petty tyrants, carrying on like "godless bloodsuckers" (Catherine), squeezing more and more taxes out of the impoverished population. By 1375, the measure was full: The republics of Tuscany exported the courage to revolt into the papal States, where the cities began rebelling against papal rule. The Florentines' blood-red banner of lilies led the way with the golden motto *Libertà*: Freedom.

Gregory XI, who had already become pope at the age of thirty six, had character. He was a conscientious priest, an admirer of Cicero and a highly cultivated man, but hesitant and easily swayed. He stood helpless in the face of this militant hunger for freedom. He adhered to a long-outdated papal feudalism that would continue to survive as a dream for another five hundred years until in our day Paul VI gave away the golden papal crown and John Paul I renounced his coronation altogether.

Now, for the first time, Rome asked the strange letter-writing woman, who, after all, came from the heartland of the revolt, to serve as a mediator. She was supposed to get Pisa and Lucca not to join the Tuscan city alliance, organized against the pope by Florence. Very cleverly Catherine turned first to the ladies of Lucca, so as to win over the aldermen by way of political discussions at home, but all she managed to achieve was a delay.

The conflict sharpened when, in a clumsy maneuver, the pope once again packed the College of Cardinals with Frenchmen. Among them was the worst of the despotic legates, Gérard du Puy, whom the people had finally imprisoned in his defiant fortress in Perugia.

Catherine was caught between two fronts. She was inwardly torn, faithful to Rome but a Sienese, unconditionally devoted to the pope but swept along by her oppressed compatriots' drive for freedom. She resolved the conflict by working out her own opinions and activities, bombarding Rome with letters and telling the pope straight out what she thought of his leadership style and his court lackeys.

BITING LIKE A RABID DOG

THE TENOR OF THESE letters is always the same: the pope must break away from his dependencies, leave Avignon, return to Rome and replace the French governors with priests who think of themselves as pastors rather than generals.

Catherine cried over the Church, deformed and besmirched with greed, pitiless cruelty, and bloodlust. "Her heart, the glowing love, is lost," she writes to Peter's successor in Avignon. "Give it back to her! Godless extortionists have sucked so much of her blood that she has gone deadly pale."

She blames selfishness for the desolate condition of the Church. She faults the egoism of shepherds who have forgotten their duty, who think only of money and honorific titles: "Wretched selfishness has poisoned the whole world and the mystical Body of the Church, it has made the garden of the Bride of Christ run to seed. Evil-smelling weeds have sprouted in it."

Catherine's tone takes on a cutting sharpness when it comes to these prelates and bearers of the purple, who were appointed to be converters and became instead "parasites and bloodsuckers of the soul." They should have been pillars, but they have shrunken to blades of straw. "You are not aromatic flowers, but a stench that contaminates the whole world. . . . You should be angels on earth, to save us from the devil in Hell and lead back the scattered sheep to the holy Church. Now you yourselves have become devils!"

If a biting dog could write letters, it would do it in Catherine's rabid style. She barks at the bishops, "bloated with pride." She tells them they should seek God's honor instead of earthly vanities and not "live like pigs." She chides priests for dealing ruthlessly with their fellow men and women and "making their belly their God."

Members of religious orders squirrel away their own private funds: "All their ambition is aimed at decorating their bodies and their cells, and walking around town, chattering away. Their fate is like that of a fish out of water: it perishes." In opposition to all these people she cites the example of the poor, humiliated Christ on the cross in the hymnlike visions of the *Dialogo*:

> He hangs his head to greet you, he bears the crown on his head to adorn you, he holds his arms out wide to embrace you, his feet are pierced through to abide with you.

"I say to you, my father in Jesus Christ, come soon and humbly as a lamb." That was her constantly repeated plea to the hesitating shepherds in Avignon. "Answer the Holy Spirit. He calls you. I say to you: Come, come, come! And don't wait for time, for time doesn't wait for you." The pope should return to his "starving flock" and set up the sign of a renewed poor Church, "of manly spirit" and without fear. Indeed God is to make Gregory "a new man," who bears within himself a glowing desire for *riformazione*—reform.

That was her whole longing, the chief point around which all her thinking revolved. "The reform of the Church is the most urgent and important task," she wrote to Dominican brothers in Spoleto. "Compared with that, everything else is of second rank. Let us help the Bride of Christ, the Church . . . Drop everything else, and come to your Mother's aid!"

Hence the high-handed, demanding tone to the pope, whom she threatened with the wrath of God when she was at a loss as to what to do: "If I were in your place I would be afraid of the threatening divine judgment." In these letters there is no malicious raving or caviling, no crowing over mystical experiences, just pain, concern, and passionate longing for a Church that Christ could rejoice in.

Dolce babbo mio, "my sweet daddy," she addresses the pope with Mediterranean tenderness, *dolce Cristo in terra,* "sweet Christ on earth." And we hear a note of something like wounded love when in the next moment she flings abuse at him. At bottom Gregory thought the same way she did (he himself wanted to return to Rome, and he ordered all bishops and abbots who were living the high life in Avignon to move back to their abandoned dioceses and monasteries). He felt the way his critic Catherine did, but he was living in a golden cage, or "like a lamb among the wolves" (Catherine).

"Get up, father, don't lie idle," she encouraged him. But soon, she was making more demands: "The wish to gloss over and quiet down everything is the cruelest of all. If you don't cut and burn the wound with fire and iron, but merely put ointment on it, it will never heal. It will get all poisoned, and often enough this brings death." No, he was to proceed strongly and consistently, no longer taking part in wars, but restoring morality and credibility in his own house.

Catherine had a keen sense for the sore points of a Church leadership intent on maintaining its power. And so she comforts the pope by telling him that if this reform program costs the Church status and possessions, that will only be a blessing, because the Church will at least have been forced to attend to its actual responsibilities.

In an enigmatic passage she argues that God has apparently granted "that his bride have countries and possessions taken away from her, in order to show that the holy Church should return to its original poverty, humility, and gentleness." And, "the real treasure of the Church is the blood of Christ shed for the redemption of souls. This blood was not shed for the sake of worldly possessions, but for the redemption of humanity. . . . So it is much better to let the gold of worldly possessions go hang rather than lose the gold of spiritual possessions . . . goodness, love, peace."

"Don't disappoint me!" she warns Gregory. "Otherwise I would have to appeal to the Crucified, the only one I have left." This is her only threat. She doesn't threaten to fall away or to found a new Church of the "pure," as others had done. She doesn't raise the specter of a popular uprising or of war with the troops of the rebellious alliance. That is not the way to renew the Church, as she knows. "Not with the sword, nor through war and cruelties will it recover its beauty, but through peaceableness, humble and continuous appeals, through sweat and tears."

During this time Catherine was constantly striving to defuse the conflict between Florence and Rome, placating the city and soothing the pope. "One conquers rebels with kindness and patience," she enjoined the pope, reminding him that in the face of the injustice of the legates, Florence believed it had no choice but to act as it did. She again asked the Florentines not to make war on God's representative. "However greatly the father may offend against the son, that doesn't give the son the right to make war upon him. . . . He is always his debtor, because he has his being from him."

Such well-intentioned images from family life were naturally not enough to dissolve the accumulated bitterness on both sides. The obstinate Gregory wanted to display his authority, and so he ordered the entire Florentine leadership to report to Avignon. When the councillors missed the deadline, he excommunicated them all and imposed an interdict on Florence: Church services and the dispensation of the sacraments were immediately forbidden in the city. Anyone who maintained contact with a Florentine would likewise fall under the ban of excommunication. Debts incurred by, or contracts signed with, a Florentine were cancelled.

In this hopeless situation Catherine went off with a group of twenty faithful followers on the difficult 430 mile journey to Avignon (it mustn't be forgotten that on its peace missions the *famiglia* fed itself through begging). She was hardly sending the embittered city leadership into the lion's den, but she did send a pair of friends or her own conscience. *Io muoio di dolore, ma non posso morire* is a line from one of her desperate letters to the pope: "I am dying of grief, and yet I cannot die."

Scarcely had the exhausted travelers arrived in Avignon than the Inquisition also put in appearance. It sent a three-man crew to Catherine's place to sound out this self-appointed church reformer from the Italian provinces. Yet, as she had already succeeded in doing before, here too Catherine dumbfounded this clutch of star theologians with her unsophisticated faith and her solid knowledge of religious matters. If she hadn't managed to convince those stern gentlemen, the pope's personal physician later divulged to

one of Catherine's companions, "This would have been the worst
trip she ever took."

Shortly thereafter she had an audience with Pope Gregory that
labored under certain language difficulties. Raymond of Capua had
to translate Catherine's Sienese dialect into official Latin. Evidently this didn't in the least impede or fluster the young visitor.

To the pope's skeptical question of how she believed she could
judge the circumstances at his court after only a few days, "Catherine, who till then had stood there looking small and inconspicuous,
suddenly shot up and aswered with a steady voice: 'Since the honor
of the almighty God is at stake, I fearlessly confess that the sins of
the papal court stink all the way to Siena, where I come from. These
sins have caused me more disgust than they do the people here,
who daily defile themselves anew with them!"

"The pope fell silent," Raimundo goes on to report. But he didn't
send this bothersome creature home.

He also listened calmly to her pleas for the Florentines. But he
didn't commit himself and showed that he didn't think much of
the readiness of the city, already harshly punished, to be reconciled with him. And sure enough, when the Florentine envoys
entered Avignon, they would have nothing to do with Catherine's
efforts at mediation. They also refused to go along with the pope's
grossly exaggerated conditions. (He is said to have demanded three
million gold florins in reparations.) The stiff-necked Gregory was
likewise not to be moved to compromises.

At first she was surprised and indignant ("With your sudden
inspirations," she wrote to Florence, you are ruining what I sow").
Catherine had once again learned that peace-loving idealists often
serve only as a front for the master deceivers of politics. She returned
downcast to Siena, preached in the marketplaces and meadows all
around the city, and made peace where she could.

Meanwhile papal troops were on the march to Florence, commanded by the hardboiled Cardinal Robert of Geneva. Cesena was
the one city in Tuscany faithful to Rome, and of all places, he abandoned Cesena to his soldiers for plundering. When the citizens

defended themselves, the cardinal called in the troops of the notorious John Hawkwood for reinforcements and unleashed a horrible bloodbath.

At least four thousand persons, men, women, old people, and little children, were slaughtered in a single night. "Things happened that would make you lose your faith," was the judgment of one chronicler on this permanent mark of shame in the history of the papacy. The poet Franco Sacchetti gave Gregory the contemptuous nickname of *papa guastamondo*, the world-wrecking pope.

She would rather be dead, Catherine confessed, than have to look on that scene. This high-spirited woman, who could dictate so self-assuredly in a state of ecstasy, felt merely small and helpless. In despair she once more asked the pope to stop waging war and to root out the "stinking flowers" in the Church's garden. Then the correspondence broke off.

In all this one might overlook the fact that by the time of the massacre of Cesena, Pope Gregory had already returned to Rome. After six years of maneuvering he had finally prevailed against the bitter resistance of his enormous family (his cousins and nephews crowded the papal court), the curia and political France, and left Avignon. Catherine had certainly strengthened his resolve with her letters and her visit to France, where she was called the "terror of Avignon" and was mercilessly fought by the pope's sisters and nieces. Yet she didn't deserve the sole credit for his return to Rome.

Although contact was broken off for a while, shortly thereafter she asked the pope once again for mediation. In 1378 she arrived in Florence—and landed in the middle of the civil war between Guelfs and Ghibellines.

The conflict with the pope had long since become a power struggle between rich and poor within the city, in which Catherine could accomplish nothing. She herself fell into danger because she was living in a Guelf house. A shouting mob pressed in upon her with swords drawn, but according to eyewitness reports it gave way before her sovereign courage. Sadly the failed peacemaker went back to Siena: "I am going away with a heart full of sorrow and care," she wrote to the Florentine councillors in farewell.

"YOUR DEAD CHILD, HUMANITY"

WHY WAS SHE continually getting mixed up in such complicated political confrontations? Why didn't she stick with the theme that she quite obviously had a better command of, namely, church reform?

Because she couldn't do otherwise. Catherine's religion was concrete. She couldn't pray in church for peace and then not hear the clatter of arms out in the street or fail to see the blood that flowed. She prayed that God might have mercy on his "dead child, humanity." She felt driven to activities that we call "political" and that are nevertheless religious to the core: peace should reign again, justice should come to stay, a "world completely enslaved to death" (Catherine) should be ordered in love and justice.

The prerequisite for this was a simple acknowledgment of the fact that all men and women are God's children with rights and dignity. God alone is the Lord, the mighty of this earth are only temporary administrators. As far back as the fourteenth century, people like Catherine already had some notion of human rights.

In Catherine's letters the partisanship for the victims and the exploited and the marginalized is striking. This mystic never straddled the fence as some pastoral letter writers do today. She did not limit herself to helpless entreaties for everyone just to keep the peace and to be content. She was biased like her Lord, she charged, her evaluations and judgments were clear. Catherine called tyrants by name and made concrete demands.

"God has made you a man, why do you make yourself a beast?" she asked her bloodthirsty contemporaries (in a prayer). She saw the root of all evil in arrogant selfishness—when politics is carried on only for one's own fame and purse, and not so that the citizens can live lives more worthy of human beings. It was out of self-love, "blind with fear that he could lose his post," that Pilate sent Jesus to the cross. "I have the impression," Catherine said, "that the whole world is full of people like Pilate."

Meanwhile under chaotic circumstances a new pope had been chosen in Rome. With the cry *Romano volemo o almeno italiano!*—"We want a Roman or at least an Italian!"—six thousand armed men from the Romagna were besieging the Vatican. The terrified cardinals asked for soldiers for protection. A scaffold stood ready in St. Peter's square for disturbers of the peace. Thinking it a clever chess move, the cardinals actually enthroned a non-Frenchman for the first time in sixty-three years. The new pope was an Italian, the archbishop of Bari, but he had proved himself in Avignon as chancellor of the Church.

Urban VI was definitely not a straw man for the French or for any Italian aristocratic mafia. He was a monkish type with a well-developed conscience, seriously trying to do something about reform: "I want to clean up the Church," he declared, "and I will clean it up!" But unfortunately in his new office he quickly turned into a real Ivan the Terrible, unlovable, surly, irascible and irritable, at odds with the whole world. Later on he displayed increasingly morbid signs. He had five rebellious cardinals half-starved and finally tortured to death.

The diminutive Neapolitan mercilessly took revenge on the high lords of the Curia, the French nobles, who had no doubt clearly shown him their snooty contempt—and came off the worse for it. A year had not passed since his election when the cardinals left him in the lurch. They explained that he had been chosen under duress; and then they made, of all people, Robert of Geneva, the "butcher of Cesena," the antipope. He resided in Avignon, and the "great western schism" began. For forty years it would tear the Christian world apart.

Catherine is supposed to have foreseen the brotherly feud. Immediately after his election, she had encouraged Urban VI in enthusiastic letters: "Tackle the work of reform boldly like a true knight and righteous shepherd . . . Cut out vice!" Urban was supposed to "sweep out the rotten stuff," that is, reform the College of Cardinals—which he did, but the newly appointed Italians couldn't prevail against the experienced power clique at the top of the Church.

When the cardinals, whom he had all too often snubbed and treated with unimaginable harshness, had abandoned him, she wrote a letter of consolation to the broken man on the Chair of St. Peter. She was invited by him to Rome, and at Gregory's instigation she delivered a fiery speech to the fainthearted cardinals—a unique event in church history.

But nothing changed. The antipope in Avignon won over Emperor Charles IV, Flanders, England, southern Germany, Hungary, and a series of other countries. Both popes excommunicated each other, both launched troops against each other. Catherine invented a council of mystics, a gathering of saintlike hermits, which was supposed to advise and enlighten the pope. It was assembled only with difficulty, and it disappeared from church history without leaving a word behind.

Catherine's letters to cardinals and princes urging them to remain loyal to the legally elected pope had no success either. "The whole world is now split," she wrote, shaken to the king of Hungary, "Hell is gaining ground . . ." Her constant appeal *Pace, pace!* (peace, peace!) was in vain. Her profound argument, that God could not dwell in a heart filled with hatred, went for nought: "Anyone who murders an enemy thinks he is only killing him, but first and foremost he is slaying himself."

When she found out about Gregory's disastrous escapades, she carefully tried to pacify him ("Action without measure devastates more than it orders") and to dissuade him from his harshness ("Justice without mercy would be darkness"). With creative irony she sent him a pair of preserved oranges in the Vatican. She asked him to please take an example from these bitter fruits: when they are handled properly they emit a sweet aroma. But Pope Urban was not ready, and perhaps no longer able, to learn this lesson.

Politically speaking, Catherine had obviously failed. She herself, to be sure, once observed quite realistically that even if the great success didn't materialize, "at least the path will have been made ready." In the short span of life that still remained to her now, she again withdrew more forcefully into silence. This points to

Thou fire and abyss of love . . . Thou fool for love, do you then need your creature? It seems to me that you do, for you behave as if you couldn't live without it. Yet you are withal the life from which everything has life and without which nothing lives? Why then are you so foolishly fond of your creature?

Because you have fallen in love with your creature, you found your pleasure and delight in him, and are as it were intoxicated with care for his salvation. It flees you and you go off in search of him, and you feel driven to get close to him. You could not get still closer to him than by clothing yourself with his humanity.

disappointment and resignation, but perhaps it also signals another activity no less valuable from a Christian standpoint.

For Catherine's "inner life," her relationship to God, her trailblazing mysticism was something extraordinarily active. It was all love, passion, longing. "What is my nature, you unfathomable love?" she asked God and answered her own question: "It is fire, because You yourself are nothing but a fire of love."

"GOD, YOU FOOL FOR LOVE!"

SHE CALLED GOD "the fire that is always burning." In Catherine's work God appears as a pulsating center of energy and not as a wearily, awaited judge of the world, "fire and abyss of love," "unfathomable love," "sea of peace," "poor lamb, bled white."

The love of God created us; God can do nothing but love. Indeed she calls him a "fool for love," who pursues his creature, "drunk with care." "Because you are completely in love with your creature, you brought him forth from yourself and fashioned him after your image and likeness."

Catherine's trust in God was enormous, because his compassion is infinite. "Out of the nothingness of guilt," she has God say about a sinner, "out of this thornbush, which wounds the soul, I unexpectedly pluck the rose of his salvation." Jesus, the sweet eternal truth, *dolce Verità eterna*, was her friend, quite unsentimentally and as a matter of course. She experienced Christ as an elementary power that shaped her life and blew sky high everything usually taken for granted, even the commandments of justice. "My compassion opposes justice," God promises the dissolute prelates, in the *Dialogo*, "in order to overcome it with the power of compassion."

Because God is "our lover," we too must "lovingly run toward him," go with him on the way of the cross and above all love people. "Whoever really loves me is a blessing for his fellows. That has to be so because love for Me and for one's fellows is one and the same love. The soul loves its fellow man just as much as it loves me, for love that it bears for him pours forth from Me." God does not save us without our cooperation.

More and more this apparently enraptured mystic learned to love the world. Catherine initially saw in the "tyrannical world" an enemy of the soul and the chief obstacle to a controlled, rational life, but she changed her mind. She wrote to an abbess from Siena: "If you say to me that you would like to cease to care about earthly things, then I answer: things are earthly to the extent that we make them so." Everything, she said, arises from the goodness of God. "Thus everything is good and perfect in its way. Therefore I don't want you to avoid taking pains under the pretext that this is a matter of earthly things. You should keep the eye of the heart directed to God and strive for souls."

The good things of this world become dangerous and burdensome only when a person misuses them. You lose some of your dignity to inferior things, if you "cling to things without orienting them to God." Those are standards that in the twentieth century we need more than ever before.

It's considerably harder for us today to deal with Catherine's "holy hatred" of herself and her wildly excessive guilt feelings. Her basic mystical experience is called (again a conversation with God): "I am he who is—you are she who is not." Of himself the person is nothing. Only love has produced him, and if God were to withdraw his love, the person would cease to exist.

Strictly speaking, of course, this total dependency of the tiny creature whom only God can make great and happy through his love is the basis for human dignity. Strictly speaking, Catherine's guilt-feelings show—sometimes she makes her own weakness entirely responsible for the fact that church reform is not succeeding—just how much God, in her opinion, thinks humans are capable of. Strictly speaking, the "holy hatred" she propagated, the "contempt for ourselves," applies only to the powerful drive to egoism. And again and again her glowing trust in the benevolent God shines through; from him she wants for herself such an excess of love that even hell will collapse under its weight.

Catherine's slow dying in Rome lasted for months. Although she was suffering from the consequences of a cerebral hemorrhage, every morning she made a pilgrimage of more than a mile to the grave of St. Peter, to pray there until vespers, "to work a little in the boat of the holy Church," as she called it. She must have suffered terribly from the condition of this Church; she pleaded with God to take her heart and press it out over the countenance of his bride, the Church. In loyalty to the Church, which is "built on love," and makes Christ visible, not for a moment, for all her clear-sighted criticism of the Church, did she waver.

She broke down a second time in St. Peter's and for the next eight weeks wrestled with death, without being able even to lift her head. She looked "like the way one paints a corpse in pictures," reports the eyewitness and friend Barduccio dei Canigiami, protruding bones under thin skin. Amid self-reproaches (she said she was "indifferent, ignorant and ungrateful") and prayers for the pope and the Church, she died on April 29, 1380, thirty-three years old.

The wake lasted three days and three nights. At her funeral in the church of Santa Maria sopra Minerva the Romans wept so loudly that the preacher never got to speak.

"A woman who wasn't silent in church" is how a modern biography calls her. In the beginning she seems to have been rather bashful.

When after years of being withdrawn, Christ sent her among people, according to Raimundo, she resisted with the argument: "But I'm just a pitiful thing and the weakest of all. I am a woman, my sex is in the way of all this, you know after all, how contemptously men think of women . . ."

To which Christ replied almost indignantly: "Am I not the one who has created all people, men and women? Can't I pour out the grace of my spirit where I wish?"

Even today this dialogue would have to put to shame many power-conscious masculine egoists in the Church. Perhaps the sign that the mystic Catherine set up with her courageous appearance can only be rightly understood now.

Back then, at any rate, it remained an isolated episode—although within the Church in those years women experienced in general an increased appreciation. In the mendicant orders around 1300, there were already as many sisters as brothers. In German nunneries a highly individual mysticism was taking shape, and the Franciscan wandering preacher movement was decisively stamped by women. But after some time, this development again came to a halt.

"This weak woman puts us to shame," Pope Urban VI is supposed to have said at that time, before the disheartened cardinals, when Catherine delivered a rousing sermon. A later successor of Urban VI, Paul VI, was no doubt paying off an old debt, when in 1970, he declared Catherine, along with Teresa of Ávila, a *doctor ecclesiae*, a Doctor of the Church, and praised her "glowing superhuman wisdom." Apart from them not a single other woman in church history had received this title of honor.

Or might there be a future in the evaluation by a still later successor of the unfortunate Urban, namely Pope John Paul II, who scarcely three weeks after his election, visited Catherine's grave in Rome? Pope Karol Wojtyla confessed, "In St. Catherine of Siena I see a visible sign for the vocation of women in the Church."

THE TORN CHRISTIAN

AURELIUS AUGUSTINUS,

TEACHER OF RHETORIC

(354–430)

Conversions Often Last an Entire Lifetime

> You have struck our heart with your love,
> and like arrows that stick in the heart,
> we bear your words in us.

*H*e wasn't *the* playboy who, unstable in his younger years, always on the hunt for adventures, wandered through bars and bordellos, changed girls like shirts and then all of a sudden—moved by the tears of his pious mother—got converted and became a strict ascetic.

He wasn't *the* enemy of the body and every kind of erotic sensation, who (as one furious critic of the Church has put it) "didn't turn religious until he was all whored out," and with his teaching on sin shaped the destiny of millions "of sexually repressed and inhibited westerners."

Finally he also wasn't *the* Church Father pure and simple, against whose work all Christian theology would have to be measured, an intellectual genius who some would say ranks right after Paul and Plato, unsurpassable, incomparable, and timelessly valid till the distant end of Church history.

Aurelius Augustinus himself would have strictly rejected such facile judgments. He knew about the fragility of his life, about the many layers of his personality. Above all, he knew about the changing nuances in his work that for all its fullness was so fragmentary, out of which, today, overhasty people still like to pick out a few details in order to draw a caricature of the author.

Augustine dealt more carefully with his writings. At the end of his life he began to work through and comment on whole books and manuscripts. At that time he quoted against himself the passage in Scripture: "Where there are many words no doubt there will be sin." And if anyone believes he'll never have to recant any of his statements, that points rather to a complete fool than to a perfect sage.

To be sure, Augustine *is* considered a great western Doctor of the Church. The legacy of antiquity came down to the Christian Middle Ages as filtered through and stamped by Augustine. He wrote an entire library about God and human nature, about the Church and the world. For hundreds of years he was invoked by the philosophy of nature, epistemology, ethics, the theology of history and scriptural studies. He is the father of the doctrine of grace; he laid the groundwork for a theology of the laity in the church; he founded disciplines such as hermeneutics and catechetics, and with his epic hymn-like style was even a shaping influence on Church Latin.

But Augustine's theology, which stamped western intellectual life for centuries, never became abstract. What he thought and wrote always had something to do with his own life story.

That probably also makes him so attractive, so interesting, and vulnerable: The man we meet here is no cool scholar, no saint up in the clouds, no plaster figurine of unreachable virtues, as perfect as he is boring, a creature from a special world.

Quite the contrary, we find a person full of passions, impetuous, vital, in love with everything beautiful and also a little in love with his own complicated soul, at times unbridled and weak, but with the strong conviction that there must be something above and behind this life . . .

This person, who radiated more fire than warmth, wasn't actually a saint to like, a saint for feeling secure. But we sense in him the brother who is familiar with our problems and who knows the tornness of the modern Christian from his own experience.

In the beginning of his famous *Confessions* he challenges the reader to praise God, the reader who as a human being is "only a part of your creation," bearing with him his mortality and weakness. And then come the words about the restless heart, so often quoted that we can hardly hear them anymore—and yet this restless heart is the actual code name for Augustine's pulsating life: *Tu excitas, ut laudare te delectet, quia fecisti nos ad te et inquietum est cor nostrum, donec requiescat in te*—"You make it a joy for us to praise you, for you created us for you, and our heart is restless till it rests in you."

The Last Gasps of a World Empire

Augustine lived in a time of upheavals and catastrophes. When he was a child, under Julian the Apostate (361–63), pagan philosophy and oriental cults were making a last tremendous effort against victorious Christianity. As an adult he experienced the establishment of the Catholic state church under Theodosius the Great, while paganism continued to scrape along among peasants and intellectuals. As an old man he saw the destroyers of the empire, to whom the future belonged: the Eastern Roman empire split off from the West, which was cut to pieces and then abandoned by the self-emancipating proletariat. Byzantium attempted to create a new edition of the old empire after the model of dictatorial regimes: omnipotent emperors surrounded themselves with incense, slavish courtiers, amd secret police (Augustine called them *agentes in rebus*).

While the Roman world Empire was breathing its last, the Western emperors transferred their court to Gaul and into the Danubian provinces, where armies secured the threatened frontier. The little people paid for this arms build-up and for the magnificent display of the upper classes with a doubling of taxes.

But for a long time a new, Christian Rome had been in the making. The broad streets were paved with smashed votive inscriptions of the pagan gods of the city. Christianity grew beyond the role of a state religion chosen out of political calculation. It also gained increasingly strong social and intellectual influence. Theological disputes heated minds in a way we can now scarcely imagine. In bakeries, in the streets and market places, people discussed the divinity of Jesus and the Holy Spirit.

The Roman province of North Africa, where Aurelius Augustinus was born on November 13, 354, in the little town of Tagaste (today Souk Ahras in Algeria) was no exception to this. For ancient Africa was Latin cultural soil, it thought of itself as the outskirts of Europe. Latin was Augustine's mother tongue. His father Patricius, a petty bourgeois official and landowner, was almost crushed by the burden of taxes. He proudly bore the title of Roman citizen, but there was such a chronic lack of money in his house that at the age of sixteen Aurelius had to interrupt his studies. Augustine accidentally reveals later in his *Confessions* just how carefully the family had to calculate their finances. He devotes an entire chapter to the sneaky Roman students who liked laying claim to his services as a teacher of rhetoric, but who disappeared without a trace when it came time to pay.

His father is said to have been a difficult, violent character and indifferent to religion. His mother, Monica, was altogether different. Canonized by the Church like her son, a dazzling figure, a mother hen, solicitous, demanding but tolerant too, understanding, discreet.

With their preference for the genius-neurotic side of St. Augustine, psychologists have seized upon the conflict-ridden family life of his parental home: Doesn't the strictly-raised Monica look like a frigid person? Didn't she evidently want her son to love God more than his father? Didn't it necessarily lead to a clash with his pious mother when Augustine identified with his father, who prized status, and tried to find success in society? Didn't Monica make a big theatrical number of her pain by continually wailing to him about one thing or other and innoculating him with a guilty conscience through portentous dreams?

On the other hand she responded with great understanding to his first experiences with girls. She showed sympathies for classical education. She reacted with calm restraint and not at all hysterically to her husband's constant adulterous escapades. Monica was in any case an enormously dominant personality. "My life and hers became *one*," Augustine noted after her death, "and now it was torn apart, since she left me."

Aurelius was to have it better than his father, who played the proud Roman in the marketplace of Tagaste and wore out wretched clothes at home. With the help of a rich benefactor he got a good education, which would open up a career for him as a rhetorician and lawyer in the emperial administration.

Back then rhetoric was the worthy art, constructed with extreme complexity and quite hard to learn, of speaking convincingly, pointedly, and correctly for classic sensibilities. A respected rhetorician like Augustine would never have dreamed of using his art for shamelessly mendacious stump speeches or of selling people expensive products they had absolutely no need for. "Words," said Augustine, full of respect for language, "are select, precious vessels."

The literary education of his time consisted of grammatical training and intimate familiarity with the classical poets. Augustine's work bristles with literal quotations and encoded allusions. He didn't know much about science, and even his knowledge of philosophy remained relatively meager.

Augustine concluded his studies in Carthage, the worldly metropolis of Roman Africa. He was quite obsessed with circus games and theatrical productions—the latter, he admits in the *Confessions*, provided continuous new fuel for the fire of his passion. Pious biogaphers like to misread this fact. Carthage's shows and circus arenas were not the same as the nightclubs and porn theaters of today's metropolises.

He "plunged" into love, he reports in the same book, "and secretly arriving to the bond of enjoying; I was with much joy bound with sorrow-bringing embracements, even that I might be scourged with iron burning rods of jealousy and suspicions, and fears, and angers, and brawls."

But even today the first passionate boiling-over of emotions sometimes sounds just as dramatic when we read of it in the diaries of young people. Upon closer inspection, the supposedly unbridled enjoyment of Augustine's early years turns out to be a transitional phase of puberty: lurid dreams with no practice worth mentioning.

Anyhow, Augustine never went beyond the standards of the era. At age of seventeen he took a concubine to whom he was faithful for fourteen years. He called the son they had together Adeodatus, "a gift from God." And as early as eighteen he was flirting with an ascetical life of discipline and self-control: "Give me chastity and continence," he prayed with appealing candor, "but not right away!"

Why didn't he marry Adeodatus's mother? We get the impression that he simply exploited the woman and then turned his back on her, in order to live a "pious" life. That would be nothing but blasphemous hypocrisy if it came at the cost of other people. But the situation wasn't quite so simple.

For one thing, cohabitation, without a marriage license was very common in the late Roman world; it was even tolerated to a certain extent by the Church. In the year 400 the Council of Toledo decided that concubinage was no ground for exclusion from the Christian community, if the "form" of Christian marriage, i.e., primarily fidelity to one's partner, was preserved. Secondly, gentlemen from the so-called better circles of late Rome were accustomed to acting just like some top managers today: they kept a mistress who was far below them on the social ladder. The famous (man-made) laws of that time didn't forbid a rising young man like Augustine from sleeping with some workman's daughter. But they did prohibit him from marrying her.

And later on he did get rid of his son's mother when Monica came up with a rich heiress from a good family. This doesn't shed much luster on either of them, nor on the morality of the Church either. Pope Leo praised it as a "sign of moral improvement" when anyone dismissed his "illegal" partner in order to enter a legitimate marriage (and thereby make a considerably better match). Adeodatus' mother bravely packed her bags and swore "never to have anything to do with another man again."

But things hadn't got that far yet. In Tagaste, Augustine began to teach as a *rhetor*; soon afterwards he opened a school in Carthage, the metropolis, which at the time was the second city in the empire after Rome. He made an arrogant, dazzling appearance. Everything came so easily to him. The young people hung on his lips transfixed. The Roman proconsuls and administrative officials needed good teachers and skilled lawyers,so his supply of future pupils was assured.

But Augustine had set his sights higher. At the age of twenty-nine he moved to Rome, and a year after that to Milan, where the emperor lived. Perhaps he could get a position as governor. He was utterly sick with ambition, he writes in the *Confessions*, and yet he wasn't really happy about it. When Augustine, the professor of rhetoric, had to deliver a speech in praise of the emperor's eight-year-old son, who had been made a consul, he clearly felt his "misery." It was a gushing piece of flattery, "in which I told lies so that the liar could share the favor of those who knew about the lie."

"I found that I was in a bad way," he would later recall of this apparently so successful, brilliant time. "And even if happiness once smiled at me from afar, I couldn't bring myself to grasp it."

"But from afar your true compassion circled over me."

"O TRUTH, TRUTH!"

OUR MANNER OF venerating the saints isn't fair. We sing songs of praise to them—and falsify their life story. We build memorials and altars to them—and distort their personality beyond recognition.

We make them into supermen—just so we won't have to walk in their footsteps.

We construct two classes of Christians: *There* the ones chosen by God, the perfect, who were at some point struck by the overpowering ray of grace. *Here* the mediocre, average, well-meaning, relatively decent ones, but without any special élan or claim to fame. We could never be saints! Nor do we have the least desire to.

But this double-decker Christendom is wrong—comfortable, false, and dangerous. There is only *one* Gospel and only *one* message of happiness. There is only *one* obligation, to come close to God, which holds true for all men and women. There is only *one* grace—though, of course,there are various personal and social conditions for starting out. And first and foremost there is no all-transforming lightning bolt from heaven, but only arduous strivings and lifelong processes of conversion—for every one of us. Even for those who later on get called "saints."

Aurelius Augustinus didn't first become a religious person with his famous "conversion experience," which can be dated exactly in 386. He was religious long before that, he was on the way to God from his early years. All his life he was filled with passion for more, "longing for the totally Other."

Even in the turbulence of his student years he believed in God; and he had a relationship, even if a vague one, with Christ. But the Catholic notion of God was too personal and too human for him. He would have liked something more abstract, more spiritualized, more philosophical. As an eighteen-year-old, he was thrilled by a reading of Cicero, whom he thanked for a "burning love of wisdom."

"O truth, truth!" he later recalled, "how intimately even then the marrow of my soul was longing for you!" His interest was aimed at the eternal wisdom in itself, not at some philosophical theory or other. But it was his own intellectual skepticism, that fear of commitment typical of an enlightened member of the educated classes, on which this piercing longing kept coming to grief year after year.

His turning to the sect of the Manichaeans has to be understood from the standpoint of this inner conflict. For the teaching

of Mani (executed in Persia in 276) was understood as an intellectually higher development of Christianity, as a religion of the elect.
It seemed to outshine and correct everything that had gone before.
It had a strong scientific coloring and a philosophical formulation,
a mixture of effective propaganda and attractive secret rites. And
it was comfortable into the bargain.

Like many black-and-white thinkers before and after them, the
Manichaeans divided the world into a "kingdom of light" and a
"kingdom of darkness." The good in man, the soul, could be released
from "lower nature" and led back into the realm of light through
sexual continence, a special diet, and meaningful rituals. Of course
only the few "elect" were bound to those responsibilities. For the second-class Manichaeans, the "hearers," it was enough to perform services for the elect. They needn't rack their brains over their sins,
because their still unpurified, compulsion-driven nature was responsible for that. Augustine: "At that time I still believed that it wasn't
we who sinned but some other nature in us. . . ."

Augustine soon understood that this was a fairly transparent,
stop-gap measure: "But in truth it was I, entirely myself, (who
sinned) and only to harm me had my godlessness divided me in
two. . . ." The skeptic began to take a position toward the evil *in*
himself. Still, he was so fascinated by the Manichaeans' image of
Christ that he continued to sympathize with the sect for nine years.
For this Christ was wisdom pure and simple, the fulfillment of his
philosophical dreams: "He came, he separated us from the errors
of the world," it says in the hymns of the Manichaeans. "He brought
us a mirror, we looked into it, we saw the universe inside."

But we can only admire this philosopher god, we cannot love
him. The Christ of the Manichaeans brought Augustine enlightenment, but no warmth. He felt homeless, driven this way and that,
torn by a thousand longings and expectations. He wanted so much
to know where he belonged, and yet he was at sea in every respect,
compulsive, hungry for experience, not satsified with anything,
wanting to make the most of everything, an intellectual adventur-
er and a hot-blooded sensualist. Later he would put all-too-vigorous

God, through whom everything that could not of itself be strives toward being!

God, through whom the Universe is perfect even with its illogical side.

God, the Father of Truth, Father of Wisdom, Father of the true high life, Father of bliss, Father of the good and beautiful, Father of the spiritual light . . .

God, turning away from whom is to fall, turning toward whom is to rise up, remaining in whom is standing fast.

God, from whom going away is dying, returning to whom is being reborn, in whom dwelling is living.

God, whom only he who is beguiled loses, whom only he who is called seeks out, who is found only by those who have become pure.

God, leaving whom is the same as going under, striving toward whom is the same as loving, and seeing whom is the same as possessing.

God, you who call us back onto the way! God, you who lead us to the gate! God, you who let the one who knocks open! God, you who give us the bread of life!

Come to me with your grace.

—*CONVERSATIONS WITH HIMSELF*

opponents of unorthodox Christians in their place: didn't they know how arduous the quest for truth was, "under what difficulties the inner eye of a person is healed, so that it finally can look on the sun?"

"Two persons are in me," he discovered in desperation. In moments of "trembling vision" he was indeed thrust forward to the Eternal, but "my weakness ricocheted and returned to the accustomed path." And the only thing left was "a recollection full of love, and something like a longing for the fragrance of a food that I could not yet enjoy."

As a professor of rhetoric in Milan, Augustine became a catechumen (candidate for baptism) of the Catholic Church. He probably did this with his career in mind (the imperial court was Catholic) and to please his mother. More decisive for his development would have been the encounter with neo-Platonism, above all, with Plotinus.

Too late came I to love you, O you beauty both so ancient and so fresh, yes too late came I to love you. And behold, you were with me, and I out of myself, where I made search for you: in my ugliness I rushed headlong upon those beautiful things you have made. You were indeed with me; but I was not with you: these beauties kept me far enough from you: even those, which unless they were in you, would not be at all. You called and cried unto me, you even broke open my deafness: you discovered your beams and shone unto me, and chased away my blindness: you did most fragrantly blow upon me, and I drew in my breath and I pant after you; I tasted thee, and now do hunger and thirst after you; you didst touch me, and I even burn again to enjoy your peace.

—*CONFESSIONS*

In the Milanese interpretation neo-Platonism was an essentially Christian wisdom teaching concerned with the immortality of the soul and judgment after death, and clearly opposed to fashionable skepticism: one can know, understand, be sure!

Incredibile incendium! Augustine raves: These books had kindled "an unbelievable fire" in him. He began to understand that God alone can satisfy every longing. In short, by laborious steps he came closer to Christ—no longer on the path of cool philosophical arguments, but with the passion of someone who has just fallen in love: "What is it that glowing there bursts into my eye, shakes the heart and yet does not wound, that I tremble and burn?"

To be sure, he was still shrinking back from the definitive decision. He would have to give up so much to make a really radical change in his life: possessions, prestige, career, a whole group of good friends (and all his life friends were as important for Augustine as his daily bread). . . . And then baptism counted for considerably more than it does today. It often meant the total break with one's previous existence and not just something that was automatically part of the entrance into life, like childbirth and baby carriages.

But it was more than just fascinating books that drove him on the path to overcoming his skepticism. On the road to Christ there were also always people, who radiated more of him than they talked about him. Books stimulate, ask questions, force you to think. People live the answer, without always being able to formulate it conclusively.

Ambrose, the bishop of Milan, was one such person, a towering figure of his epoch. Authoritarian, radiant, inexorable, intolerant, and at the same time a brilliant and very practical-minded theologian, aside from being a hymn writer and composer. He fought with the court ("The emperor is in the Church, not over it"). He defended the civil rights of the individual against the power of the state posing as absolute. He excommunicated the emperor on the spot when, in an act of revenge, he had seven thousand people killed.

At first Augustine was impressed only by Ambrose's rhetoric. But soon he was struck by more than the beautifully framed words: the skillful chain of arguments, the brilliant marshaling of ideas. He understood in amazement that this man *believed* with every fiber of his being what he preached with his brain and heart and nerves.

Stirred, he asked an old priest for help. He felt that he had already delayed too long. "Tomorrow I shall find it. Then it will clearly show itself, and I shall know how to keep it . . . No, I will rather seek still more zealously than before and not despair."

Hitherto, the Bible had seemed to him a piece of vulgar literature, a collection of fairy tales—and not an especially artistically-written collection at that—for undemanding plebeian readers. The intellectual pride of Augustine, the professor of rhetoric, no doubt matched up with the timeless incapacity of the people's church to understand the problems of skeptical academics. But now to his shame and confusion, as he listened breathlessly, he discovered the earth-shaking contents of Holy Scripture, which turned him upside down.

Still he hesitated. He was sleeping, he accuses himself in the *Confessions*, he heard the call to get up, and knew only the weary answer: "I'm coming, I'm coming! Leave me for a little while longer."

He learned from the strange, hard life of the desert monks, and again he was ashamed. He cried in desperation to his best friend: "Have you heard? The uneducated rise up and bear the Kingdom of Heaven away, and we with our heartless wisdom, see, how deeply we are entangled in flesh and blood."

And now finally, after years of struggle and wandering about, it came to that all-transforming decision, which Augustine stylizes in his confessions in accordance with the ancient and biblical model. Filled with pain and discouragement, he lay under a fig tree and tormented himself with gloomy thoughts. Then suddenly he heard the singsong of a child from the garden next door: *Tolle, lege! Tolle, lege!* "Take up and read, take up and read . . ." Augustine stood up, took a volume with the Letters of Paul, and upon opening the book, he came across the passage:

> Let us conduct ourselves becomingly as in the day, not in reveling and drunkenness, not in debauchery and licentiousness, not in quarreling and jealousy. But put on the Lord Jesus Christ, and make no provision for the flesh, to gratify its desires (Rom. 13:13).

He calmly went over to his friend and told him what had happened. "All the night of doubt was scattered." Immediately thereafter he informed the happy Monica. The endearing legend concentrates as if in a burning glass, what actually lasted for years.

CUTTING THE UMBILICAL CORD

THE RESULT OF the long history of conversion must have been radical. Augustine consistently broke loose from all previous connections in order to live a quiet life close to God, devoted to study and contemplation. He gave up his teaching post, renounced his wedding plans and—once again—dismissed the concubine that he had taken because his future wife was too young to get married right away. Here too there was little trace of consideration for the feelings of his partner. Instead, in his readily theatrical language, he describes the process of cutting the umbilical cord in this manner: "Let us put aside all empty duties and take on useful ones!"

Of course, how could the former Manichaean and obedient pupil of the Neoplatonists have acted otherwise? Their common goal, after all, was to free themselves from everything sensual and to control the needs of the senses.

On the other hand, he seems to have held on to his son: On Easter night of 387, Augustine, thirty-two years old, was baptized along with his son Adeodatus and his boyhood friend Alypius. Shortly thereafter the seventeen year-old boy died, and not long after that Monica followed him into eternity.

Augustine went back to his African homeland. He sold his father's estate in Tagaste (the proceeds went to the poor) and tried to realize his dream of being a hermit, in order, he tells us, "to become deified, free from business." To be sure, his new life was as different from that of the African desert monks as it was from later western monastic existence. With a few friends he built up a community of people living together that was like a monastery and yet entirely different. It was a circle of like-minded individuals, who plunged like wild men into the most adventurous intellectual games. But they also quite soberly devoted themselves to reading the Scriptures and intensive prayer. Augustine read a lot and wrote his first philosophical treatises.

Unfortunately this peaceful time, in which he could work out and deepen his radical change of direction, lasted only three years. In the port city of Hippo Regius, he had the bad luck to enter the basilica at the precise moment that the old bishop Valerius—a Greek who didn't even understand the dialect of the African peasants—was telling his community that he absolutely needed a preacher. Naturally, a few of the churchgoers recognized the famous rhetorician. So they dragged him to the altar and gave him no rest until he had promised to let himself be ordained. Such was the spontaneous fashion in which this impetuous people chose even its bishops.

Augustine's dreams of a quiet life in the country were finished. Overnight he saw himself thrust body and soul into the pulsating life of a Church pregnant with the future.

Because, for Christianity, Africa was by no means missionary territory. On the contrary, the African Church had already produced highly respected theological writers such as Tertullian and

Cyprian, an enormous number of martyrs, and ecstatic forms of piety. In Augustine's day there were six hundred bishops in Africa, and the Bible was probably available in Latin translation here earlier than in Italy.

Hippo on the Mediterranean was the second largest city on the continent. It had a gigantic basilica (the remains of its walls are still impressive), a generously laid out forum with countless statues, and a theater with five thousand seats. To be a priest here was at once delightful and difficult. Valerius protected his new co-worker so much that he made himself unpopular, but even without such support, Augustine won considerable fame, as a brilliant debater. At a dispute in the portico of a bathing establishment, he made such a fool of one Manichaean that the man left Hippo in headlong flight. And in a street song, he wrote he launched an attack on the very popular sect of the Donatists.

Before long Valerius made Augustine his coadjutor bishop, to prevent another diocese from wooing away the beloved preacher. Five years after his ordination Augustine himself became bishop of Hippo—and remained in that post for almost forty years until his death.

This was surely not his dream profession. He once admitted that there was nothing more beautiful to him than "to explore the spiritual treasure without noise and jostling." Having to preach and admonish, "having to feel responsible for every one of you— that is a great burden, a heavy load on me, a hard task."

But he knew that it all depended upon "happily uniting the quest for truth with ministering love" and not forgetting one's fellows in the sheer intensity of self-discovery and contemplation. And then—he was so happy because he had found God, found the one whom people restlessly fled from, only to find him suddenly in their hearts "and you kindly brush away their tears."

For this reason he gave himself to his community with complete commitment, threw himself uncompromisingly into pastoral care. Augustine, the high-flying thinker, dealt with all the unnerving odds and ends that managing a diocese brings with it. He organized,

conferred, soothed, spoke powerful words, dealt with the authorities, boosted charitable work, prepared catechumens for baptism,
preached, often twice on Sundays and feast days (about a thousand
carefully elaborated sermons have been preserved), often sat in the
judgment seat all morning wrestling with small-time business matters, disputes over legacies or problems with guardianships. In those
days the administration of justice was just one more of the bishop's
jobs. He seems to have intervened with special courage for the victims of political persecution.

But becoming converted means not yet being perfect. Finding
God doesn't simply mean getting an immediate feeling of happiness and satisfaction. Bishop Augustine remained a torn man. Till
the end of his life he yearned mournfully for the fruitful leisure of
those few withdrawn years that he had spent with books and friends.
And now? On the anniversary of his consecration as bishop he
declared to the assembled community that he was simply overwhelmed. What didn't he have to do? "Straighten out troublemakers, console the fainthearted, help the weak, refute adversaries,
guard against intriguers, teach the uneducated, wake up the lazy,
check the contentious, put the conceited in their place, calm down
rows, aid the poor, free the oppressed, encourage the good, endure
the bad, and, ah, love them all . . ."

What did he get out of being a nuisance to his listeners by
admonishing them and feeling responsible for others? "It is the
Gospel that causes me terror."

On the other hand, he made a sincere effort to fulfill his sometimes, unloved duties conscientiously and not just mechanically.
The once-so-arrogant individualist succeeded more and more in
seeing his fellow humans as fellow "pilgrims," as contact points
with Christ: "They are your servants, my brothers; you have chosen them to be your children and my lords and commanded me to
serve them, if I wish to live with you and from you."

He had a similar notion of office: "Not to preside but to serve."
Bishop Augustine's accomodations were not those of a prince of a
city. He lived among his priests, in a poor community that he established right next to the episcopal church. Whoever wanted to enter

had to give up his possessions, take a vow of chastity, and oblige himself to a brotherly lifestyle.

Relentlessly honest with himself, he also put on no theatrics for other people. Instead of hushing up painful episodes, in his sermons he imparted to the people of Hippo a realistic image of the Church. As he warns in his commentary on the Psalms, one shouldn't wax so enthusiastic about the "tremendous Christians," while hushing up the "evil mixed in." Otherwise one might come to the Church with completely false expectations, and soon take to one's heels in disenchantment. Augustine knew that in the monastic community there were "pearls," but also "garbage."

Battle against the Deviants

Various passages in his writings show that the job of bishop with its daily duties was a burden to Augustine. But we also clearly see how much he learned from the deep-rooted, unaffected faith of the people and from their vital piety.

The monumental theological work that marks these almost forty years as a bishop is, for all its classical perfection of form, unusually alive and written in a way that even simple people could understand. In more than a hundred books, countless voluminous letters, burning sermons, and relentless discusssions, Augustine fought a single-minded battle against all those who deviated from orthodoxy.

"His writings," his friend and disciple Possidius attests, "are so numerous that scarcely any scholar can read them through and become cognizant of them." Augustine obviously knew the Scriptures by heart (patient experts have counted 42,816 quotations from the Bible in his manuscripts) as well as the Latin classics. Hundreds of trains of thought and thousands of themes are heard, often standing unconnected one to another like meteors flashing quickly across the sky and burning up. Many book projects were left half-finished.

Two burning problems of the time dominate Augustine's literary work: the confrontation of the still-relatively-young Christianity with surviving pagan traditions, which were still out in the open, and the contrary tendencies that divided the Christian camp itself.

Augustine did indeed take a position on every question; his enormously broad mind was capable of picking up and processing stimuli everywhere. But when it came to doctrine, he increasingly became a fanatic for order. The individual who entrusted himself to the Church has to know what he or she is about. Reliable orientation is everything.

In all this one may doubtless suspect a little bit of fear of the free play of the mind. This is only too understandable in a man who had so painfully experienced in his own life the effects of a lack of connections and clear orientation. And then, too, Augustine did not grow up in the freedom-loving climate of the Enlightenment but in the mental world of Roman antiquity, which was intent on solid, conclusive arguments and intellectual certainty.

Hence it comes as no surprise that the onetime skeptic turned into a strict advocate of discipline and church order. He wanted to speak only *voce ecclesiae*, with the voice of the Church. He went so far as to claim that he wouldn't even believe the Gospel if the authority of the Church didn't bring him to it. "But if we threaten," he demands, "then there must be pain involved, as we point to the imminent penalty according to Holy Scripture."

He fought relentlessly, for example, against the originally pagan custom, now deeply rooted among Christians, too, of having meals for the dead. On certain memorial days the survivors assembled at the grave for a sort of funeral banquet. However the custom gradually degenerated into real orgies with drunken carousing, lewd songs, and wild dances. This was particularly the case in the crypts of the rich, which were furnished with chaise lounges, kitchens, and stoves. But it also happened in the churches that had been built over the graves of the martyrs.

"The martyrs hate your jugs, your kettles, your feasting," Augustine chided the participants in these not-very-pious gatherings. "One sees people run to the funeral chapels, consecrate their cups there and go home drunk. Since they can no longer persecute the garlanded ones (i.e., the martyrs in heaven) with stones, they stay close on their heels with wine glasses!" Such admonitions proved very unpopular. Augustine succeeded in stemming the abuses through tough struggles, partly because he didn't condemn the banquets outright, but accepted them in small family circles.

He tried to understand seekers and the misled from the standpoint of his own biography. He wanted to bring order into the diffuse juxtaposition of religious convictions and doctrinal opinions—in his time there were dozens of heresies—but he preferred convincing to extorting. To begin with, he also took a decisive stance against forced conversions; he had no use for mere "seeming Catholics."

Later, of course, when the dispute with the so-called Donatists had already been smoldering for years, and there were bloody excesses on both sides, murders and destroyed altars, he did an about-face and agreed with state sanctions. He justified this change of mind with the weak argument that everything depends on what one is being forced to, whether good or evil. But he asked the imperial commissar, who was in charge of the criminal prosecution of the Donatists, to treat his opponents gently.

Augustine loved the Church and would give everything for its unity—for through the Church, God is in the world, and whoever splits it up tears Christ apart and has no love. But the institution of the Church, according to Augustine, may not simply be equated with Christ or even be placed over him, because humans go astray far too often.

What Augustine says on this subject is multi-layered and contradictory, like many of his statements. On the one hand he asserts stiffly and solidly that outside the Church there is no salvation. On the other hand he insists that God alone knows who really belongs to him: "Because in God's ineffable foreknowledge many who seem to be outside are inside and many who seem to be inside are outside."

Anyone who critically observes himself as Augustine did, is forced to such modesty. For he had to go on fighting against himself. Meanwhile he did know where he had to go, but the path was still a hard one. "You, o Lord, have *begun* my conversion," he prayed twelve years after his baptism. "You never leave off from what you have begun. Lead what is still incomplete in me to completion."

And he wrote this too: Anyone who thinks he can possess the "unclouded light of changeless truth" understands neither what he is looking for nor what he is. *Desiderium sinus cordis*, desire is the depth of the heart. We are called to seek, to believe, and to hope—not to possess.

He complained about the power of custom, which "sculpts" at his mind, and about the ineradicable "fantasies of the flesh." He suffered from a tormenting instinctual build-up, that with alluring remembered images broke into his dreams. He still hungered for recognition and admirers. Arrogance and intellectual vanity remained burdening character features. For years he couldn't get over the famous Jerome—himself quite arrogant and more a man of the world than Augustine, always surrounded by a swarm of noble women. Jerome once called him a "little upstart."

Sometimes a hard, cold undertone creeps into his writings, even when he speaks about God: God alone, he says, is an end in himself. All men and women are just means to this end. The covenant between God and man, which the Old Testament paints with glowing colors and at times in distinctly erotic terms, became a one-way street: God suffices for himself, he apparently takes no joy at being with people. Only with some theologians and mystics of the high Middle Ages was this narrow approach overcome.

Augustine the passionate, warmblooded, sensuous person was also a sober, sometimes cool intellectual. Indeed he was very much both of these things—that was part of his inner tornness. Christian theology owes to this second side of his nature the clarification of the indispensable role that falls to reason in believing: "One must understand," he says, "in order to believe," but he stresses the fact that faith shows understanding the way. He asks God for "knowledge and understanding" and confesses his impatient longing "not just to believe the truth, but to come to understand it."

Augustine maintains that in order to be happy, one must have certainty: reliable information about what really counts, enduring values that don't alter with every shift in philosophical fashion.

Against the skeptics, who maintain that only questionable, sub-jective sense impressions are possible, he emphasizes that: there is truth. There are things that are true and certain. This much at least is certain: I am, I know, and I love. Even if I doubt or deceive myself, someone who doesn't exist can't deceive himself. If I doubt, at least I know that I'm doubting and thinking.

Thus Augustine, basing himself on the simplest basic certain-ties, builds up his argument for the deepest truths: Humans must reflect on themselves, must know themselves, become conscious of their minds. Yet the mind, too, is dependent on something indis-pensable; it needs a guaranteed foundation that bears everything. If it is certain that we are and think when we doubt—and when we rely in our thinking, which changes, on unchanging norms, then there has to be a final unchanged truth: God.

"For he is above me, who made me, no one reaches him with-out transcending himself."

It was precisely in intellectual confrontations with unorthodox theological opinions that Augustine saved a bit of humanity for the Christian faith. For example, in the dispute over the status of human freedom vis-à-vis grace. The point of departure was the endless question of why, if God is in fact almighty, all people aren't saved. The British monk Pelagius had an answer: A person can carry out God's will from his own strength, and thus work out his salvation. The grace of God *does* make this easier, but it isn't necessary. Peo-ple are fully responsible for their actions, and if they sin, they do so consciously.

By contrast, Augustine held that sins can often be committed out of ignorance and weakness. Freedom of the will isn't given beforehand; it has to be fought for and won. Man needs God's grace, which is a gift and can't be merited. In principle, freedom of the will remains unaffected by this. God doesn't dispense us from action, he gives us the strength for it.

At the synod of Mileve, the African Church followed Bishop Augustine and condemned the Pelagians. On the other hand his far-reaching conclusions—that God rejects some people in advance in order to teach the others—were accepted neither by the Roman

What are you, my God?

... Constant and incomprehensible; immutable, yet changing all things; never new, and never old; renewing all things, and insensibly bringing proud men into decay; ever active and ever quiet; gathering together, yet never wanting; upholding, filling, and protecting; creating, nourishing, and perfecting all things; still seeking, although you stand in need of nothing. You love, yet are not transported; are jealous, but without fear; you repent, but don't grieve; are angry, but remain cool.

Who shall enable me to repose in you? Who shall enable you to enter into my heart; and so to inebriate it, that I may forget my own evils, and embrace you, my only good?

Answer me for your mercy's sake, O Lord my God, what are you to me: Say to my soul, I am your salvation. Speak it out, that I may hear you. Behold, the ears of my heart are before you, o Lord, open them, and say unto my soul, I am your salvation. I will run after that voice, and take hold of you.

—*CONFESSIONS*

magisterium nor the Church as a whole. Augustine, too, was wrong more than once.

We can also find a humane theology in his explanation of evil, which among the Manichaeans could deploy an eerie power, an overwhelming active force. Manichaeism viewed evil essentially as a material substance, which bursts destructively into the realm of the good. Augustine demythologizes evil by interpreting it as the subversion of uncorrupt, good nature, as a lack of being. Ultimately he takes evil to be pure nothingness, unthinkable without the good.

Finally, in the case of the Donatists, Augustine had to deal with harsh Puritans who for a time were represented in every African episcopal city and who disqualifed the priests who had weakened and betrayed their office in the last persecution of Christians. Donatism argued that the Church was supposed to be a community of the pure, in which no sinner could take part.

But for Augustine, the Church was also and especially the homeland of sinners, the weak and the cowardly, as long as they found themselves in the condition of pilgrims. "We don't leave the threshing floor of the Lord on account of the chaff," he objected to the self-confident dividing of the world into the just and reprobates. "We do not break up the Lord's flock because of the goats, which are to be separated out only in the end."

The holiness of the Church was for him independent of the human qualities of its officials—because it came from the power of God, which is always stronger than any human troublemaking. And besides, a missionary Church has more important things to do than get involved in such fruitless quarrels. Augustine notes sarcastically: "The thunder rolled through the clouds, proclaiming that the house of the Lord was to be built all over the earth, and these frogs squat in their swamp, croaking; 'We are the only Christians!'"— What would Augustine have said to those Catholics who today make some liturgical service the crucial criterion of faith?

On the other hand, in these constant struggles with heretics or mere dissenters, the bishop of Hippo became visibly harder, more aggressive and dogmatic. This may have had something to do with the ongoing conflict with his own sexuality, which he probably never overcame. Augustine was a man who would have preferred being all mind, pure discipline, untouched by physical needs, and yet he was continuously tormented by his desires. The frustration and self-hatred this caused swung around to aggression.

In the end he defended the forced conversion of the Donatists. He argued that it would certainly be the better ones who, led by love, would find their way to the faith. But the number of those "whom fear improves" would be greater. And as an old man he would express pride and contentment in a theology that "can show the just God in so many pains and such agonizing death struggles of the smallest children."

Is this the same Augustine who, as a spiritual leader of the African Church, its theological inspiration and mentor, remained at bottom a child before God? "We shall find, when we have been compelled to go on searching," he writes modestly about the zenith of all theological knowledge.

Is this the same Augustine, who, according to an old legend was put to shame by a tiny tot whom he saw trying to scoop out the ocean with a shell? When he smilingly questioned the boy, a voice told him that the child was more likely to succeed than he—Augustine—would in his attempt to grasp the nature of God.

Is this the same Augustine who, the older he got, developed an increasingly powerful sense of an incredibly living God—a God who was all heart, all warmth, all closeness? "From your fire," he shouts out with joy, "from your good fire we burn and we head upwards!"

Yes, this is the same Augustine who vacillates back and forth between zealous intolerance and careful benevolence, who wants to love everyone—and for the sake of pure doctrine believes he has to be merciless. This is the same man who suffers from his human limitations and instinctual obsessions but nevertheless bravely holds fast to the path started out on: "Sing and walk on," he encourages himself, "God himself is at the end of the road."

There he waits, no gloomy judge, no heavenly bureaucrat with the register of human achievements and missteps in his hands, but one who encourages, who starts humans off on the path and can give them an incredible amount of power.

"Give what you demand, than demand what you will."
Seldom has anyone put more trust in a profession of faith.

THE MEDICAL HISTORY OF AN EXHIBITIONIST?

AUGUSTINE'S *Confessions* are a prayer too, a poetic song of praise, a dramatic story of interaction between God and man. This is no sober piece of spiritual bookeeping. The book is quite different from the many self-justifications history is familiar with: proud, coquettish, and peppered with tingling amorous details. This irritated Nietzsche. The "mixture of humble servility with a courtly-plebeian pushiness" with which Augustine here "wallows before God" suggested to Nietzsche that man's religious feeling for God resembles that of a dog for people . . .

Augustine stood squarely in the tradition of pagan philosophers who enjoy describing their life as a thorny path to the truth. Yet while the educated person of antiquity would recount spiritual

"I am," said Christ, "the way, the truth, and life" (John 14:6). If you want to walk, I am the way. If you want to be without disappointment, I am the truth. If you wish not to die, I am life. That is what your redeemer says: You can go nowhere else except to me; and you can go nowhere except through me.

If the Lord, your God, had said to you: "I am the truth and life," and you longed for truth and wanted life, then you would seek the way there. . . . If you seek the way, then hear his word: "I am the way." Before he told you whither, he said through what: I am the way.

He was hungry and thirsty; he became weary, slept, was captured, beaten, crucified, killed. That is the way: Go humbly forward, so that you can arrive at eternal glory. Christ our God is the fatherland toward which we go; Christ the man is the way on which we go. We go to him, on him we go—why do we fear to go astray?

processes of knowing, at most from a noble distance, and would speak reluctantly and very sparingly about feelings, Augustine delivered an unsparing medical history of his soul. His almost relishing contemplation of his own inner world must have struck his contemporaries as exhibitionism.

For, instead of the familiar classical ideal figure on its serenely unerring path to perfection, they found a broken person tumbling from relapse to relapse. He portrayed his life as an "unremitting temptation," as a never-finished story of reconversion, continually caught up with by the merciless past. In the words of Augustine's biographer Peter Brown, the *Confessions* end not with the "certificate of a cure," but with the "self-portrait of a convalescent."

In tormenting images and almost epic detail this eternally dissatisfied soul painted his desperate struggles with himself and God: "I bore in myself my tortured and bleeding soul, and it would not endure that I bore it . . . And if I wished to lay down my soul, so that it might find rest, then it slid off into the void and fell on me once more, and I was an unhappy place for myself, where I couldn't be and when I nevertheless couldn't leave. Whither could my heart have fled away from my heart? Whither would I not have run after myself?"

Some people think that in this book, which became a classic of world literature, Augustine was merely sublimating his sexual problems. Is this so?

To be sure he told of the violent pressure exerted on him by his soul. But the actual goal of the *Confessions* was neither self-observation nor self-justification, but God alone, who "is deeper in me than my deepest self." Augustine spoke of him in powerful images, as the "God of my heart," as his "late joy" and the "life of his life." He doesn't want to confess his guilt so much as God's power. He wants to show how God's love can take hold of a life and change it.

The *Confessions* are more, much more, than the sex-obsessed revelations that superficial readers expect of them. Sexual needs and problems with relationships play a rather subordinate role in the book. The mistake that tormented Bishop Augustine most in his life was—the pointless plundering of a pear tree in his young years. "As if," he laughed long afterwards, "the only sins that you can commit were those for which you need your sexual organs."

Nevertheless, scattered throughout the life work of the most productive theological author of late antiquity, which fill up several bookshelves, there do recur such bad sentences as the warning: "Whether she lies hidden in a wife or a mother, it is always Eve the seductress, from whom we must be on our guard in every woman." For Augustine it's always the women who get the men, even as they strive for continence, to surrender to "the weakness of the unbridled flesh."

To the end of his days Augustine dreamed of a world where there would be no more sexual intercourse, with all the dangers it posed for the peaceful ascent of the mind. But then, someone objected, the human race would die out. Augustine's spontaneous answer—and we can imagine it accompanied by a deep sigh: "Oh, if only everyone were willing!"

Such statements expressing a pitiable fear of his own body, of women, of temperament and feeling, of the not-always-controllable demands of a partner, have deeply engraved themselves in the moral consciousness of the Christian West—up to those Puritans who invented the witch trials out of fear of the threat posed by the feminine and their own instinctual structures.

Was Augustine the mastermind behind this? It doesn't help at all to play down the disastrous actual history of his statements. But, like everyone who makes mistakes, the bishop of Hippo has a claim to our effort to understand his motives and the fixations to which he was exposed and which he could not escape.

There was first of all the whole tradition of Roman antiquity, which scarcely conceded any rights to women and which took a pessimistic view of sexuality, though it also sometimes looked on sex as tragicomic. The last years of antiquity were generally shaped by a feeling of the exhaustion of a world grown old and tired, of expectation of a purifying catastrophe.

Then there were the intellectual trends that one and all took a highly skeptical view of the body and sensuality. For the Platonists the body remained second-class; the important thing was to become independent of it, and elevate oneself into the spiritual sphere (the late Jewish and Christian teaching about the body that will rise again in glory protested against this notion). The Stoics wanted the mind to master the emotions. The Manichaeans, to whom Augustine belonged for nine years, looked upon the soul as the archenemy of the body, which burdened it. And the oriental-gnostic ideas that were greedily snapped up were likewise convinced of the inferiority of raw, coarse matter.

Augustine's own biography powerfully strengthened this omnipresent dislike for the sensuous and corporeal. The structure of his theological thought is stamped by a struggle of resistance against his past life, which he looked upon as profoundly sinful—whether rightly or not we can't judge. Guilt complexes keep running into repressive mechanisms.

For Augustine it seems to have been impossible to cultivate sexuality. He thought he had to take a radical distance from every erotic feeling—and naturally that led him to throw out the baby with the bath water. He could view sensuality and eroticism only as a threat to his peace of mind, as disobedience of the flesh to the all-controlling spirit. How could any thought, he asked reproachfully, much less wisdom, be accessible to someone in bed?

Augustine couldn't imagine a genuine partnership with a woman. He waxed enthusiastic over male friendship: "How much better two friends are for living together and spiritual exchange than a man and a woman!" The latter was obviously created only as a "help in begetting children."

He didn't waste a single tender word in the *Confessions* on the mother of his son. This relationship had been a "union of lustful love"—although it lasted fourteen years—nothing more. And of Adeodatus he wrote: "I had no share in this boy except for the sin."

Or, beneath the hard-frozen surface of total renunciation, did some of the old feelings break forth after all when upon the departure of Adeodatus's mother he noted in one short sentence: "My heart still clung to her, and when she went away it was wounded and bleeding?"

But the fact remains that in a sexual relationship Augustine could see no personal exchange, only an arrangement for relieving physical needs. This led to his highly unsatisfying theology of marriage.

To be sure in Augustine's vast oeuvre the bad sentences with their fateful effects stand over against statements with other nuances. For example he made some initial moves toward sexual equality when he wrote that, "Both partners should be aware of their dignity." He stubbornly demanded fidelity from men as well—a challenge to the timeless double standard; and he even encouraged them to take a leaf out of their wives' book.

In looking back on his own life, he condemned not so much his sexual practices as the unrestraint and lack of commitment expressed in them. Did he have any sense that in this way he was demeaning and objectifying his partner? Behind his concept of sensuality there suddenly looms the real opponent: self-love, egoism, the exploitation of another person.

And in his late work *The City of God* Augustine can suddenly intone a song of praise to the "wonderful power of sex"! Up to the end Augustine maintained an alertness to the beauty of creation and a sincere admiration for the achievements of human understanding, from architecture and navigation to the theater and music. At Bishop Augustine's house there was always wine, and he deliberately used silver spoons at table to set himself off from joyless ascetics.

THE MEANING OF HISTORY

Augustine worked for fourteen years on *The City of God*. It contains the first wholesale sketch of a Christian theology of history and a comprehensive answer to the fall of Rome. The conquest and plundering of the "Eternal City" by the Germani of Alaric (who behaved in a rather civilized fashion when they took it, by the way) had seemed as world-shaking to contemporaries as the destruction of Jerusalem centuries before. "If Rome can go under," Jerome exclaimed, "what can be secure?"

The adherents of the old gods held Christianity responsible for the fate of Rome. The exiled gods had avenged themselves, and despite all the prayers, Christ hadn't helped. Augustine resisted the temptation to hit back with attacks on the lifestyle of ancient Rome. Unlike the pious zealots in our days, he didn't explain the downfall of Rome by the immorality of his society. If anyone was guilty, then it was the entire human race. He put the alarming events of 410 in a larger framework—an overall view of history.

Augustine's goal was to understand history from the standpoint of faith. Christ was to bring order into the pulsating turmoil of battle and blood and greed for power and unappeased longings. World history, the frustrating, continually disappointing story, was to get a meaning. Augustine wanted to show that the earth rolls through sin and suffering, through sheerly unbearable human meanness and brutality, unstoppably homing in on a shining goal: the good God, who created the world and carries it.

He once compared history to a wonderfully beautiful symphony directed by God. But Augustine the realist also heard the discords in this symphony and the countless mistakes at the rehearsals.

From the theological tradition of Africa he borrowed the image of the two kingdoms, the *civitas Dei* (the kingdom of God) and the *civitas terrena* (the earthly kingdom). Both exist on earth alongside each other, indeed in one another, indivisibly woven and mixed together even in one and the same person. Wheat and tares grow together and will be separated by Christ only when the day of his harvest comes.

In this ongoing struggle between the *civitas Dei* and the *civitas terrena*, between the orientation to the spirit and clinging to flesh (to put it in a highly abbreviated way), the case of Rome was no more than a mosaic chip. From his two-kingdom doctrine Augustine developed a healthy skepticism vis-à-vis the state and its tendency to make of itself an almighty idol. The state must, it is true, wage wars and pass death sentences but it must also submit to the same commandments of God that apply to the individual person. That sounds rather conservative, but today's arms race politicians, including the "Christian" ones, would likely have difficulties with such guiding principles. Politicians, we know, always raise the objection of "practical constraints" to the peace campaigns of concerned Christians.

At a time when the crumbling superpower of Rome was increasingly tempted to divert attention from its inner disintegration through warlike adventures, Augustine warned against the usual imperalistic expansionary politics: "Why should the kingdom rob itself of rest in order to become great?" Lust for conquests, greed, the politics of violence, and the subjection of foreign nations finally turned states into nothing but "large bands of robbers." Of course, he also gave the Church very clear warning about claims to omnipotence and striving for political power.

In 429, when 80,000 Vandals under Genseric had advanced through Gaul and Spain into Africa, and were approaching Hippo, old man Augustine was busied with the correction of his writings. On the side he was writing a new work about *The Gift of Perseverance*, even as the alien conquerors were extinguishing the spiritual elite of the land and delivering an annihilating blow to African Christianity.

When the Vandals besieged Hippo, the seventy-five-year-old bishop sank into a lethal fever. He had the cult vessels melted down to buy wheat for the hungry populace and ordered his priests to be the last to leave the city, which had been locked up for fourteen months when the barbarians invaded it: "If the people remain and the pastors flee and withdraw from their service, what is that but the damnable flight of the hirelings who have no care for the sheep?"

Such a position called for courage, of course. Augustine's biographer Possidius attests to the besiegers' "every possible cruelty and wildness." They had plundered, tortured, and murdered. "The enemy spared neither sex nor age, neither priests nor the other church servants."

Augustine died on August 28, 430, with the mellow words of the pagan philosopher Plotinus on his lips: "There is no greatness in anyone who considers it very important when trees and stones fall and humans, who have to die, actually do die."

"Thus if we get to you," Bishop Augustine had written some years before in his book on the Trinity, "then the many things that we say and to which we don't get will be at an end, and you alone will remain, who are all in all."

And he closed his *City of God* with a request, that can stand for his whole powerful work:

> To whom too little or to whom too much is said—may they be indulgent with me. But to those who have gotten enough, let them rejoice with me and thank—not me, but God with me.

THE IMPOSSIBLE ARISTOCRAT

ELIZABETH OF HUNGARY,

LANDGRAVINE OF THURINGIA

(1207–1231)

A Princess Shares the Life of the Plundered

How can I wear a golden crown,
when the Lord wears a crown of thorns?

A princely marriage had seldom produced so much head-shaking and snobbish indignation. "What can the young landgrave see in this wild gypsy?" puzzled the Thuringian court ladies at Wartburg, the great castle near Eisenach. They cast poisoned glances at the young Hungarian woman, who was once again running through the high halls, laughing out loud, instead of—as courtly etiquette prescribed—tripping in short, measured steps.

This Elizabeth most definitely didn't look as stiff and boring and etheral as she does in the old paintings and sculptures. According to the historical sources she must have been a fiery-eyed Magyar, blueblooded, scintillating with life, with beautiful dark eyes, raven black hair, a dusky skin, and a soft timbre to her voice.

She was merry and spontaneous. She liked to laugh aloud, much preferred riding out for hours in storm and rain to the monotonous round dances in the fortress. She strikes us as a wilfull, self-conscious, critical person, with intelligence and depth. She was no more cut out to be a wily intriguer than to be the subservient cajoler, a forever presentable conformist.

A decade before this, the little Hungarian woman had been brought as a child to the Thuringian court. Back then a gigantic baggage train with her trousseau and gifts of extravagant splendor rolled down the ancient trade roads to Germany. At the time people were still enthusiastic over so much exotic magnificence. *Vita Ludovici* noted that there were "countless gold and silver drinking vessels" among Elizabeth's dowry, along with gold brocade garments and canopies, bedding of purple silk, "a tub of silver, in which the little maid was to bathe," in short a treasure so rich that "its like was never seen again in the province of Thuringia."

Yet now it turned out that the courting of the bride in Hungary hadn't been such a good move after all. The noble young ladies at Wartburg resented more than the foreign woman's temperament and her slight accent. With her stubborn attempts, as a member of the upper class, to lead an alternative life, Elizabeth was behaving in a way that was simply impossible.

The young princess clearly showed her distaste for official social functions. She preferred to wear simple wool clothing, took off her finery in church, strewed generous alms about, and thereby lured continually growing swarms of beggars and wretches into the castle courtyard. Instead of embodying the splendor of the crown as the mistress of the country and observing a majestic distance, she joked with her maids, addressed them as "friends," and seriously asked them to call her by her first name.

An early chronicler, to no one's surprise, took note of "bitter invective," "shameless insults," indeed open persecution by the displeased courtiers and relatives.

"But among them all Elizabeth blossomed like a lily among thorns."

Carnival and Cathedrals

Erzsébet (Elizabeth) is a name still found in many Hungarian families. In its original Hebrew form it means something like "God swore" or else "God is fullness." The name could serve as a code word for that period of soaring Gothic culture that people like to imagine as the perfect city of God, as a Christian universe. The reality looked different. In the shadow of the heaven-storming cathedrals and behind the omnipresent Christian façade, there was hardly more authenthic faith in bloom than there is today—with the difference that the façade of that period was splendidly decked out, while nowadays it is crumbling. Nothing proves the the fragility of this façade better than the hatred and scorn with which an officially Christian environment reacted to the challenging, uncompromising piety of the landgravine Elizabeth.

While little Erzsébet was growing up in the fortress of Saros-Patak or perhaps in Pozsony—historians aren't quite certain which—the cathedrals of Rouen and Lincoln were being built, Pope Innocent II was calling for a crusade against the southern French heretics, Francis of Assisi was heading though Umbria with his poor companions, Genghis Khan was spreading fear and terror through Asia, Walther von der Vogelweide was composing his lovesongs, King John was sealing the Magna Carta at Runnymede, and for the first time Gottfried of Strassburg was representing in his epic *Tristan und Isolde* the purely earthly fulfilment of love: redemption through one's lover, not by God.

Mourning penitential processions and boisterous, obscene carnival frolics, ecstatic enthusiasm for heaven and cruel joy in executions and tortures shape this period of extremism. It was a time that often united the most extravagant extremes—like the tradition-rich house of the Arpad dynasty in Hungary and the Bavarian counts of Andechs-Meran, which Elizabeth's parents came from: regents, rebels, commanders, bishops, murderers. The saintly duchess Hedwig belonged to this family, but so did the bewitchingly beautiful Agnes, who drove the queen of France from the throne, and Elizabeth's power-obsessed mother

Gertrude—struck down by Hungarian nobelemen when Elizabeth was six years old.

Yet at the time of the bloody deed the king's daughter was no longer in Hungary. As early as four years of age she had been engaged to the oldest son of Landgrave Hermann of Thuringia. This was the preliminary stage to a "political marriage" (which was of course the norm), and was supposed to strengthen the alliance between Thuringia, Hungary, and Bohemia against the German king Philip. When her intended bridegroom suddenly died a few years later, Elizabeth remained in Thuringia with Ludwig, the younger brother of the dead man, to whom she had long been like a sister.

The two grew up in legendary Wartburg, where sunny poetry and cultivated ways of living were at home. This lordly manor, whose palace displayed a splendor unusual in a medieval fortress, magically attracted the courtly singers with their knightly epics and tender love songs. In the year Elizabeth was born the famed "war of singers" had taken place, and Wolfram von Eschenbach is supposed to have composed part of his *Parsifal* at Wartburg. Landgrave Hermann loved power and using singers as his propagandists. "Even if a barrel of good wine were to cost a thousand pounds," Walther von der Vogelweide was amused to remark, "none of Hermann's guests would have an empty barrel before him." But sensitive ears should rather avoid the bustle at Wartburg: "One crowd leaves while another is entering, day and night. It's a great wonder that anyone is still listening."

At first the mercurial child from the land of the Magyars must have felt just right in this continuous hurlyburly. The little bit of tradition that we have sketches a quite normal girl, playful, and a bit vain. She prayed that she might win at games, and was overjoyed at the presents that Ludwig had the habit of bringing: little mirrors, ribbons, and coral chains.

But even as a child the reflective, inner-directed side of her nature broke through. Then Elizabeth would suddenly break off her games and fly like a whirlwind across the fortress courtyard into the chapel. She liked to dance but often turned down the invitation to a second round with the explanation: "Once should be

enough for me; when it's best, I want to renounce for God's sake."
She liked to join her girlfriends in playing "poor"—children of
rich parents generally find that quite romantic. And even in her very
early years she provoked bitter discussions with the young count's
mother because she simply refused to wear her crown in church.

"What splendor there was with tournaments and dancing and
courting of lords and ladies in the city and suburbs up to the grove
for three days, there is just no describing it in a few words." That
is how the chronicles from 1221 portray the magnificent wedding
of the twenty-one-year-old Ludwig, now a landgrave, and the barely fourteen-year-old Elizabeth. One year later her first son was born.

What the historical sources say about this young couple is far
more reminiscent of the story of Romeo and Juliet than of the sober
purposeful unions that were so common in the thirteenth century
between the children of princes. They addressed one another as
"dear brother" and "dear sister." At table, contrary to courtly custom, she sat beside him. When he rode off for long stretches of
time, she dressed in mourning, which she replaced upon his return
with a festive dress. And when he came home after such weeks of
separation, she would run up to him and kiss him "more than a
thousand time heartily on the mouth," without caring about the
nettled spectators.

The "great love" between these two vivacious, but also very sensitive, young people was obviously—and exceptionally—no sen-
timental schmaltz. He preferred his Elizabeth to a mountain of gold,
said Ludwig. There was nothing on this earth dearer to him. This
was an extremnely unusual attitude for relationships back then.
On their journeys noble knights were accustomed to taking their
pleasure with maids and farmers' daughters, and otherwise to make
a sharp distinction between the boring lady of the house (who in
fact was often treated as a serving maid) and the object of their
"courtly love." One chose for oneself a desirable woman, usually married but by no means always inaccessible, sang her beauty and carried out heroic feats in her honor. In his *Tristan* Gottfried von
Strassburg criticizes this devaluation of marriage and the evasion
into guilt-laden extramarital love affairs.

For his part anyhow, Landgrave Ludwig dismissed the playmate, discreetly sent to his room after a festive banquet by a prince friend of his, with a silver thaler. He said he didn't want "to sadden" his Elizabeth. And his wife had to hear herself mocked by an uncomprehending noble lady: "She loves her own landlord." This relationship, full of passion and tenderness, in no way faded over the course of the years. Elizabeth was not the would-be nun, as invented by anemic legend-writers, who simply had the bad luck of having bound herself too early to a man.

Of course it was also part of the mystery of this partnership that each one let the other be himself or herself. Elizabeth didn't torment him daily to live the way she did. And he had enough self-consciousness and respect to accept her uncommonly intense relationship to God—even if it sometimes worked out in ways disturbing to marital life, for example, when Elizabeth dashed out of bed at night to pray. Ludwig wasn't jealous of God because he knew that this love took place in another dimension and that Elizabeth's love for God supported, animated, and enhanced her love for her husband. God was no competitor. God never impoverished people, he enriched them. Elizabeth said: "I include Ludwig in my love for God, and I hope that God, who sanctified marriage, will grant us an eternal life."

This is not contradicted by the fact that she once is supposed to have wanted to die unmarried and a virgin. There's nothing wrong with tensions and inner conflicts in a person's life, if they are settled honestly.

Alms from a Bad Conscience

The landgravine also urgently needed the tolerant, warmhearted sypport of her husband because her alternative lifestyle increasingly made her enemies among nobles and conspicuous consumers. The more harshly her own troubles tormented her—her mother was murdered, her future bridegroom died while practically a child, and the old landgrave died too—the more sensitive she became to the needs of the peasants and day laborers.

At first her charity was still prompted by a bad conscience. She acted out of spontaneous sympathy without reflecting much about it. She threw her alms among the people like a graciously condescending princess, like a lady who finds it chic to be a benefactress.

But then she began to draw altogether personal conclusions from the constant confrontation with the hunger and misery on the streets. She traded her expensive robes for a simple dress, took off her rings and neckbands when she went to mass, often ate from a common bowl with her maids, forbade them to call her "mistress," and had them address her as "Elizabeth." These were little gestures, not very important in themselves, but they expressed a great deal, could have a consciousness-altering affect, and also cause a corresponding amount of scandal at court.

Sometimes she dreamt quite naively of "being poor"—just as nowadays the daughters of well-to-do families dream of raising sheep in Sardinia. Ludwig was amused by her wish "that we had only enough land to be worked with a single plow and two hundred sheep, that you could work this land with your own hands and I could milk the sheep." Whereupon Ludwig is supposed to have corrected her: "Ah, sister, if we had that much land and two hundred sheep, we'd be rich, not poor."

But Elizabeth wasn't just dreaming. She gradually realized where the money was coming from to pay for maintaining the feudal court at Wartburg. The Thuringian landgraves had never hesitated when it came to enlarging their own territory. Wars and feasts were financed by fleecing their subjects and raising their taxes. Up in the fortress one gave out the thalers with full hands and asked no questions about the oppressed farmers and day laborers who had to slave away for them in the wretched villages below.

As late as the nineteenth century, Thuringia, with its thickly wooded hinterlands, was considered Germany's "hunger corner." The bad harvests that plagued all of Germany in the years from 1224 to 1226, along with a raging cattle plague, must have had devastating effects here. Apart from that, all of Europe was suffering from the consequences of a mighty population explosion (it is estimated that between the eleventh and fourteenth century the population of Germany doubled). Masses of people streamed into the cleared woodland areas and the rapidly growing towns, but even there the jobs couldn't be multiplied at will. The ranks of the underclass spread far and wide.

And then, of course, the Middle Ages had no health insurance or social security. Every stroke of fate could plunge a person into hopeless misery. The threadbare social "safety net" consisted of pious almsgiving and a few hospitals or leprosariums. Most members of this constantly growing, many-layered proletariat loitered around the squares or the church steps or crowded the highways: There were fired day workers, defrocked clerics, down-at-the-heels pilgrims, war invalids, cripples, the handicapped, abandoned orphans, dowryless girls, whores, knights forced to mortgage their estates, peasants whose farms had burned down, victims of robbery, desperate people with no hopes or chances.

Back then it never occurred to anyone to question this murderous division of society into haves and have-nots. The bronze pyramid of medieval class society—with the crown vassals and their retinue and the higher clergy on top, and the peasants who belonged to them at rock bottom—was considered just as divinely willed as the poverty of the masses. "Perhaps you would like to be a knight or a lord," preached the famous Franciscan, Berthold of Regensburg, "but you have to be a weaver, a shoemaker or a peasant, just as God made you. . . . He has given each of us his office, as he wills, not as you will!"

No one, as mentioned, thought that these conditions might be changeable. There was always the appeal to better oneself or one's own class—but there was no notion of economic restructuring or reforms. The alms thrown to the poor out of one's superfluity did not have the purpose of evening out the unjust distribution of goods, but of paving the donor's way to heaven. The alms purse was one of the indispensable accessories of aristocratic ladies; and their gifts shamed and demeaned the wretched poor more than they helped them. Fine society delighted in the sufferings of the cripples and half-starved. The *Liber vagatorum*, a widely disseminated "beggars lore," warned of false pity. It claimed that many of those with amputated arms and legs had lost their limbs in prison "for bad reasons," that countless blind men had had their eyes put out "because of their misdeeds."

Elizabeth didn't fit into this picture at all. She began to experience the needs of the poor as a shameful judgment on her own luxurious lifestyle. She was stunned to realize that she was living on what had been taken away from others. She revolted against the idea that there should be privileged individuals and people of lesser value. With increasing urgency she felt the necessity of overturning this class-bound society which the good Lord couldn't have wanted—and because she didn't know how that was to be done (no one in the thirteenth century did), she tried to change the life in her personal domain.

And radically. There are beautiful stories of the landgravine walking along in procession with the poorest women, barefoot and wearing simple wool garments and, in the same outfit, without an escort of riders and her retinue, bringing her children for the blessing after childbirth. But that's not all. There is her shocking behavior with the maids, with whom she joined as an equal in the chore of spinning and forbade respectful forms of address. But that's not all. Probably the most stunning symbol for us today is the "food prohibition" to which, upon the advice of her confessor, she subjected herself at the prince's table.

Four years after her death her faithful servants went on the record that "at table at the side of her husband she disdained everything that came from the collections and exactions of court officials. She helped herself only when she knew that the food came from the lawful property of her husband. But if dishes were served up from extorted contributions, then she would merely break bread in front of the knights and lords, cut up the food, and pass it around here and there, so as to give the impression that she was eating."

No wonder that she often got up hungry from such a spread. She rigorously limited her herself to victuals that came from the actual properties of the landgrave's house. In addition, according to the statement of her women servants, she also did her utmost to see that the people plundered by unscrupulous stewards and tax-collectors were recompensed.

Were these the quirks of an eccentric aristocrat, bored by life in the fortress with its rigid ceremonial etiquette? Were they the arrogance of someone desperate for admiration, who had to get attention at any price?

Elizabeth's motivation was much stronger: She had met the poor, crucified Christ—as have many other people. And she didn't shy away from drawing the uncomfortable conclusions—as not many have.

On the way to Eisenach, in the middle of a frightful storm, she is supposed to have seen a child in rags on a woodpile, looking at her with great, disappointed, old man's eyes. "Where is your mother, child?" Elizabeth asked. The legend goes on to report that where the woodpile had been, a cross shot up, on which hung the dying Christ. He looked at her, and his eyes were the eyes of a child.

The Erfurt Dominican, Dietrich of Apolda, who used the oldest sources in his *Life of Elizabeth* (1297), tells a similar story. Elizabeth was in church with a large retinue. Suddenly her glance fell on the cross with the life-sized, shattered body of the crucified Christ. Then "she began to reflect" and came to the conclusion: "See, there hangs your God naked, and you, a useless person, go about in costly clothes. His head is wounded by thorns, and yours is embellished with gold. Thus gripped by inner compassion, she fell to the ground like a corpse."

The truth of such stories doesn't lie in their detailed precision, but in their underlying point. In the Man of Sorrows on the cross Elizabeth recognized the wretchedness of the poorest of her people, she saw the outcast Christ in the cripples and beggars of Thuringia. There is no better way of understanding the Gospel.

It's idle to discuss the possible dependency of Elizabeth on the Franciscans, who were just then showing up in Germany (there were Friars Minor in Eisenach as early as 1224). It's superfluous to draw parallels with the Beguine movements, to those women from all levels of society, mainly the nobility and bourgeoisie, who

> How can I wear a golden crown, when the Lord wears a crown of thorns? And he bears them for me.
>
> Look, I have always said, one must make people gay!
>
> We have to give what we have gladly and gaily.
>
> I am not angry at those who deny and despise me, for God is all my love.*

(starting in 1216, with official approval from the Church) had been founding communes and living on manual labor.

No one lived evangelical poverty so clearly and radically as Elizabeth did, and above all no one bound up a simple, undemanding private life with an effective social practice as much as she did.

"HER RELATIVES THOUGHT HER INSANE"

FOR THIS REASON the supposed quirk of a peculiar countess very soon turned into an attack on the hitherto-prevailing self-evident truths of the social order. And the people around her got a clear sense of this danger—especially since Elizabeth was not accustomed to keep quiet about her opinions. One time poor nuns wanted to do her a favor and proudly showed her the richly gilded figures of saints in their little chapel. Contrary to their expectations Elizabeth wasn't at all enthusiastic: "You would have done better," she said, "to spend the money on feeding and clothing yourselves than on decorating the walls. You should bear in your heart the image of God, which these figures represent."

The court of Thuringia reacted to such protests, sometimes silently, sometimes vocally, with hostility, intrigues, and open contempt: This Ersébet, this gypsy from who knew where, was impossible. How could one be so tasteless as to forget all courtly

---

* Only a very few sentences by Elizabeth have been handed down. We have nothing at all written in her own hand.

composure, and climb down in such a way beneath the level of a princess? To be sure, as a Christian aristocrat she was obliged to do good and to give something to the poor. They had nothing against that—but within limits, please! In the final analysis there had to be a difference between the privileged race called by God to lead and the primitive rabble. The way this Elizabeth carried on with maids and beggars—ugh, no, one couldn't put up with that; the man of the house really did have to step in.

Once again to quote the absolutely reliable statements of her servants Guda, Isentrud, Elizabeth, and Irmingard at the canonization trial, "She had to bear scorn, curses, and great contempt from the mighty ones of the country. Her relatives thought her foolish and mad, because she rejected the riches of the world. They annoyed and calumniated her in many ways, and wished neither to see her nor speak to her."

"Elizabeth, you are not behaving like a ruling princess, but like a serving maid," indignantly exclaimed her mother-in-law, Sophie (a very pious woman, by the way, and no more the resentful dragon than her son Ludwig, who had no qualms about warlike quarrels, was a complete saint). The black-and-white version of events in old legends isn't always quite honest. In any case, although she had the highest rank, Elizabeth's situation at Wartburg was by no means easy. Above all, whenever she could, Ludwig's sister Agnes sneered at and stirred up hatred against her supposedly sanctimonious sister-in-law.

Only Ludwig stood unwaveringly by her side. "The holy angel was often a messenger between them," wrote the poetically gifted court chaplain, Berthold, about this tender relationship; and we know that many of Elizabeth's relief actions were co-sponsored by her husband. All intrigues came to grief on Ludwig, so long as he lived. Nowhere does his attitude toward Elizabeth shine out more clearly than in the legend of the leper whom the langravine had put in her marriage bed so as to take better care of him (as a matter of fact, she was capable of taking the most wretched creatures from the hospitals into Wartburg): Ludwig, who was informed about this latest escapade of his foolish wife, raised the blanket—

and saw, because God had opened his "inner eyes" (Dietrich of Apolda) the crucified lying there.

"Elizabeth, my dear sister," he murmured in embarrassment, "you should often put such guests in my bed . . ."

Elizabeth's piety, put into practice in her dealings with the poor, was as radical as it was pragmatic. She met Christ not only by appointment at mass and prayer; she lived in his continuous presence. She turned aside loveless, thoughtless remarks with the comment: "The Lord is there! Don't grieve him."

This sense of the nearness of God seemed to immunize her against the stench of misery, with which she—unlike the charitable ladies in her environment—dealt very closely. She personally took care of her leper friends, washed their purulent wounds, and applied bandages to them. From the report of her woman servants: "Although foul-smelling air was otherwise repellent to her, she bore without any disgust the worst sickroom air, which her maids could endure only with difficulty and grumbling. She served the sick lightheartedly and with her own hands. With her kerchief she wiped away saliva and spittle from their faces, as well as filth from their mouths and noses."

With especially loving devotion she cared for feeble, handicapped, and incurably sick children. She bought them glass rings and toys. "One has to make people gay," was her regular expression.

The landgravine took care of orphaned children; together with her maids she spun wool, from which clothes were woven for the Franciscans and needy people. With her own hands she sewed baptismal dresses for newborns from poor families, and stood as godmother. Otherwise these poverty-stricken individuals couldn't even afford the churching ceremony. "With her own hand she made shrouds for the burial of the poor," the account by her servants adds. "She washed and dressed the bodies herself, and took part in their interment. . . . She would also not allow the bodies of rich dead people to be wrapped in new bedsheets or new shirts. Rather they were to be buried in old ones, and the good ones were given to the poor." As we see, charitable care can get dangerously on the nerves of social norms.

Every day ragged beggars, misshapen creatures, and the riffraff from the highways gathered in the fortress courtyard, to get a warm meal from the countess and her maids. But because many old and debilitated people couldn't make the difficult ascent to the fortress, Elizabeth set up a house for them down below at the foot of the mountain and visited it twice a day (at the time noble ladies were accustomed to ride out only rarely). She founded a second hospital in Gotha.

Again and again there was this striking urge to lend a hand herself, not to delegate charity to some organization, but to help with her own hands. Once she even wanted to milk a cow, her maids relate, to meet a sick man's request for fresh milk. We can well imagine that the countess must have gone about the job clumsily, for the report dryly notes, "but the cow kicked, and would not let her."

The decidedly practical feature of this "guardian of the poor" became clear in 1224, when Thuringia suffered through a very hot and dry summer, and a strong wind, which blew for several days, so completely battered the wheatfields, "that for two whole years grain was dear."

Then the landgravine, who was barely seventeen years old, didn't limit her efforts to almsgiving, but thought up the most productive measures for creating jobs. She put the needy to work building bridges and improving roads. Earlier, when harvests were still fairly good, she had given shirts and shoes to those capable of work, as the four serving women report, "so that they wouldn't injure their feet while gleaning, and sickles, so that they could reap and feed themselves with their own work."

Here too we see that this teenaged "mother of the poor" wasn't using the wretched for the sake of her own perfection. Elizabeth didn't want to earn heaven with her alms through cool calculation, but to deal humanly with the outcasts. She discovered the *human being* in the cripple, in the neglected old harlot, in the "unpersons" who loitered in throngs in front of churches and fortresses. "She didn't give just money," a Hungarian biographer observes, "but tools and work. She didn't give alms, no humiliating donations,

Lord, I thank your grace and compassion, that you have ful-
filled my great longing. You have done this for me, your poor
handmaid, and you have kindly consoled me in my affliction so
that I have seen and looked upon the tender remains of my
dearest brother and friend.

Yes, I have loved him with all my heart above all earthly
things, yet I feel no hatred that he has sacrificed himself to you
and through your will, in order to help the Holy Land, he has
met his end in foreign lands.

Lord, you know well, if it might be possible with your
holy divine will, his life, his loving, joyful presence would be
dearer to me than all joy, bliss, honor, and voluptuousness of
this world. I would be willing to go begging in humility with
him, if only I could see his amiable face again and enjoy his
company.

But now, dearest Lord, I do not wish to resist your divine
will. I commend him and myself to your divine will. If it should
be against your will, I would not buy him back into life for the
price of a single hair.

—PRAYER OF THE WIDOW BEFORE THE MORTAL REMAINS
OF THE LANDGRAVE LUDWIG

but work that gave people a sense of themselves—and a fair salary
for that work."

Two years later the starvation that had been feared broke out
all over the country. Ludwig was abroad, in Lombardy with the
Emperor, and the nineteen-year-old lady of the fortress had the
sole responsibility for his estates. Hunger had never raged so greatly in Thuringia before. People reduced to skeletons fed on roots, rose-
hips, crab-apples, and herbs; they fought over the flesh of dead
animals. In addition to the lack of food, the people driven half crazy
by the distress were plagued by epidemics, floods, and an overwhelming cattle die-off—people who had become completely dependent on grains in their agricultural economy.

Elizabeth didn't bother having long consultations with the
prince's financial advisors. She opened up her private granaries
and all the storehouses of Ludwig's family throughout the country.

Nine hundred poor people are said to have been fed every day in Wartburg. She plundered Ludwig's treasury, which contained exactly 64,000 gold pieces, down to the last penny. And, of course, she also pawned her few remaining jewels and festive robes. When Ludwig returned from Italy, the provisioning of Wartburg was evidently already endangered. Both hate-filled sycophantic courtiers and responsible financial administrators accused their mad mistress of having brought the princely house to the edge of ruin.

Yet Ludwig shook his head with his peculiar amiable sovereignty: "Just let her do good. Let her do everything she wants, as long as she doesn't pawn my two castles, Wartburg and Neuenburg."

Was all this just a fig leaf or a pious veneer covering up a thoroughly unchristian social order? The lonely saint as an alibi, while the majority of Christians once again neglect the distress of the time? "What had really changed?" ask the skeptics. Some critics would pigeonhole people like Elizabeth of Thuringia or Mother Teresa of Calcutta as minor reformers who are part of the system. They would argue that there has to be total revolution and a fight to the finish in order to get rid of the causes of poverty.

But in so doing they repress the infinite value of every individual human life that Elizabeth and Teresa and all the other "insiders" have saved or at least helped to a humane death. The skeptics forget that the great revolution of structures and programs is of no use whatsoever if people don't at the same time learn a completely new way of dealing with one another and, above all respect for the weak and the broken. In their chilly arrogance they look past the fact that there is also a quiet revolution without watchwords and shouts. A silent poverty movement like Elizabeth's can thoroughly change the fatalistic recognition of "above" and "below"—determined by the good Lord and untouchable for all eternity.

Not to mention the exemplary effect of this life, which even back then was attested to here and there—Mechtild of Magdeburg has Christ say in a vision that Elizabeth was a "a messenger whom I have sent to the unhappy women in the fortresses," and a number of those women followed her example. Not to mention the many hospitals and parishes, both Catholic and Protestant, that invoke the memory of the landgravine, from the Elizabethan Sisters of the fifteenth century through the Gray Sisters all over Europe to the organization *Caritas*, which employs approximately five hundred thousand volunteers in Germany alone.

"DEAD? NOW ALL JOY IS DEAD TO ME!"

"LET US REDEEM the Tomb!" With this battle song on their lips the Crusaders set forth again in the year after the great famine, hoping to win back the Holy Sepulcher and the other Christian sites under Moorish domination. The pope had called for a thousand knights, one hundred fifty ships, and 100,000 ounces of gold from Emperor Frederick II. At first the landgrave of Thuringia hid the red cloth cross—the mark of the Crusaders—from his wife, who was now pregnant for the third time, "so that his dear lady St. Elizabeth would not be aware of it, and would not be troubled and terrified, since she loved him dearly beyond all measure and with her whole heart."

When she accidently did discover the tell-tale cloth cross, she fainted in terror. In vain she begged her beloved husband: "Dear brother, stay with me!" For three days' journey she accompanied him across the borders of Thuringia, and when she finally managed to tear herself away, she returned home, "weeping like a widow, with tears on her cheeks" (Dietrich of Apolda).

Elizabeth never saw her husband alive again. At the age of twenty-six, before embarking from Brindisi, he succumbed to an epidemic. Then barely twenty years old herself, Elizabeth was left a widow with three children. When she received word of Ludwig's death, according to the old sources, she reacted like a madwoman: "Dead?" she cried out, "All the joy and honor in the world is dead to me!" Crying aloud, she stormed through the halls and struck her head against the wall, "as if out of her senses."

This outburst of passionate love can certainly count more on our sympathy and no doubt corresponds better to a humanitarian religion than the remarkable ice-cold "words of comfort" spoken by her father confessor: "Is that your piety, Lady Elizabeth? Do you no longer know resignation to the will of the Creator?"

No, even now, when He had taken away her beloved, she wouldn't hate God. But she wanted at least to be allowed to cry out her pain. Even in her famous prayer composed six months later, when Ludwig's body was shipped to Germany, and Elizabeth looked shudderingly at the professionally prepared remains of her husband, even in that prayer, for all its admirable strength of faith, we can still hear the tremors of boundless pain: "I wanted to go begging with him all my days, if only I could see his amiable face again and enjoy his company. But now, dearest Lord, I don't want to resist your divine will. . . ."

Up on Wartburg now, as was only to be expected, the hatred against the young widow broke out openly. Ludwig's successor as landgrave, his younger brother, Heinrich Raspe, took away her widow's property, despite her protests—although not without offering to maintain her out of the budget of the new lord of the fortress. Moreover, Heinrich Raspe had good reason for doing what he did. With her urestrained joy in giving she might have squandered her widow's legacy, and then her children might have had to suffer need. Still, this assault on Elizabeth's rights was, of course, illegal; and her few remaining loyal relatives energetically intervened to get Heinrich to reverse his stingy policy toward his sister-in-law. "He saw that she was well cared for and looked after," chaplain Berthold assures us.

For that reason all the legends picturing her brutal expulsion from Wartburg, in the dead of winter, with her little children shivering in her arms, are likely just a dramatic touch, though doubtless a masterly one.

This sort of black-and-white portrayal—here the heartless family, there the noble outcast—belongs in a mediocre novel. It's also easier to accept than the idea of freely renouncing one's usual standard of living and family ties.

The "expulsion" by "certain vassals" is mentioned in the deposition by the four women servants in a single dry sentence and without further explanation. But all the evidence suggests that this was more a gradual process of freezing out than a spontaneous booting out. Life for the widow in a hostile environment, which barely tolerated her as a burdensome guest, but likely made her feel the rejection more clearly than ever, can't have been especially appealing.

Besides, even as a princess, Elizabeth had always longed for a still more radical change in her life. Chaplain Berthold probably explains her motives better than the expulsion legend, when he notes: "She reflected that the poor have to pay for what the princes and lords consume in their sensuality. Therefore she thought from day to day about heading off from there, and preferred to suffer deprivation with poor, godly people than to commit sin and vice in princely power and lust. Therefore she returned to poverty and privation, which she gladly endured for God's sake."

She wanted to be radically poor, no longer a princely benefactress and helper in a secure position. All or nothing. Hence she left Wartburg. That is why she categorically rejected all the attempts by her relatives to get her to remarry. She threatened her uncle, the warlike archbishop, Egbert of Bambert, that she would rather cut off her nose, "then doubtless no one would come wooing me." Elizabeth's stubbornness takes on a special importance when we realize that among her suitors was the Emperor Frederick II. Later he would lay a precious crown on her coffin.

But, now that her beloved Ludwig was dead, the widow wanted to belong to only one person: the one whom she had seen in a vision after leaving Wartburg, during a Lenten mass, with an enchanting smile, in the open sky: "If you want to be with me," she heard Christ say, "then I want to be with you, and never to part from you."

We find her again in Marburg—far away from Wartburg— where along with her two faithful servants, Guda and Isenrud, she lived in modest conditions and in 1228 or 1229 took a momentous vow. Her already-mentioned confessor, Conrad of Marburg, reports: "Precisely on Good Friday, when the altars were stripped bare, she laid her hands on the altar of a chapel that she had given over to the Franciscans, and in the presence of some brothers she renounced parents and children and her own will, all the splendor of the world and everything that in the Gospel the Savior counsels us to abandon. When she also tried to renounce all her possessions, I tore her away from the altar."

This short text already contains the two main difficulties that the following, final section of Elizabeth's life causes us: her conflicting relationship with her confessor and the no-less-problematic choice between her role as a mother and a sort of nun's existence.

This Conrad of Marburg, Master of Arts, preacher to the Crusaders and persecutor of heretics, is one of the most unpleasant figures in early thirteenth-century church history. He was highly educated, frugal, and ascetic; but in dealing with others he displayed inhuman harshness. He was utterly frigid, tyrannical, narrow-minded, and obdurately cruel when it came to deviations from pure orthodoxy. In the year Elizabeth died, Pope Gregory IX made him the first Grand Inquisitor of Germany, directly subject to the Apostolic See and beyond the reach of episcopal jurisdiction. There was no way to appeal his judgments. With a network of spies, extremely dubious legal procedures—all sentences were death sentences—and grisly forms of torture, Conrad set up a regime of terror in Germany.

Brother accused brother, wife accused husband, the archbishop of Mainz wrote in horror to the pope. In the end this fanatical heretic-hunter increasingly issued verdicts without any hearing. He had people arrested randomly without proof and burned at the stake, with the cynical justification that: "Let us burn a hundred innocent people if there is only a single guilty person among them" (Annals of Worms). Barely two years after his appointment, some relatives of his victims struck him dead like a mad dog near Marburg. No one mourned him.

How could such a fundamentally good and sensitive person like Elizabeth, full of tender love for the little and the weak, seek out this dark figure, of all people, for her spiritual guide? How could she, in the presence of her husband, swear obedience to him? Conrad must have had his good sides too. In those days he was considered upright, austere, and wise. Elizabeth was no doubt fascinated chiefly by his life of absolute poverty.

Of course, it soon became clear just how he understood the spiritual care of Elizabeth, which had been personally assigned him by the pope: He wanted to make her a completely passive instrument in God's hands. In the process he constantly ran the danger of simply twisting her into his own marionette. He supported her wish for radical poverty with commands and rules, some of which were thought through very practically (the "food prohibition" was his idea). But once Elizabeth had been freed from possessions and courtly convention, his tyranny plunged her into new dependencies. Once when she missed one of his sermons (because she had to receive an important guest at Wartburg), he punished her with the most severe penances. And in other cases he didn't shy away even from thrashing the princess, in order to give his words emphasis.

There is a telling story about the nuns of Altenberg that has been handed down by Elizabeth's servants. The nuns very much wanted to get to know Elizabeth, who was already a widow; and so they asked Master Conrad. "She may enter, if she wishes," he answered ambiguously, in order to test her. Elizabeth misunderstood this as permission to visit the nuns, which she did. But she was immediately called out by the infuriated Conrad, who threatened her with excommunication and had her so brutally beaten by his servant with a strong rod that the marks could be seen on her flesh for more than three weeks.

MASOCHISM OR FAITH?

HE WAS AN UNHAPPY creature, this merciless priest, who obviously didn't like himself and believed that one came closest to God by renouncing human feelings. A broken person who in his role of taskmaster fastened on a woman who with her tenderness and tranquil kindness had everything he lacked. Elizabeth feared him, she subordinated herself to him to the point of completely losing her ego ("I am only a part of you," she confessed to him three days before her death). But she was much too strong and too much her own character to let herself be shattered by this meanspirited thrashing pedagogue with his fundamentally ridiculous harassment.

She ingeniously got around his draconian prohibitions. When he tried to put a stop to her boundless joy in almsgiving and bade her distribute small change instead of copper coins, she expressly had tiny, but precious silver pennies coined. After the beating scene in front of the Altenberg monastery, where she was gasping with pain, she compared human life to a reed: When the water rises, the river presses it down and flows over it without snapping it; afterwards it straightens itself up and grows as it did before. "Thus we too sometimes have to bend and humble ourselves and afterwards arise again in love and beauty."

Behind such words (which are based on an old Hungarian proverb) lies not just masochism, but rather a highly realistic attitude to life. Elizabeth's ascetical self-surrender didn't arise out of pleasure in being humiliated. She became little so that others could get opportunities in life. For in order to make others happy, she chose poverty; and in order to grow more consistently into this poverty, she betook herself—quite literally—to Master Conrad's switch. It was precisely in this priest who was so often unworthy, railing, and contemptuous of people that she saw God at work. And in the final analysis God was the only one she obeyed.

All this may have been a great mistake, but historical fairness demands that we take seriously Elizabeth's admirable intentions. We should not prematurely label as "sadomasochistic" the many-layered relationship between two religious radicals such as Elizabeth and Conrad, whose natures were so different and yet in some ways similar. That would bar the way to authentic understanding.

All the more so as the merciless Master Conrad played the crucial role of a reality check in her life. Often enough he met her dreamily enthusiastic desires with convincing rational arguments. As the description of her vow shows, he prevented her from becoming a beggar. If that had happened, who would have paid her husband's debts from the Crusade? And how could she have helped the poor, if she renounced even the few properties that remained to her as a widow? Conrad forbade her to touch the lepers, so that, with her delicate health, she wouldn't get infected.

Conrad certainly had a share in Elizabeth's evolution into a ecstatic mystic, who recklessly whipped herself, undermined her health, and saw things that one doesn't know whether to call the visions of a passionate believer or morbid hallucinations. But his "life rules" for the princess, which have been preserved ("Be compassionate to your neighbor . . . Always have God in your heart and in your thoughts. What you want people to do to you, do to them as well. . . .") reveal understanding, tact, and a sober realism.

Nowadays we find it considerably harder to understand the fact that under Conrad's influence Elizabeth abruptly separated from her children, "so as not to be hindered in serving God through too much love." Before this, "in the knowledge that she wished to become perfect," he had already taken away her maids, who voluntarily accompanied her into exile and became true friends to her. Instead of this she had to live together with a deaf, surly widow and an ugly lady's maid. Conrad explains that he did this so that "her humility would be increased through the maid, and her patience would be exercised through the unpleasant widow."

True, one might point out that back then the raising of children by nurses was customary, and the close ties between mothers and children common in later times were still unknown, particularly among the nobility. It's surely also correct to add that the children were doubtless raised better at Creuzburg and in the monastery of Altenberg than they would have been with the landgravine who was living in misery and longing for a beggar's existence. (Her son died as landgrave, one daughter become a duchess, and another an abbess.) Almost all her biographers say that she gave away her children to spare them poverty and to guarantee them an education befitting their station; and then they drop this ticklish theme— although this motive of an "educating befitting their station" is totally inappropriate for Elizabeth.

No, we really must confront the unhealthy features in this development. It is also extremely disturbing if it is true, as her servants report, that she prayed God "to take away from her her exaggerated love for her children," and if she indeed said to her maid

Isentrud: "I am concerned for my children only as a neighbor. I have entrusted them to God. He may dispose of them as he pleases." The question must be permitted, whether very real "earthly" duties weren't being repressed here for the sake of a dream of a nun's existence, and whether the solution might not have been to remain at Wartburg for the children's sake.

But there of course she wouldn't have been able to reverse Above and Below so effectively and to live like one of the poorest—that is why the erstwhile princess longed so much for the beggar's staff. She refused to live in the citadel in Marburg (which she would have been allowed to do). Instead, with the money from the redemption of her widow's estate and with what was left of her dowry, she founded the Franciscan hospital in front of the city gates. Together with the two overseers appointed by Conrad and a helpless boy suffering from a hemorrhage, whom she had to take care of and carry to the latrine as many as six times a night, she lived in a little room and earned her meager daily bread by spinning and weaving. She spent every free moment in the hospital.

Even without begging she had reached her goal: the princess had become a poor, despised woman, standing on the lowest rung of the social ladder, cut off from her former compeers and in no way honored by her new milieu as an angel come down from heaven. Many of the embittered, wretched creatures who had become hard and spiteful thought the former mistress of the country, who had now voluntarily renounced money and power, was quite simply cracked. And they also probably avenged themselves on the now defenceless Elizabeth for the violence and injustice that they had once endured from the prince's overseers and tax collectors. The painters were happy to take this story of the beggar woman as a model: Once the princess had lavished alms on her, and now she sadistically shoved the nobleman-turned-pauper into the dirt on the street.

Here we also have to keep in mind that Elizabeth's zealously used organizational talent fit badly into her age. This was a time when the image of women *was* being gradually and doggedly upgraded. In monasteries and "secular" religious communities, but also in groups of heretics, women were discovering new and relatively free modes of life. For well-bred knights and charming minstrels they suddenly moved into the midpoint of courtly society. But this was also an era,when at the the University of Paris, scholars were still discussing in all seriousness whether women had a soul just as men did. And what Elizabeth did in her hospital was for the most part considered men's work anyway.

She took care of stinking lepers, bound up their purulent sores, and washed off the discharge. "How well off we are," she airily said to her maids, "that we are allowed to bathe our Lord and put him to bed in this way!" She made the patients' beds, changed the soiled linens, helped carry the feeble to the bath, and encouraged them all. Children in particular loved this always cheerful, uncomplicated nurse, who, to the astonishment of her confessor, had acquired detailed hygienic and medical information. But she still couldn't cook, as her servants dryly remark in the canonization trial. "On account of her extreme poverty she often settled for watery soups from pulse or leaves of herbs. This already wretched food, which was carelessly prepared because of her praying, then tasted burnt into the bargain."

Envoys from Hungary wanted to bring the king's daughter back home with all honors, but she amiably sent them back. Instead she took a girl with leprosy back home with her, fed and washed her until Conrad discovered the unbidden guest, and once again made Elizabeth feel the rod.

But by now her body was already exhausted and used up. Her soul had aged and her *joie de vivre* had disappeared. Elizabeth fell seriously ill, gave away her very last possessions, lay down on her deathbed at the age of twenty-four, and, in a fever, dreamed of Bethlehem: "Now let us speak of God and the child Jesus," she whispered on her last night. "Midnight is approaching, the hour when Jesus was born, when he lay in the manger and in his omnipotence created the new star, which no one had seen before!"

No, she didn't feel sick, just very weak. She began to glow with joy and announced in a very low voice, "Now the time is near when the almighty Lord will call his friends to him." When she passed away, she lay, according to the report of the servants, "as if slumbering." At her bedside sat a bald-headed boy suffering from scabies, whom she had recently been taking care of.

This was on November 17, 1231. Just four years later she was declared a saint. The canonization had been pushed by the enterprising Conrad of Marburg—who may also have been bothered by a guilty conscience. Pope Gregory IX announced that this woman had been "a work of almighty God." To enshrine the precious reliquary containing her remains, covered with gold and silver, they built the splendid church of St. Elizabeth in Marburg, the first purely Gothic house of worship in Germany.

Yet it's almost as if, even in death, Elizabeth wanted to protest against such feudal gravesites. During the Reformation her bones disappeared, and no one knows whether and where they were reinterred. Her splendid coffin is empty. Elizabeth's stormy love for poverty had conquered one last time.

DAZZLING SIMPLICITY

JEAN-MARIE VIANNEY,
THE CURÉ OF ARS
(1786–1859)

What God Can Make of a Wretched Human Life

| Among the other priests
| I'm like an idiot!

*I*t was an exciting, promising time. The winds of radical change were blowing through European culture. The same year that a peasant woman named Marie Vianney gave birth to a son in the mountains near Lyon, Schiller's classic "Ode to Joy" was published, Mozart's *Marriage of Figaro* was premiered in Vienna and Prague; and in Great Britain, Robert Burns breathed fresh new life into the stiff love lyrics of his time with his *Poems, Chiefly in the Scottish Dialect.*

While the son of peasants, Jean Vianney, was herding sheep in his little village, hearing and seeing nothing of the wide world, cultivated citizens of France were reading the Enlightenment writings of Voltaire and Diderot and laughing at religion. With the breakdown of belief in a just God, the Marquis de Sade saw the crumbling of all moral barriers. While remaining a prisoner in the Bastille, he shocked his contemporaries with novels that showed vice triumphing over virtue. In *Dangerous Liaisons*, de Sade's contemporary, Choderlos de Laclos, announced that the truly wise person will know how to satisfy all his or her desires without being hampered by burdensome ethical considerations.

It was a time when vanity, and pleasure in fashionable display, which had previously been reserved to courtiers, spread to the middle class. But the same ladies who could choose between two hundred different kinds of hats were visibly warming to a simpler, more natural way of life; so they gave up wearing corsets and being attended by servants, and moved to the country.

In 1783, Joseph and Étienne Montgolfier—near Lyon, not far at all from the Vianney's farmstead—launched the first hot air balloon to a height of 1,300 feet. Within two years people were flying in similar balloons from England to France.

Even the crusted surface of social relations began to move. The year Vianney was born, strikes were reported from Lyon among silk workers who couldn't support their families even by working eighteen hours a day. The city authorities announced a wage increase then brought in a batallion of artillery to fire upon the strikers and took back the raise when the silk weavers returned to work.

The shy and not especially bright peasant lad from Dardilly took precious little of all this in. When he finished his seminary studies, with great difficulty, and was assigned to a tiny country parish, the culture and politics of the time remained a mystery to him. He had no interest in the intellectual upheavals of his day, for exciting discoveries and pioneering scientific achievements. He didn't think he was capable of understanding it all.

"I am like the zeros," he said of himself, "that have value only when put after the other numbers." He hadn't studied anything in particular, and he couldn't even "hammer Latin into my wretched head." There was no calculating coquetry in his admission that, "Among the other priests I am like Brodin"—Brodin being the local village idiot.

But the simplicity that this modest priest so disarmingly concedes exercised a dazzling effect. People came from all over to hear his simple sermons and to get his advice in the confessional. This village pastor, whom some of his confrères still considered a halfwit and who fully concurred with their judgment, became the most famous priest in France.

From Vianney's wretched and yet so shining life we can learn what God can make of a weak person who radically commits himself or herself to Him.

The curé of Ars himself had the clearest realization of this. "God uses me as a tool," he once said, "the way a carpenter uses a plane." "If God could have found a priest even more stupid and less worthy than me, he would have used him instead of me, in order to make known the greatness of his compassion."

A Thrashing for His First Sermon

EVEN AS A SMALL BOY he struck people as a little strange. One day a troubled neighbor in Dardilly came to farmer Vianney's wife and hesitatingly informed her that her son Jean-Marie must have been taking him for the devil. "Every time he sees me, the rascal makes the sign of the cross." Whereupon the empathetic woman admonished her son to carry out his pious exercises a little less conspicuously.

If we are to believe the rapidly growing legend, the peasant boy from southern France was a complete angel from the cradle. He supposedly enjoyed praying as much as other boys did scuffling and fighting. When he and his little sister watched their parents' paltry herd (three sheep and a donkey), he often left her alone knitting at her stockings, while he stole off to his "altar." In the hollow of an old willow tree he had placed a statue of Mary, adorned with moss and flowers.

His amazed biographers report that he would do anything to "play church." He arranged solemn processions with his friends, with Jean-Marie always taking the part of the pastor, of course. He preached to his comrades that it was a sin to beat animals in anger—and for his trouble he himself got a thrashing by a lout who was stronger than he was.

All this no doubt testifies less to a "born saint" than to a thoroughly Christian upbringing in the house of the Vianney family. His mother, an arch-Catholic, intensely spiritual, affectionate, seems to have been fixated on him. "If your brothers and sisters were to offend the good Lord," she told him, "I would be sad, but much more if you did."

Besides, most children in good Catholic homes will enthusiastically play "church" at one time or another. At least that's how it used to be not long ago. For these young boys at a certain stage of their development, being a priest is just as much one of the dream professions as being a locomotive enginer or—nowadays—an astronaut. In fact, such lads will generally go no further than altar boys and later wind up as tax consultants.

Fortunately, we have a number of accounts of young Jean-Marie's "exuberant character" that identify him as a merry little devil. Nonetheless, even back then, his piety was beginning to display unhealthy features.

He fled tenderness like the plague. His shining blue eyes pleased Marion, the seven-year-old daughter of his neighbor, and she uninhibitedly asked him if he would marry her later on—with their parents' permission, of course. "Never, no," the seven-year-old Jean-Marie refused in horror, "Let's not talk about it anymore." Later, he wouldn't let himself be kissed, not even by his three-year-old cousins. In his rectory he wouldn't pat the girls on the head, and occasionally even boasted of having foresworn embracing his mother, "although that is permitted."

One important point, if we are to understand some of Vianney's narrow-mindedness and timidity in his later dealings with the "world," is that as a little peasant boy he experienced the Church as a *persecuted* Church. In 1789, Jean-Marie was three years old, when the great revolution began to shake France to its foundations. In 1790, a state law, the *Constitution civile du Clergé* turned the priests into salaried officials of the state and bade them take an oath to the new constitution. 130 0f the 134 bishops refused, but only 46,000 of the 70,000 curés did so.

Over the next few years these priests could be found in flight all over France, disguised as peasants and artisans, hiding in barns and stables. The Vianneys' farm became a meeting point for a catacomb Church, where those who refused to take the oath went in and out, where Christians met who had heard too much about the virtues and freedoms of "citizens" from the pulpit.

That is how the great revolution had begun: as a cleansing bath for a society filthied by injustice, as a social liberation movement, prepared with the help of progressive nobles, enthusiastically greeted by the bourgeoisie, longed for by the poorer classes—and supported by the lower clergy. The French Revolution by no means started out as the God-hating, demonic phenomenon from the deepest abyss of hell that lives on in one popular, but untruthful, Catholic version of history. The revolutionaries were not fighting against heaven but against heaven's earthly administrators in bishops' palaces and the royal court.

The princes of the Church owned an estimated one-fifth of all the land in France. While they vigorously demanded payment from their tenants and small farmers, they themselves were exempt from taxes. The yearly income of the French Church amounted to around 150 million livres (around 185 million dollars). Poor rural pastors saw little of that. They had to pay their tithes to My Lord the Bishop just as every other peasant did. While the noble clergy—among whom, paradoxically, Enlightenment unbelief and decadent laxity proliferated—hung on tightly to the old order, and the pope in Rome prepared a condemnation of universal human rights, a crowd of little curés and monks were making common cause with the revolutionaries.

When the Revolution degenerated into a fanatical reign of terror and devoured its own children, it was often enough Catholic children who saw their pious dreams of freedom and justice drowning in the bloodbath of the omnipresent guillotine. In Paris, drunken sailors went whoring in Notre Dame, the howling mob killed imprisoned priests by the dozens. Robespierre tried to replace Christianity with an insipid cult of the "Supreme Being."

Not far from Dardilly, in Lyon, civil war was raging between republicans and royalists, and the guillotine worked busily away like a blacksmith's hammer. Within a few minutes more than 1600 executions were carried out. Radical Jacobins led a donkey dressed up as a bishop through the streets, with the miter on the animal's head and a Bible and crucifix tied to its tail. A bonfire was lit with missals and statues of saints, and consecrated hosts were thrown into the blaze.

Needless to say, the provinces did not go unscathed by such excesses. Even in Dardilly, revolutionary soldiers went hunting for the non-juring priests who celebrated secret masses at night in the Vianneys' farmhouse with their conspiratorial followers. The family was taking a big risk. Anyone who granted asylum to such priests could be executed without trial. Anyone who denounced the outlaw received a reward of 100 livres.

Little Jean-Marie enthusiastically participated in these adventurous nightime services, and dragged crowds of beggars and homeless people into the house of his hospitable parents. He hid the statue of Mary—his dearest possession—under his shirt.

The education that the peasant boy picked up was limited to the most basic elements: a little reading and writing, clandestine religious instruction with nuns who had been driven from their convent. Behind closed shutters the children from Dardilly received their first Holy Communion, while outside the men busily unloaded a hay wagon to camouflage the services. Jean-Marie remained a strikingly pious child. Every time the clock struck the hour he prayed a Hail Mary and recited aloud, "Time passes away, eternity is coming. Let us live as though one day we shall die. . . ." Some of his companions laughed at him: "Look at him, wrestling with his guardian angel."

On November 9, 1799, General Bonaparte led a coup against the bourgeois regime, and the Revolution was over. Although at bottom he took himself for God, egocentric, cold, vain, and totally skeptical in questions of religion, Napoleon needed the Church. "With its belief in heaven," he said, "religion gives hope for a compensation that protects the rich from being massacred." In 1801, when Jean-Marie was fifteen years old, Bonaparte signed a concordat with Rome. The persecuted priests were allowed to return.

DESERTER FROM NAPOLEON'S COLORS

JEAN-MARIE, WHO had worked as a boy on his parents' little farm, digging up the vineyard, plowing the field, and sleeping in the stable, now saw his dream of the priesthood suddenly move into graspable proximity. The energetic resistance of his pious but realistic father, who feared losing his best worker and didn't know how he could pay for his son's studies, made little impression on him.

But the same Napoleon, whom the Church had to thank for its recovered freedom, put a thick spoke in Jean-Marie's wheel. Since he needed soldiers for his wars against Austria and Spain, he recruited the last reserves. And young Vianney was called up too. This was quite clearly an error by the authorities, since his pastor had already put him down on the list of candidates for the priesthood, who were exempt from military service.

Confused and frightened, he stayed only two days in the barracks; then he got seriously ill and was sent to a municipal hospital. "I ate up only one of the government's field rations," he joked later. Then, when he was supposed to march with an infantry battalion to the Spanish border, he missed his unit. At first Vianney ran after the rearguard, but on the same day, without much reflection, he joined a deserter who brought him to a remote village hidden away in thickly-forested mountains.

Jean-Marie lived here for two years on a farm in the wilderness under the assumed name of Jérome Vincent. He taught the children reading, writing, and the Mass prayers. With his intense piety he disturbed the family life of his hosts (thirteen-year-old Louis didn't want Jean-Marie to sleep alongside him because he spent half the night praying). Still, he so enchanted the family that, to be on the safe side, they had a cassock tailored for him. To be sure, his father, who remained loyal to the state, was annoyed with his deserter son. Then, a few weeks after an amnesty made it possible for him to return, his careworn mother died.

His biographers have always been voluble in covering up and finding excuses for this apparently embarrassing episode in the life of a saint. They claim that Jean-Marie slipped into this underground existence only because of his naiveté and without doing anything on his own. Or if they do take Vianney the deserter seriously, they chide him for being a bad patriot.

Why can't it be conceded that, like many of his contemporaries, he was simply disgusted by the war-mongering, tyrannical Napoleon and the imperialism of the French upper classes? Many others deserted and, like Vianney, never regretted it. As a parish priest he loved to tell his catechism pupils with sparkling eyes how he hid himself from the gendarmes in a haystack and went through agonies of fear as they poked through the hay with their bayonettes.

The pastor of Écully, a cultured man named Charles Balley, now took over the fostering of Vianney, the candidate for the priesthood, and accepted him in his parish school, which was a sort of pre-seminary. But though Jean-Marie was fascinating as a human being, though his intuition and will-power were pronounced, on the intellectual level he proved to be rather limited.

His memory was like a sieve, and grammar caused him insuperable difficulties. "I couldn't force anything into my wretched head," he later candidly admitted. The twenty-one-year-old was given a twelve-year-old whippersnapper as a tutor, but his behavior so vexed the boy that he once boxed Vianney's ear in despair.

Prayer and fasting were of no use, not even a pilgrimage of over sixty miles that he made on foot with high hopes. Jean-Marie was continually tempted to chuck the whole thing.

At the age of twenty-six he was finally admitted into the seminary, where he couldn't follow the lectures in Latin, and even had problems with extra instruction in French provided for the weakest students. Philosophy above all proved to be a book with seven seals. Soon his professors gave up even asking questions of this hopeless case, and advised him to leave.

Balley talked him him out of following his resigned intention of becoming a simple monk. Balley practiced with him and managed to get him admitted to the examination. But Jean-Marie failed miserably. When he saw the severe faces of the board and heard the questions in Latin, it was all over. Everything got jumbled in his head, and he couldn't come out with a single clear sentence.

Was the game up now? Paster Balley, energetic and unwavering in his faith in the hidden talents of his problem child, ran to the bishops' office in Lyon. He talked, implored, and begged until with a sigh they let Vianney be tested once again—this time in French and in the presence of Balley. The candidate didn't do brilliantly, but his examiners were satisfied.

Vicar General Courbon thought of the ominous lack of priests, asked about Vianney's piety ("Can he say his rosary?") and admitted him to ordination: "The grace of God will do the rest." In the document there is a cautious proviso that Vianney would be authorized to hear confessions only when his superiors should see fit.

This was one more humiliation at the end of a time of formation that won for Jean-Marie Vianney the reputation of a saintly halfwit among many of his confrères. He himself drew his own conclusions from it. "When I think how the good Lord has taken care of me, I am altogether beside myself." All his life he considered himself a poor idiot; and this was no flirtatious game with a modest image. He was fully convinced of it. He claimed no credit for anything that he set in motion and achieved; everything was God's grace.

The Church of France had gotten the sort of priest that comes along once every hundred years: a person without the faintest glimmer of intellectual vanity and free of the unpleasant consciousness of moral superiority that, unfortunately, so often marks the Catholic leadership.

Jean-Marie Vianney was in fact nothing but a pure vessel, clear as glass, in which heaven shone through to Earth.

To be sure, a lukewarm Christian still regularly meets his obligations, at least to all appearances . . . But he does it all so reluctantly, so carelessly and indifferently, with so little inner readiness, and he changes his way of life so little, that we can see quite clearly: He's just meeting his obligations, routinely, out of habit, because just now it's a feast day and because he usually does that around this time.

But this is a faith without zeal, a hope without perseverance, a charity without ardor . . . a passive and powerless charity. Ah, my brothers, this poor soul in its lukewarmness is like someone lying half asleep.

A lukewarm soul, if you will, commits no bad sins. But vile gossip, lies, stirrings of hatred, loathing, jealousy, a little dissimulation—that costs it practically nothing. If you do not pay it the attention that it thinks it deserves, then it clearly lets you know this, because it no doubt believes that this is an offence against the good Lord. It would be more correct if it admitted that the lukewarm soul had itself been offended.

Everything that is not quite a serious sin is good enough for these people . . . They wish to do good, but they don't want it to cost them anything—or very little indeed. They would be glad to care for the sick, but the sick have to come to them. They have enough money for alms, and they know people who need it. But they wait for them to come and ask them for it . . .

The lukewarm soul locks its God up in itself as in a dismal, dirty prison. It doesn't kill God, but God finds in this heart neither joy nor consolation.

The simple folk of Écully obviously had a keener feel for this than the episcopal authorities and the harsh examiners in the seminary. When he was assigned as vicar to his friend Balley they flocked en masse to the church. And when he finally got the right to hear confessions, they besieged his confessional.

Two years later Pastor Balley died. Yet, even though a delegation from Écully pleaded with the archbishop to have Vianney appointed his successor, the hierarchy still had a low opinion of him. He was sent to Ars, on the high plains of Dombes, a Godforsaken place twenty-one miles from Lyon with only 230 parishioners. It had been without a priest for some months. A few hunched

brick houses with thatched roofs in a forest of fruit trees, a delap-
idated church, an empty tabernacle—but full taverns. The clergy
considered this region a kind of Siberia, and an assignment there
a punitive transfer. No doubt the idea was that even a Vianney
couldn't do much harm there.

"You won't find a lot of love for God," Vicar General Courbon
told him frankly, "You'll have to bring it with you."

WHAT DOES THE RIDICULOUS CHARACTER WANT?

TO BE SURE, the village *was* wretched, and its inhabitants a little dissolute, but Ars was no penal colony. The people seemed insecure,
hardened, sobered up, embittered. They had lost their faith in God
and humanity. A typical postwar generation, they set themselves
no lofty goals.

"No one in Ars would have stolen a penny from his neighbor's
pocket," reports an early biographer of Vianney, "but few of them
had any scruples about cheating when they sold animals or packing bundles of hemp in such a way that the bad pieces were cleverly hidden. The fathers laughed when their children came home
from school with their pinafores full of stolen turnips."

Vianney made his entrance into Ars with a ramshackle cart containing a wooden bedstead, a few books, and clothes. The shepherd
boy who had guided him there was given not the tip he had hoped
for, but a pious promise: "My little friend, you have shown me the
way to Ars, I will show you the way to heaven." Naively trusting in
God, Jean-Marie Vianney had no notion of what awaited him. He
knew nothing of the world outside the farm and the seminary.

The first Mass said by the new pastor was attended only by a
few old women. Instead of dissolving in self-pity, Vianney proceeded to clear the junk out of his much-too-comfortably furnished
residence: the handsomely turned out, velvet-covered chairs, the
dinner table, bed linens, and frying pan. He had no need of such
things. The rectory was turned into a meager, shabby cell.

That done, he attacked his real goal, which was simple enough
yet beyond all human capacity he wanted to convert 230 persons.

He became the curé of Ars, that is, he was responsible for the eternal happiness of every single inhabitant, period. No elaborate strategies, no cautious weighing of who might be in the least interested in his pastoral services. Here was Ars with its 230 souls, who had been entrusted to him; there was heaven, waiting for those 230 people. And he, the curé of Ars, was in the middle, with a giant reponsibility on his shoulders.

A few individuals joined in from the beginning: mayor Mandy, one or two families, the aging Mademoiselle des Garets, who lived in a castle with her much older servant. Of course the great majority scarcely took notice of this ridiculous figure, who behaved like a missionary and staked out such mighty claims after he had barely landed in the village.

What did this ridiculous character want anyway? Barely over five feet, two inches tall, an emaciated figure, on whom his worn-out soutane hung loose, his eyes hidden behind thick, bulging glasses, Vianney shuffled across the village square in his bulky peasant shoes, which he mended himself. He certainly wasn't very imposing. "He didn't have the charm of youth," an abbé friend of his remarked, "His face was pale and bony, his body small and thin, his gait clumsy, his expression shy, even embarrasssed, the whole cast of his appearance was common rather than fine. . . ."

But his eyes could flash fire. His penetrating look—not scrutinizing mistrustfully, but open, vulnerable, and refusing all masks—remained in the memory of everyone who met him even once. "Sometimes his eyes shone like diamonds," one recalled.

This lively look unsettled and fascinated the people when he called upon them at work in the fields or suddenly appeared at the door during lunch (because at that hour he could be certain of finding the whole family at home). He came crashing in on his parishioners, asked questions, recruited, told stories, inquired about the harvest and the children. As a pastor he was tiresome. He looked as if he couldn't count to three, and he didn't even leave people in peace at mealtimes.

And then those sermons. What has been preserved of his homilies forces us to the conclusion that Sunday after Sunday he led a regular military campaign from the pulpit, combative and uncompromising. Often enough his tone was aggressive and sometimes downright unfair. The main targets of this Sunday campaign were religious ignorance, breaking the Sabbath, cursing, drinking, and—dancing.

"A religiously ignorant person," the pastor argued, "doesn't see the evil he does nor the good he gives up by sinning." Since he held ignorance on matters of faith to be the deepest cause of the religious tepidity and indifference that had sunk deep roots in Ars, he fetched the children into his catechism class. In the process he by no means disdained little tricks such as promising a lovely holy picture for the first ones to arrive. Later on he took the older people immediately afterwards.

"You work! You work! But what you earn destroys your soul and your body," he snapped at those who in summertime preferred to go off to the fields with their scythes instead of observing the Sabbath and attending Mass. "When I see people who drive around in their carts on Sunday, I think to myself that they are driving their souls to hell!" he thundered from the pulpit, belligerently and irascibly, like Giovanni Guareschi's Don Camillo, but without his humanness and conciliatory spirit. He had nothing in common with the homey, hard-drinking, deeply pious village pastors who were highly indulgent to the sins and weaknesses of their fellows, of the sort produced in the nineteenth century, notably in Bavaria.

In the process he wasn't simply fighting for some canon law, but defending a healthy rhythm of life and the non-material needs of people, who do not live by bread alone, but by adoration and love: "Man is not just a working animal, he is made in God's image." Sunday should be a feast for the inhabitants of Ars, otherwise overwhelmed with drudgery, an occasion "to rest a little with our Lord."

Vianney was physically pained by the curses that were part of his coarse parishioners' everyday vocabulary. How could they express such blasphemous thoughts as, "Devil take me," or "God damn me"? How could they be so full of hatred as to wish death on one another? How could a man say to his wife, "Goddamned woman, I'm sorry I ever met you." How could they curse their children as "a brood of Satan" and wish them in hell? The pastor didn't hesitate to quote from the pulpit the fecal language used in the village, and he warned: "You unfortunates! Your curses take effect more often than you think."

He made bitter enemies of the local tavern-keepers when he branded their guesthouses as "workshops of the devil," as places "where souls are bartered away, where families go to ruin, where health is undermined, where quarrels are instigated and murders committed."

Here he was thinking not so much of an innocent group of regulars having a drop as of rampant alcoholism with its devastating consequences for families who were already going hungry as it was: "The bartenders rob women and children of their daily bread by getting the drunkards to splurge their entire week's wages on a single Sunday. . . . Believe me, friends: The devil doesn't bother to take many pains with the the tavern owners; he despises them so thoroughly that he just spits at them."

But the curé of Ars would get worked up most of all over the villagers' passion for dancing. For twenty years he waged embittered guerrilla warfare, which we can understand only if we know what loose morals prevailed back then at the rural dances, which went on into the early morning hours.

In an age where contraceptives were unknown, and a double standard allowed boys everything, but the girls very little, an honest conventional country priest, with his unworldly moral training, doubtless had little choice but to throw up his hands in dismay and warn of "the hellish joys" (Vianney) of the dance floor. And finally, Ars was known all through the region for its lusty young people.

Still it strikes us today as disconcerting, indeed as frightening, with what dark aggressiveness Vianney led this struggle against all village festivities, "where boys and girls drink at the source of vice." He even forbade his parishioners to watch. He categorically explained to a father that under no circumstances was he allowed to take his daughter to the (open air) dance floor, because "if *she* doesn't dance, her heart will do the dancing." Those who came to him for confession and were unwilling to give up dancing sometimes had to wait for months at a time for absolution.

He mercilessly railed at the parents who let their children go dancing just to be left in peace because they wanted them to have fun. Why shouldn't they leave their daughter alone with a man just once for a few hours? To which Vianney replied, "Tell me, good mother, were *you* sensible when you were in the same situation as your daughter?"

And then these mothers still rejoiced "that Miss So-and-so is marrying Mr. So-and-so, and has made a good match." These mothers who covered their daughters with jewelry, plunging themselves into debt to do so, and who encouraged them not to be so shy and to get busy making acquaintances . . .

But you can't throw dry straw into fire and naively admonish it not to burn. "Blind mothers!" is Vianney's resigned judgment.

Of course, this moral preaching has unhealthy features. Instead of teaching young people tact and restraint in their pleasures, instead of training them to have more responsibility, the pastor came rushing in with his thunder and lightning, and wouldn't rest until he had totally banished dancing from the region (in the course of the years he actually succeeded in this). Vianney didn't just plead for non-alocholic drinks in the bars. No, the taverns had to disappear completely (and he managed that too).

Vianney was an anxious enemy of the little joys, a man who saw the table of regulars not as a place for well-earned relaxation but as the gate of hell. He was a dogged ascetic, who probably never understood that the soul, too, can express itself in dancing, and never dreamed that nowadays attempts would even be made here and there to introduce a danced prayer into the liturgy.

Vianney stubbornly maintained that Jesus Christ himself condemned the world and its pleasures—as if Jesus hadn't been a cheerful person, a lover of humorous parables, glad to attend weddings and banquets, and for that reason denounced as "gluttonous and a winebibber" (Matt. 11:19, KJV). Vianney saw things differently: "Didn't he say: This depraved, this miserable world! Look, my brothers, our Lord did not say: Blessed are those who laugh, blesssed are those who dance. On the contrary, he said, blessed are those who weep, blessed are those who suffering!"

No, the authoritarian pastor (he once said, "Queen Victoria rules in England, I rule in Ars") who offered musicians twice their usual wages if only they would stay out of Ars, this intolerant abbé threatens to forfeit our sympathies through such scenes.

But who said that saints always have to be right?

It's a wonder that the incensed young people didn't chase him away or at least lock him up in his wretched rectory when the *vogue*, the village dance, was announced. In fact wild rumors were spread about him. A girl who lived near the rectory had an illegitimate child and accused him of being the father. At night there was a hullabaloo beneath his windows, and the bishop received anonymous letters of accusation. But why did nothing else happen to him? Why did more and more people stick by him?

Evidently the word began to get around that this wasn't just a frustrated, embittered celibate who wanted to poison young people's *joie de vivre*. People realized that Vianney's inflammatory sermons were only a part—perhaps the least important part—of his pastoral program. Much more crucial for him was what could be called in modern theological language "substitution": Vianney prayed and did penance for his community and, to an unimaginable extent, he tried to make up with his own body what Ars was missing in faith, hope, and love.

"SAVING SOULS HAS TO COST SOMETHING"

SOON THE PEOPLE knew, and they were enormously impressed by the fact: Our pastor "lives" in the sacristy and in the church. He works there, he spends whole days and half the nights there. He used to get up at two o'clock in the morning and say his breviary before going over into the church before dawn. There he knelt for hours before the tabernacle, in a silent conversation with God, interrupted only by early Mass and a visit to the sick. He seldom left the church before the noon Angelus. Sometimes it was evening before he was finished with his prayer.

And even when he went for a walk through the fields in the afternoon to visit the farmers, he had his breviary with him. One day someone discovered him deep in the woods on his knees, continually sobbing and stammering, "My God, convert my parish!" Shaken, the accidental witness went away, intent only not to tread on any fallen branches.

Under his soutane, which in its tattered condition certainly didn't tempt him to vanity, Vianney wore a large hairshirt. He forced his upper arms into prickly chains. At night he beat himself bloody with a whip. "You preached?" he once asked, not without mockery, a desperate confrère, who complained about his unresponsive parishioners, "Have you also prayed? Have you fasted? Have you slept on a hard bed? As long as you haven't, you have no right to complain."

Vianney did not flaunt his poor lifestyle like a church banner. He tried to prevent anyone from learning of his penances. But a good deal was bruited about anyway—like the regular dealing with the whip, whose uncanny whistling and smacking sound was no secret to his neighbors.

The people were taken aback, and reflected: He's actually doing what he says, he's not just preaching. Gradually what the pious mayor had said right from the start became the public's opinion: "We have a poor church, but a holy pastor."

This simple Jean-Marie was thus quite different from some of the perfectly trained parish managers of our day. He wasn't the kind who senses nothing in his community, because he doesn't look after people, and because he doesn't give himself, but simply offers his services. Vianney, the naive, clumsy, theological ignoramus, followed no strategies and had no promising methods. He had only his humanity, his authenticity, his indescribable love. He was always there, always alert, always ready to listen. He had no office hours or scheduled appointments. A free evening? A vacation? Unthinkable. He was there, every morning and evening, until his death fory-one years later.

Even back then no one understood his insane penitential practices, but the people of Ars sensed *why* he was doing it: because he infinitely loved all of them, every single one, and because he wanted them to believe. Therein lay their happiness.

> Good Christians are like those birds that have large wings and little feet and never set down on the earth. If they did, they couldn't rise up anymore and they would be caught. They build their nests on the peaks of high cliffs and on the roof ridge of houses. So too the Christian must always dwell on the heights. As soon as we direct our thoughts to the earth, we are captured.
>
> Man was made for heaven. The ladder leading up it has been shattered by the devil.

The pastor gathered young girls around him into a loose community that regularly prayed the rosary—no doubt he thought it would distract them from dancing. He reactivated the forgotten confraternities in the parish, he led vespers in the church, and tirelessly campaigned for common prayer in the families.

To raise the educational level he set up a school for girls alongside the church. Vianney himself dragged stones, mixed the mortar, and sketched out plans. He invested the whole legacy from his father into the project, and when that ran out he went begging.

The school was closed to the more well-to-do families, as Vianney concentrated on the poor. Soon the house became an asylum for orphans and foundlings from the street. The pastor called the house *Providence*. For himself this house became the only place of refuge where he could rest a little. He tenderly called the girls "my little family." For twenty years he took his modest breakfast there—a little jug of milk. At times more than sixty adolescents were accomodated in *Providence*. There they learned to knit, sew, wash, cook, and in the one available classroom get a not-very sophisticated education. The pastor later helped them look for a position and advised them when they got married.

This sort of practical pastoral care pleased the people in Ars. But they were pleased still more by how modestly their pastor lived although it already seemed downright uncanny how this emaciated, hotheaded bundle of energy apparently had no needs at all.

He slept, at most, four hours a night. As a rule one meal a day was enough for him. Such "meals" consisted of a nearly indigestible bread cake, or one or two cold, and often enough moldy, potatoes.

What would you say about a person who plowed his neighbor's field and left his own lie fallow? That's exactly what you do! You constantly push your way into the conscience of others and leave your own by the wayside. When death comes, you will be sorry that you have busied yourself so much with others and so little with yourself. For we shall have to give an account of ourselves and not of others . . .

As soon as we hate our neighbor, God turns against us. The tables are turned. I once told someone: "So, you don't want to go to heaven so you won't have to see this person?—"Oh yes, I do . . . but we want to stay far apart so that we don't see one another." That won't be hard for them, because the gates of heaven remain closed to hatred.

The characteristic feature of the elect is love, the characteristic feature of the damned is hatred. No damned soul loves another damned soul. . . ."

As an antidote for his nervous attacks (no surprise, given his way of life) the doctor prescribed nourishing food, with veal, chicken, fresh butter, and honey. But he heedlessly set the tempting diet aside and (merely as a sign of his good will) asked his benefactress, Mlle des Garets, for a packet of tea leaves.

"Whatever he has he gives away," good pastor Balley had sighed long ago, shrugging his shoulders. Vianney never had an overcoat. He mended his tattered soutane himself and wore it almost his entire life, until it hung from his body in bizarre twists. When his sympathetic confrères gave him a pair of new pants, he exchanged them as soon as possible for the rags worn by a beggar he ran into. But he did change his underwear often, because he thought a lot of hygiene.

"It's good enough for the curé of Ars," he retorted obstinately to all reproaches, and generously swept aside the dress code of the episcopal authorities. Cardinal Fesch of Lyon, for example (Napoleon's uncle), thought it highly important for his priests to present an impeccable image, and he ordered them to powder their hair and wear buckle shoes.

Jean-Marie no doubt only smiled indulgently to himself over such wishes of his superiors. He had a keen sense that the mundane lifestyle of France's elegant princes of the Church had little to do with the alternative that the poor Jesus had brought to a world dominated by power, money, and boastful hypocrisy. In any case, Vianney never lingered over such ridiculous problems. He gave his mattress and pillow to a beggar and shifted his sleeping quarters to the floor of the attic, bedding his head down on a beam.

Now it was no surprise that the parish of Ars opposed the transfer of such a strict and yet so beloved a pastor to Salles-en-Beaujolais. As Vianney was en route with his wretched little wagon, the Vicar General reversed his decision.

"Ars Is No Longer Ars"

Jean-Marie himself said so after nine years of pastoral activity in the Dombes high country. Ars had admittedly not become a colony of saints, but its social and religious climate had noticeably changed.

The people were no longer leery of kneeling down in public at the sound of the vesper bell. On Sundays most of them went three times to church for Mass, catechism lessons, and evening prayer. A traveler passing through Ars once expressed his astonishment that out in the fields during heavy harvest-time work he hadn't heard a single curse. To which he received the thoughtful answer: "Oh we're no better than the others. But we'd be shamed to death if we'd commit sins like that alongside a saint."

The fame of this curé had long since pressed beyond the limits of Ars. All his confrères in the neighborhood treasured him as an ever-ready helper, and they called upon him during missions. "He works hard and eats almost nothing," one of his highly satisfied colleagues attested. Once he supposedly almost froze to death when he lost his way in a blizzard one night and was found unconscious. In Trévoux the impetuous pressing crowd nearly overturned his confessional. And in Saint-Bernard, the day laborers and vineyard workers dropped everything and even offered to pay their employers for the time they missed if only they could hear Pastor Vianney.

Regular pilgrimages to Ars are reported to have begun in 1827—when Vianney was just forty-one. People flocked from the

We are in this world as in a fog. But faith is the wind that scatters the fog and makes a splendid sun shine over our soul. . . .

See how gloomy and cold it is with the unbelievers. There a long winter prevails. With us everything is cheerful, full of joy and consolation.

Pull a fish out of the water, and it will no longer live. So too a person without God.

"Why, my God, have you put me into this world?"—"In order to redeem you."—"And why do you wish to redeem me?"—"Because I love you."

Up, my soul! Speak with the dear God, work with him, go, fight, and suffer with him! You will work, he will bless your work. You will go, he will bless your steps. You will suffer, he will bless your tears.

In this world we have to work and struggle. We shall have time to rest in eternity.

neighboring villages to make their confessions to him and hear him preach. "The curé of Ars" gradually became a fixed concept like "the pope in Rome."

Curiosity and pious sensationalism may have played a part in this as with the thousands of people who visited the controversial tailor's daughter, Therese Neumann, in the Bavarian town of Konnerstreuth, to see her stigmata bleed and to experience her visions of the sufferings of Christ. But many people *were* sincerely looking for advice and consolation or, quite simply, contact with a fundamentally good person.

They were hungry for his sermons. This is astonishing, because they were terribly long, neither original nor intellectually appealing, and over broad stretches simply boring and banal. The preacher obviously lacked any rhetorical talent. It is reported that he almost continually spoke too loud. "I'm speaking to deaf ears and to sleepy people," was his excuse.

For his entire life, preparing his Sunday sermons must have been the hardest thing he did. He wrote up to seven hours at a clip, only to fall exhausted on the cold floor of the sacristy. Still worse was learning by heart the thirty-to-forty page text every weekend, year in and year out. Needless to say, Vianney's sievelike memory, which had driven him to desperation even as a young seminarian, didn't improve with age.

In the pulpit he often got muddled; more than once he lost the thread in the midst of excited gesticulations, and couldn't go on. Then he had to step down in shame, while (in the early days at least) the congregation surely traded smug whispers.

But even here Vianney's secret lay not in artful techniques or intellectual brilliance. The people who streamed from all over to the tiny village church in Ars weren't looking for a divinely gifted speaker, but for a person whose every word they could believe, who put his passionate personality in those sermons. They were full of anxiety and concern, helpless excitement, defiant mistrust, and a love that accepted no boundaries.

"We have to go to heaven, all of us! What pain if one of you were on the other side!" That is how simple his message sounded, like a child's prayer. He told his listeners about Paradise as glowingly, as disarmingly, as he had once spoken to his little sisters and his playmates: "There we shall see God. How happy we shall be! If the parish becomes good, we shall all go up as in a procession and your pastor will march at your head."

At the Last Judgment a fragrant soul will rejoin its body, in order to enjoy God for all eternity. Vianney describes the body freeing itself from the earth with the unspoiled sharp eye of a French peasant: "pure like linen after the last bleaching." And in heaven these bodies will shine like diamonds.

So what was there to do on Earth but love God and work for him? "Everything else that we do is a waste of time," Vianney said. Three-fourths of Christians—"It makes one shudder!"—busied themselves simply with satisfying their bodily needs and without thinking of their poor souls. Yet the whole world could no more satisfy an immortal soul "than a fingertip of flour can satisfy a hungry man."

Now we understand better what fascinated his audience about his sermons. They are as far removed from the unctuous, sweetish homelies of that period as the little church in Ars was from the cathedral of Notre Dame. And if their content, too, is hardly original, and the grammar leaves something to be desired, Vianney speaks with enormous concreteness, robustly, vividly, in images from everyday life.

After communion, he advises his parishioners, they should keep the Lord in their hearts as in a well-corked bottle. In their love for God they should behave as the shepherds do in the cold winter fields: "They light a fire, and from time to time they busily fetch wood from all sides, so that it doesn't go out." By wood he means love for one's fellows and the prayer that lifts up the soul, "as fire does a hot air balloon."

Prayer is like a fish that "first swims near the surface of the water, then dives ever deeper." And a fish, by the way, never gets annoyed by too much water. "Thus a good Christian never complains of being too long together with God. Whoever finds religion boring does not have the Holy Spirit."

Vianney also had a quick, not-always-forgiving sense of humor. A well-nourished lady once asked him what she had to go to get to heaven. "Keep the fasts, my daughter," he dryly replied.

He informed another pious Madame, who absolutely had to have relics, that she could manufacture her own (i.e., by becoming a saint). And he posed the question to the worst gossip in Ars: "In which month of the year do you gossip the least?—I'll tell you: in February, because it has only twenty-eight days."

May a pastor be so merciless? Even in the pulpit he took on people in an unsparingly personal, indeed a nasty, way: "Isn't it true, mothers, you have nothing to give the poor?" he asks pointedly. "But one has to buy lace handkerchiefs for one's daughters. They have to wear three collars, one on top of the other, one has to buy earrings, chains, and ruffles. . . ."

The sharpness of his speech ("A shepherd that wants to do his duty must always wield the sword") sometimes drowns out his deep love for all these dull, limited people. He had to shake them up, drastically, relentlessly, in order to save them. He wept unrestrainedly in the pulpit because God finds so little love among humans—and immediately afterwards he shouted down at this parish: "It's just no use. You're all booked for hell! You've long since bought your tickets."

Once he is said to be spent a full fifteen minutes doing nothing but gasping, "O you accursed in God's eyes! You accursed in the eyes of God, who is love himself!"

Actually this sort of emotional outburst reassures those of us who have problems with this saint's ranting, seemingly heartless style. It shows after all that behind Vianney's wrathful threats of hell lies hidden the good news of God's love, along with the helpless despair that in many cases people perhaps just don't want to hear this message.

Over the course of the years he must have become gentler and more considerate. The effort to make God's love graphically perceptible played an increasingly powerful role in shaping his program. "The good Lord wants to make us happy. His hands are full of graces. He seeks someone to give it to, and, ah, no one wants it." After death there remains only love: "We shall be drunk with it, we shall drown in it, lost in the ocean of God's love. . . ."

Such a tender, caring God can also write straight with crooked lines. Vianney thought and encouraged his listeners to approach their Father uninhibitedly, instead of constantly intimidating them with gloomy visions of the future: "If he sees us, his little creatures, coming his way, he bends down to us, as a father does, to listen to his child, who wishes to speak with him."

Each and every time the curé of Ars inevitably comes to his favorite subject: Everyone has to be a saint. Like Vianney himself, by going without sleep, doing extreme penances and praying for hours and hours? The curé had no intention of declaring *his* way a model. He warned mothers never to neglect their domestic duties merely so they could keep running to church. When it came to religious practice, Abbé Vianney, who seems at first blush so fanatical, proved to be highly sensitive and understanding: "People misunderstand religious life," he declared quite calmly. "Look, my children, there for example is someone who has to go to work in the morning. But he's haunted by the idea that he has to take upon himself mighty works of penance, which consume half the night with prayer. Now if he is sensible, he'll tell himself: No, I have to drop that, otherwise I can't fulfill my duty, I'll be sleepy in the morning. The tiniest trifle will get on my nerves, I'll be unbearable the whole day long. . . ."

Holiness grows in the everyday routine. Vianney says that to the exploitative lords of the manor ("There too we shall find enough thieves. How many lords give their servants less than they had agreed on!") just as directly to their faces as to the notoriously litigious types: "How many souls bring upon themselves the sentence of damnation with their perjury, their hatred, their cheating, their acts of revenge!" And he doesn't at all see it as a misuse of the pulpit when he admonishes husbands to be considerate of their pregnant wives and warns the women themselves not to lift heavy loads.

"THIS WRETCHED CARNIVAL!"

BIGGER AND BIGGER crowds of pilgrims kept making their way to Ars. Soon they came in regular processions, led by church banners and first communicants, four hundred and more every day. During the year 1830, thirty thousand visitors came to the remote little village outside Lyon, a number that would later be quadrupled. A daily mail service was set up between Lyon and Ars.

The masses of people pressed into the side chapels of the little church, sat on the steps, jammed between the tombstones in the cemetery, waited for hours and days at a time for the most famous confesssor in France. In the slowly moving queue, bishops stood alongside Parisian ladies, peasants from Provençe next to professors and intimidated street walkers. Marshals had to be hired to control the crowd, which surged day and night.

In all this hurlyburly, Jean-Marie Vianney maintained a stoic calm. He slept even less now so that he could meet his penitents at an early hour. He endured with clenched teeth the way the crazy souvenir hunters tore his soutane to pieces and cut up his hat. When he got wedged into a crowd, hyper-pious women snipped at his thinning hair.

He got furious only when he saw the sugary holy pictures with his own portrait that were sold everywhere in the shops for two sous. "This wretched carnival!" he snorted. Once and only once a sculptor succeeded in doing a sketch of him. The photographers didn't cover their own expenses until he lay on his deathbed.

Understandably some of his colleagues didn't at all like it that their flock wandered off to this peculiar guru, with his deliberately wretched appearance. They chided his sloppiness and hunger for admiration. At a conference of priests one confrère refused to sit next to Vianney because his hat was too dirty. And then this very halfwit, whom they knew only too well from the seminary, now had the gall to bewitch their parishioners.

It hurt Vianney to see how unbrotherly his colleagues behaved. For all his self-discipline he hadn't turned to stone; he remained a vulnerable person. But he tried to take the defamation from clerical circles (even today envy among priests, *invidia clericalis*, is considered an occupational hazard) as a salutary warning against arrogance. "They burn incense to me—and they kick me" was his sober assessment of his image.

Some of his colleagues threatened to deny their charges absolution if they visited that damned Ars. The bishop assigned his vicar general to investigate Vianney; and the abbé Borjon from nearby Ambérieux-en-Combes wrote him an outrageous letter ("When one has so little theology in one's head, one should not sit down in the confessional"). The simple Jean-Marie found all such behavior quite in order.

"My dear and highly esteemed confrère," he wrote back to Borjon, "I admire you, for you are the only person who really knows me." He went on to say that he, Vianney, was in fact intellectually limited, and wondered whether the highly esteemed abbé couldn't help in getting him transferred to some quiet corner. . . .

Thereupon Borjon is supposed to have rushed to Ars and gone down on his knees to ask Vianney for pardon.

His bishop backed the much-ridiculed country preacher anyway and cut short the resentful enviers: "Gentlemen, I wish you had a little of this folly that you mock so much; it wouldn't harm your wisdom."

Besides, Vianney had no time at all for such confrontations. The stream of people to his confessional wouldn't let up. During the final decades of his wretched life he literally inhabited this box made of three boards. He left it only to celebrate Mass, to teach catechism, to visit the sick, or to pray a little in front of the altar, motionless as a statue, kneeling on the stone floor.

One has to see Vianney's confessional, which has been preserved in the sacristy of Ars, to get some notion of the torments that this service on the edge of the humanly possible meant for the aging priest. This was no roomy miniature chapel with a finely upholstered seat for the priest, as is customary today, but something from the junk room shoved into a corner of the sacristy: a shed made of three boards and a piece of wood awkwardly stuck in as a seat, unbelievably narrow and uncomfortable.

In this torture chamber the curé of Ars spent up to sixteen hours a day. That has to be read twice: up to sixteen hours.

Around one o'clock in the morning Vianney appeared, a lantern in his hand, to close up the church. At around eight or eight thirty at night he dragged himself out of the church. With a stiff back, his legs numb, his feet turned into heavy lumps, his soul torn apart and plunged into the world's distress, he felt his way up the stairs to his little room. "When I leave the confessional," he once confided to a friend, "I have to grope for my legs with my hands to make sure I still have them."

During this period Vianney seems never to have slept more than three hours a night. He often fainted in the confessional—especially in summer, when the oppresssive heat turned the shed into a sauna. For years now there had been no pauses to catch his breath, and no more walks through the blooming fields, which Jean-Marie, the peasant's son, so dearly loved. "We will rest in the other world," he said with a sigh, as he saw the never-ending column of people coming to make their confessions.

We don't know what specifically happened between those boards during all those years. There are reports of spectacular cases of people being touched, about enlightened wiseacres from the big city who wanted to make fun of the little priest—and left his confessional in tears, moved to their inmost being. Vianney is credited with wizardlike abilities. He is supposed to have called sick people out of the line with a knowing look, to have told notorious sinners to their face details from the life they were leading.

But most of these confessions were likely exhausting and monotonous, a repetitious stammering of standard sentences learned by heart, "I lied," "I missed mass on Sunday," "I was furious with my wife and children." Always the same confessions, day after day, year after year. How was it that people went with these things to Abbé Vianney and not to their priests at home?

We may presume that Vianney succeeded in transforming the monotony of the same old self-reproaches into an act of religious reformation, into an encounter with God and the powers of one's own inner soul.

Jean-Marie Vianney treated his penitents in a decidedly intuitive fashion, with a sleepwalker's sureness, which came from a long experience of life, especially from concentrated devotion. This village priest who had no idea of the world, who had never gone farther than the plain of Dombes and Lyon, who had hardly ever read a newspaper, knew people through and through.

And above all he suffered with them. When he burst into tears in the confessional, as he often did, God seemed to be crying in him over the missed chances, over the lovelessness and hardheartedness of his interlocutors. "My friend, I'm crying because you're not crying," he told one man—and shook him to the core.

His words of comfort, as we can reconstruct them, were terse, but urgent. Lovingly and accurately he advised people to change their lives. Once when he was given a long list of itemized sins and errors, he simply clutched his hands together and after every point of the indictment remarked, "How sad! How sad!" Something like that offered more food for thought than a long dressing-down.

As a confessor Vianney was very strict. If he saw that a penitent lacked a firm will to behave differently, he denied absolution. Some people came five or six times for thorough discussions before the priest was prepared to absolve them. As he said: "The good Lord is not cruel, but just." He considered it of the highest importance not only that the sin be regretted but that the damage done be made good.

FLEEING UNDER COVER OF NIGHT

THIS COUNTRY PRIEST who had become a national celebrity did not, God knows, enjoy living in a goldfish bowl. He longed more and more for solitude, for a quiet monastery cell, "where I can weep for my wretched life and do penance for my sins." Vianney, who was venerated by the simple people as a saint, had a terrible fear of dying and appearing before the judgment seat of God. "Now that I am laboring over souls," he sighed, "I wish I had time to think of my own."

In vain he bombarded his bishops with requests for a transfer. The authorities played deaf and dumb, and drove the desperate priest to panic. It has been documented that on at least four occasions he fled from Ars under cover of night. In Lyon he begged without success to be accepted into the Capuchins.

In 1840, when he ran off for the first time, he forced himself to return. He stopped at a roadside crucifix in shame and asked himself: "Doesn't the conversion of a single person weigh more than all the prayers that I could say in solitude?" Later, parishioners and pilgrims had to fetch him back—a strange combination of a procession and a posse.

Typical for Vianney was the way he did penance for his attempted flights: he came to church still earlier and stayed even longer in the confessional.

Despite this incredible ruining of his health, despite his almost suicidal penitential practices, there must have been a tough life hidden in that emaciated body. True, he was deteriorating; at seventy he looked like a centenarian, white as a corpse, a bundle of skin and bones. But while the doctors had already given him up, and all Ars gathered in the church to say the prayers for the dying, he overcame a lung infection with attacks of fever and asphyxiation.

He drew his strength from his great intimacy with Christ. On the feast of Corpus Christi, the seventy-two-year-old man carried the heavy monstrance for two miles through the fields, staggering and bathed in sweat. When people asked him how he was doing, he replied: "How should I be tired? The one I'm carrying has carried me too."

Even as an old man he clung to his poor man's way of life. Once the bishop wished to pay his respects. He came unannounced to Ars—otherwise Vianney would surely have taken to his heels again. And at a reception at the church door, before the assembled parish, he conjured up the cape of an honorary canon from under his cope. It was a splendid sight, trimmed with ermine and made of shimmering red and black silk.

Poor Abbé Vianney, completely surprised, thought he would have to sink into the ground. He resisted the well-intentioned masquerade so forcefully that the mayor and vicar general had to hold his arms. The bishop managed to pull the garment of honor over his head only with gentle violence. Thus decked out, he trotted unwillingly behind the bishop into the church. "Our good curé," noted Mlle des Garets, "was like a condemned man, led to the gallows with a rope around his neck." As the bishop went up the steps to the altar, Vianney escaped with lightning speed into the sacristy. There he pressed himself in the doorframe and for the rest of the service was not to be budged into reappearing before the parish.

Scarcely had the bishop left than Vianney sold the hated cape for fifty francs and passed on the money to the poor of Ars. When Emperor Napoleon III awarded him the cross of the Legion of Honor, he immediately locked it away in a drawer.

Jean-Marie: "When death comes, and I present myself with this trinket, what if God tells me: 'Begone, you have already received your reward?'"

The last summer of his life, 1859, brought a murderous scorching heat. The seventy-three year-old Vianney wept in his confessional from pain and inner spasms. In the pulpit he could hardly utter a single word. One day he collapsed and whispered: "My wretched end has come." On August 4, he gently fell asleep—for good.

For the first time he had no longer showed any fear of death.

Pope Pius X, who himself had been a village pastor in Sarzano, beatified him. In 1929 Pius XI, who canonized him, made him the patron of all curates in the world.

Was Abbé Vianney a model for everyone? His unique recklessness toward himself, his contempt for his own body and any need for rest, his crazy asceticism—can they be a universally valid standard? He is supposed to have worn out twenty-four little whips every year, in his effort to beat the last earthly longings out his body. To this day shuddering pilgrims are shown the traces of blood on the walls of his bedroom. He even chided himself for his three short hours of sleep. The pictures of saints over his bed, he told people, looked down at him and admonished him: "You lazybones, there you are sleeping, and meanwhile we are awake and praying before God." He was sorry when he had to break off his attempt to nourish himself entirely on the sorrel that grew in the rectory garden. He wanted to live like a horse, he once said.

No wonder that for decades he felt that he was persecuted by demons, and ultimately he cultivated an almost familiar relationship with the devil, whom he mockingly called "grappin" (that was the name of the three-pronged pitchfork used by farmers). Vianney explained the devil's roaring and raging—as a matter of fact there is evidence of inexplicable noises around the rectory in Ars—in his laconic style: "Grappin is angry, that's a good sign. We'll get money and sinners."

Vianney suffered from a morbid fear of eternal damnation ("He continually saw hell beneath his feet," reports a priest friend of his, "and a voice told him that a place there had been set aside for him"). He developed a kind of self-hatred that could only be called masochistic. At such moments his faith in Christ, the conqueror of all evil, seems to have been weak.

But does this person, who gave himself to the very last drop, this miracle of love and commitment, really need our lame justifications?

Even a saint—a human being and not an angel!—may have neurotic characteristics, even though those words stick in our throat. Wanting to defend Vianney's way of life is, in the final analysis, as impertinent as defending the sun for shining.

It was *his* way, and he never tried to pressure others into imitating him. He didn't get burned out. He didn't become nasty and embittered as he pursued and unwaveringly maintained a course that is so hard for us to understand.

It was the path of the poor idiot who knew nothing about modern pastoral care and psychology—and most likely wouldn't even want to know anything about them. But the people streamed to him and went back home happy. There weren't turned into fanatics, they had calmly decided to change their lives. They had come a little bit closer to Christ.

What finer thing could a poor priest want?

The Emancipated Nun

Teresa of Ávila,
Carmelite Reformer
(1515–1582)

The Hard Path to Friendship with God

For you are not a judge like the judges
of this world . . . nothing but men!

On a cold May night in the year 1569, two old women in Toledo, Spain, thought the devil had been unleashed: Powerful poundings on the wall shook their bedroom. The plaster started to crumble in big chunks. Finally half the wall came crashing down. Out of the huge hole in the wall stepped a pair of dust-covered figures dressed in black. They cheerily wished the trembling matrons good morning and apologized for dropping in unannounced. They were Carmelites from the new order of Mother Teresa of Ávila.

That was the way Teresa founded her convents. Dilapidated buildings and well-meaning sponsors weren't especially hard to find. But because sponsors often changed their minds after the agreement had been reached; and city authorities, rival orders and skeptical neighbors make difficulties—What, another convent waiting for alms and subsidies?—without a moment's hesitation, Teresa proceeded to occupy her newly acquired house under the cover of darkness.

Thus, during those years a suspicious band of muffled-up persons could be seen in Spanish cities. Loaded down with straw mats, brooms, images of saints, and costly golden church paraphernalia, they moved through the streets at night and then began to hammer and scrub away in some remote building. When day broke, a cheap little bell, bought in some flea market, called the nonplussed neighbors to early Mass—at a convent no one even knew existed the night before. Granted, in many places the mayor and police tried to drive off the unannounced guests. But they had to retreat with embarrasssed faces when Mother Teresa showed the safe-conduct from the general of her Order, which entitled her to found convents throughout Castile. The two women in Toledo who were nearly scared to death were the ones to suffer from this sort of founding, for the entrance to the provisional chapel in the new little convent passed through their house.

Mother Teresa, whose motto was "Know no bounds in the service of God," and whose favorite word was *determinación*, was a high-spirited bundle of energy, vehement, unbending, always inclined to extremes, a restless soul. She was the sort who wanted to charge through walls—and, surprisingly, was almost always successful at it. She was infectiously impulsive, eloquent, charming, and stubborn, an irresistible person. One confessor laid down his arms before her with the unnerved outcry: "Good God! I'd rather tangle with all the theologians on earth than with this woman."

Teresa of Ávila, stubborn as an ox, thickskinned as an elephant, and sly as a fox, was both a victim of the Inquisition and a Doctor of the Church. She was guilty and rebellious, the incarnate counterproof of all those dreadful clichés of how saints, nuns, and

Catholic women in general have to be: "good," modest, not too intelligent, and above all, obedient to men. "The world is wrong," Teresa commented, noting with relief that God is no judge like men, "who think they have to suspect every good capacity in a woman."

When someone mentioned to a bishop that this insatiable nun was now planning to found a convent in his diocese, too, he is supposed merely to have sighed: "Then it's already founded!" The more problems, the better. Teresa saw in them a sign that her work must be pleasing to God, which hell was seeking to hinder. And what about those devils?—Teresa hadn't the slightest fear of them. "They must be afraid of *me*! . . . Can one say 'Satan, Satan,' when we can always say, 'God, God!' so that they tremble. Come on, all of you! I am God's servant, and I'd very much like to see what you can do to me."

Teresa's proverbial power to stick it out till the end has, however, little of that unpleasant, cold harshness that tends to mark successful types. "She stole hearts," said someone in the course of the canonization process, about her winning charm.

For God's revolutionaries laugh and dance. They bring love and rebellion together. Christians are supposed to be radical—but not grim.

IMPERIALISM AND MYSTICISM

SIXTEENTH-CENTURY SPAIN was not, to be sure, an ideal nurturing soil for rebellious spirits. After the definitive expulsion of the Moorish occupiers and the successful campaigns of conquest and looting by the *conquistadores* in Central and South America, the nation was feeling satisfied. Spain had managed to climb to the status of a world power. From Mexico and Peru the conquerors brought home boundless riches. In maritime trade the Spaniards and Portuguese drove the Italian commercial cities from their place at the top. People talked about the *siglo de oro*, Spain's golden age.

With a mixture of business spirit, missionary élan, and imperialistic arrogance, the nation looked westward, to its newly acquired colonies; northward, where the Dutch provinces were still fighting for their freedom; and eastward, where struggles were still going on with the Turks. There was little room for self-criticism and efforts at internal renewal.

Fortunately, Spanish Catholicism—which had been steeled by centuries-long resistance to the Moors in the *reconquista*—did not limit itself to providing a religious garnish to the political successes of the monarchy and the annexation of "heathen" kingdoms overseas. On the contrary, the *siglo de oro* became a brilliant period in the history of Spanish mysticism, with powerful inner-directed energy, away from merely external forms of religious practice, toward a personal experience of Christ.

Even today Ávila, the city of Teresa's birth, on the high plains of Castile, strikes the visitor as a miniature image of that old Spanish society: proud, combative, and devout, the city of *santos y cantos*, saints and stones. A wall ten feet thick, laced with parapets, with eighty-eight circular towers, gives Ávila the appearance of a massive fortress; even the cathedral, with its battlements, was more like a castle than a church.

The warlike patrician families of Ávila, the Bracamontes, Barrientos, de Velada, Villalobos, and the rest of them, enjoyed an almost legendary fame for bravery in Castille. A certain Sancho Sánchez Zurraquines, an ancestor of our Teresa, is supposed to have slain sixty fleeing Moors simply with the battlecry *Ávila, caballeros!*. The motto of this city, so uncompromisingly loyal to the king, was *Antes quebrar que doblar*, "better break than bend."

Teresa's family history shows her to be a scion of age-old Castilian nobility, but also a member of a discriminated-against minority. Teresa's parents were the rich, distinguished Don Alonso Sánchez de Cepeda, who liked to pray the rosary and refused to have slaves, and Doña Beatriz de Ahumada. Their marriage united two of the most resounding names of that time. For centuries, Teresa's biographers have luxuriated in this glow, which lay over her protected childhood in the *Palacio de la Moneda*. But this glosses over the fact that her grandfather, Juan Sánchez de Toledo, was a converted Jew. In 1495, according to the latest research, he had to appear before a tribunal of the Inquisition to answer charges of "relapsing" into his old faith.

This seemingly minor detail takes on importance if one knows how much the *conversos*, the baptized Jews, played the role of outsiders in Spanish society. Above all, those who had become rich were persecuted by the disfavor of the little people and still more by the omnipresent Inquisition. Toward the end of the Middle Ages, the previously tolerant atmosphere among Christians, Jews, and Muslims in Spain had gotten harsher. Hunger, epidemics, and social problems favored a violent form of anti-Semitism. The Jews were driven out or forced to convert. Religious orders and cathedral chapters accepted only those candidates who could prove their *limpieza de sangre*, the "purity of their blood"—a regulation that fatefully reminds us of the racial laws of the Third Reich.

Thus, Teresa was the descendant of an outlawed minority—if nothing else—that makes us see more readily why she developed such a strong spirit of contradiction and cared so little about the prevailing majority views.

No traditional saint's life lacks those early indications of extraordinary piety that turn little children into blessed heavenly beings. Upon closer inspection, these are usually examples of a playful imitation of adult behavior, of the development of fantasy and the spinning out of fairy tales. At the age of nine, Teresa reacted accordingly, after grown-ups had read to her at great length gruesomely beautiful tales of the martyrs. With her favorite brother Rodrigo, she ran away from home and set off to the east, to the land of the Moors, in hopes of being beheaded there. Instead of the longed-for martyr's death, she got only a thrashing, because an uncle of hers nabbed the two pilgrims on the road to Salamanca.

"Since I now saw that it was impossible," Teresa informs us in her autobiography, "to go where we could suffer death for God, we decided to become hermits." The two set up a jerry-built hermitage in the garden of the Palacio, and with her friends Teresita liked best of all to play "founding convents."

But a few years later we find this same Teresita swallowing one novel of adventure after another, reading them under the covers (her father had naturally forbidden her that sort of rubbish), and even writing one such bit of wildly romantic pulp herself, called *The Knight of Ávila.*

And again a short time later, Doña Teresa de Ahumada y Cepeda became an adored midpoint of the society of Ávila with her flawless figure, her expressive black eyes, and her splendid hair. She was well-groomed, charming, and intelligent, with a dislike for shallow party-talk. She "turned every head," one of her first biographers recalled.

Even as a nun she must have radiated a certain erotic aura, for a flatterer once complimented her on her elegant feet. Teresa (by no means indignantly) rejected the suggestive remark, but replied with a laugh: "Take a good look, Caballero, because it will be a long time before you can gaze on them again."

What Teresa alludes to in her autobiography mysteriously as "unjust things" and "threatening dangers," can no longer be scrutinized. Her bitter self-accusation shows nothing that wouldn't be completely normal for a young girl: "As soon as I sensed that I pleased a man, and he had won my favor, I conceived such a inclination to him that I had to think of him constantly." Behind the stings of conscience there probably lay the fear of damaging her own good name—honor meant more to her than anything else—and of causing her family difficulties.

It's also unclear to this day what moved this effervescent, much-wooed young girl suddenly to decide for a cloistered existence. It couldn't have simply been her conversations with the Augustinian nun María de Briceño—a beloved teacher in the convent of Our Lady of Grace, which for a time served as a sort of boarding school. Nor can it have been the letters of St. Jerome to young Roman ladies, which had been given to her by an uncle disappointed with the world.

For Doña Teresa vacillated far too much, and her entrance into the order took place without real enthusiasm. She later told how she had fought a "true battle" within herself, with nightmares from hell and a very realistic appreciation of her own weakness: "I am afraid of myself!"

In the end, biographer Marcelle Auclair writes, Teresa entered upon a "marriage of convenience" with the heavenly bridegroom, which hits the nail on the head. She seems no longer to have thought herself capable of a life close to God in "the world." And so out of an anxious, private faith, she sought the seclusion of the convent: God and my soul, and nothing else. Teresa herself says: "More than love, slavish fear drove me to take the veil." For the pains and woes of convent life couldn't be worse than Purgatory, whereas, after all, hell was threatening her in "the world."

Perhaps the self-conscious young girl also simply took no pleasure in subordinating herself to a husband. In sixteenth-century Spain, men were accustomed to think of their wives as slaves valuable for breeding and of themselves as proud protectors. "Sisters, look from what subjection you have freed yourselves." At the time the convent *was* the only alternative to marriage.

THE "PAINFUL LIFE" OF AN AVERAGE NUN

ON ALL SOULS DAY in the year 1535, as dawn was breaking over Ávila, the self-willed girl again stole out of the house—her father had categorically refused to let her go—and knocked on the door of the Carmelite convent of Santa María de la Encarnación. Her father later gave in, but the nineteen-year-old Teresa compared her pain at leaving home to an agonizing death: "Every one of my bones seemed to be torn from the rest."

For the next eighteen years Teresa was a good "average nun." She committed no sins worth mentioning, but also lived without taking any great spiritual flights or making any great demands upon herself: "It seemed best to me to go along with the majority, because I considered myself one of the worst. . . ." She lived in a smartly furnished two-story apartment, had thoroughly delightful religious experiences, had a vision in prayer of an "extraordinarily handsome Christ," periodically imposed harsh penances on herself, took care of another sister who suffered from horrible abcesses, secretly mended the threadbare shawls

Vuestra soy, para vos nací,
qué mandáis hacer de mí?
I am yours, born for you,
what do you want to do with me?
I am yours, you have created me,
yours, you have redeemed me,
yours, you have borne me,
yours, you have called me,
yours. you have preserved me,
yours, you have not let me be lost—
what do you want to do with me?

Give me death, give me life:
give me health or sickness,
Give me honor or shame,
give me war or peace,
to all of it I say yes before you!
What do you want to do with me?

Give me riches or poverty,
give me consolation or sorrow,
give me gaiety or sadness,
give me hell or give me heaven.
Sweet life, sun unveiled,
I lost myself in you completely—
what do you want to do with me?

Whether you want my silence or my speech,
whether you want me empty or rich in fruit,
the law may weigh me down
or the Good News lift me up,
should I rejoice or tremble—
what do you want to do with me?

I am yours, born for you,
what do you want to do with me?

of the sisters at night and still often found herself feeling utterly miserable.

For the inner strife had also remained with her after she entered the convent. Joy at the nearness of God alternated with longing for the world outside, which also kept putting out its feelers toward Teresa. For the convent of the Incarnation was a *beaterio*, an aristocratic foundation for maintaining unmarried daughters, in other words, a lady's seminary with loose rules. At the time of Teresa's entrance, it was bursting at the seams with 180 nuns, and was just then on the way to a regular life of a religious order.

There was no mention of a strict enclosure or undisturbed peace. In the *locutorios*, or parlors, the noble idlers of Ávila held rendezvous; and the nuns regaled themselves with gossip and sweetmeats. Ahead of all the others, Doña Teresa de Ahumada, whose charm and wit made her the convent's "showpiece sister," was always swarmed around and idolized.

In this way the new life that she was doubtlessly striving for kept faltering. Teresa felt like someone sailing on a stormy sea, "constantly falling and raising myself up again," and she cried out in grief: "O long and painful life! O life in which one doesn't live, in which we find all sorts of desolation but never help." She dissipated her energies, stumbled from "pastime to pastime," could hardly force herself to participate in Mass anymore. She felt herself hopelessly torn, "as if every part was going its own way."

For these unvarnished notes we have to be eternally thankful to the unhappy nun. For they show us that the way to sanctity is not a high road irradiated by mystical heavenly light but the everyday beaten path of our anxieties and frustrations. Teresa was not a bad nun. She honestly tried hard, but she made too many compromises. She loved God, but she hadn't made a radical decision for him. She kept looking back, and so she missed the connection. She had indeed heard the call, but she dawdled with the answer— exactly like us "well-adjusted" twentieth-century Christians, whose greatest sin is a sluggish lack of decision. This was a nonchalant faith, working with the left hand, so to speak—just don't exaggerate, just don't stick out, God will be satisfied.

Aren't we amazed to find ourselves in these entries: "For years I was preoccupied by my longing for the hour of prayer to be over. I listened more to the striking of the clocks than to good thoughts . . . I yearned for life, for I saw very well that I wasn't living, but fighting with a shadow of death. Yet I found nobody to give me life, and I couldn't give it to myself."

This unsatisfying condition lead to a nervous breakdown (all her life Teresa was susceptible to psychosomatic symptoms), to a slow wasting away—worsened by extreme penitential practices, the wrong food and treatment—and, in the end, to a four-day-long muscle spasm with all the signs of death. The grave was already being dug for the woman laid out on her bier, when she once again awoke to a wretched life: three years of complete paralysis until finally she could move—at first going about on all fours.

In this period of forced rest, God himself must have turned her around. Teresa was meeting a God who comes near to us in the broken body of Christ: that's one way of formulating her crucial experience, which she herself sums up in a shattering vision before a statue of the Man of Sorrows: "I sank to my knees weeping, and begged him to give me the strength once and for all not to bother Him any more."

Teresa was about forty years old when she began to experience the nearness of God so irresistibly. "Hitherto the talk was about *my* life. Now God lives in me. . . . Praised be God, who has saved me from myself!"

The consequence was, at first, an enormous process of internalization—"I wanted to flee from people and withdraw completely from the world"—and a longing to be totally "immersed" in God and to have mystical experiences, about which she writes with her unerring humor: "My soul seemed to me at the time like a little donkey at its feedbag."

Finally, the slowly healing woman even believed she heard a divine voice: "In the future I want you to consort no longer with humans but with angels."

God and the soul, God and the ego and nobody else—a misunderstanding that has a long tradition among Christians and was later vehemently attacked by Teresa herself. But the withdrawal phase was probably needed to store up energy for her later activities. How can anyone dare to try to reform an Order if she hasn't reformed herself? As Teresa put it: "It's clear that no one can give what he doesn't have; he has to first possess it himself."

This was only a transitional phase. Soon Teresa could no longer keep her joy to herself (which is characteristic of Spanish mysticism in general). It drove her to turn everyone into "fellow lovers," to tell all of them how happy friendship with God made her. She wanted to "speak only of him." That, of course, didn't go over well with her fellow sisters. For the most part they took little pleasure in the life of radical love of God that Teresa was preaching. They didn't want to be deprived of their harmless pleasures in the parlor and the dining room.

What did this faker want anyhow? Was she so addicted to recognition that she pretended to be ecstatic before them, fell in a swoon at early mass and, deathly pale, called out for Christ? Was this idol of the playboys of Ávila suffering from the fact that she was getting older? Was that why she was trying to make herself important with her supposed spiritual graces?

At first the theologians didn't trust her either. Don Francisco de Salcedo, who was considered a luminary in Ávila and was by no means ossified or hard-hearted, got a precise description of her rapturous states.

He classified them as the "work of the devil" and sent the frightened nun to the Jesuits. They ordered her, once again, to undergo strict penitential practices. However, to their consternation, they recognized her visions as the work of God. This was lucky for the persecuted woman because at that time the Inquisitor's guardians of the faith had covered all of Spain with a network of distrust and fear.

But all that no longer seemed so important to Teresa. She willingly let herself be swept away by a love that burned up her heart: "I was no longer with myself. It seemed to me as if my soul were being ripped out of my body. . . ."

That didn't mean that she didn't also have experiences of abandonment and despair. What Christian lives in a permanent psychic high? On the contrary, the saints experience inner emptiness and human insufficiency at their most painful level—the constant failure to live up to their self-imposed ideal.

Anyone who senses God's crazy, boundless love, would like to respond to it and can't accept the fact that his or her own love is so weak.

"Love is like a great fire," Teresa said on that score. "It always has to have something so that it doesn't go out. Unfortunately, the situation with me is that I would often be glad if I could throw a few straws into it. Sometimes I laugh at myself, sometimes I'm sad." And again we rediscover ourselves with our supposedly unique problems, in Teresa: "Faith then feels as if it had faded away, if not lost as well. . . . We get so depressed and lazy that the knowledge of God seems like something that we have only heard from afar. If we wish to pray freely, it's a torment. . . . When we are in such a state everything gets even worse when we meet with other people. The evil enemy then provokes me to such a rage and ill-temper that it seems to me as if I wanted to swallow up everyone, and I couldn't master this ill feeling."

Ah, Santa Teresa, you sister of us "moderns." But unlike us, you didn't give up, but bravely went on slogging.

As Teresa said, we shouldn't try to fly before God has given us wings. *He* has to give us what we long for. Once we have recognized this, we don't need constantly to torment ourselves with our own incpacity. If our inner self seems "withered and without water," then it's time for God to pull out all the weeds and for us to see ourselves as we really are—small and weak. "Then we become humble, and the flowers grow again."

Yo que soy ruin, "I, who am wretched," is a recurrent turn of phrase in Teresa's letters, "In this I am not a woman: I have a hard heart," she confesses and accuses herself of self-destructive tendencies. But she doesn't give up. We can learn from this incredibly tough woman how one can feel burned out, drained, exhausted, and comfortless, and nevertheless remain a Christian. For nothing in the world would she give up Christ, even when he seemed ever so far away. She knew that he was there, and held on tight. "We want to go together, my Lord. Wherever you go, that's where I have to go too."

"THE WORLD IS GOING UP IN FLAMES!"

TERESA DIDN'T INVENT monastic reform. At that time many people in many Spanish monasteries were striving to return from affluent Christianity and the flexible morality of Christian conformists to the uncompromising poverty and simplicity of the Gospel. At almost the same time that Teresa entered the order, the new communities of the Ursulines, Barnabites, and Hospitalers were founded, and the radically poor Order of the Capuchins grew out of the Franciscans.

And in the Convent of the Incarnation, Teresa no longer stood alone with her rebellious ideas. Around forty like-minded nuns had joined in the course of the years, and from her circle, from the very young María de Ocampo, the idea came (this thought was like music of the future): "Why don't we get up and get out of here? Why don't we arrange a life for ourselves the way the hermits did?" But Teresa was the one who actually realized this dream, in the teeth of bitter resistance, and gave the new Order its unmistakable shape.

In all this, her strongest motive, which is sometimes overlooked, was to make a contribution to the Catholic Counter-Reformation. She probably had only very nebulous ideas about Luther. She knew nothing of his motives; and as for the French Huguenots, it's likely that the only news about them that crossed the Pyrenees came in the form of distorted horror stories. As far as Teresa was concerned, the Reformation could only be the menacing, yawning gates of hell that unleashed bands of heretics and enemies of the faith to attack Christendom. "The world is going up in flames!" she cried out. "It's as if they wanted to put Christ on trial again, by stirring up a thousand false witnesses against him. They want to destroy his Church."

But clear-eyed and critical as she was, she readily recognized the connections between the successsful dissemination of the new teaching and the tragic condition of Catholicism. For that reason one had to begin with the centers of spiritual life (which often enough had degenerated into mere caretaking institutions). To renew the Church the monasteries and convents had to be turned into "fortresses of reform." In that way, "with the great number of God's enemies, at least his few friends would be truly good."

That was the reason for an about-face to the old rule of the Order, as it had been given to the first hermits of Mount Carmel in 1209 in Palestine. Two hundred years later, in the emergency times after the great plague, this Rule had been mitigated. Teresa and her friends wanted to go back to the old strictness: cloister instead of a dovecote, coarse wool clothing instead of jewelry and elegance, straw sacks instead of feather beds. One unmistakable sign of the change, of course, as with the other reform Orders, would be walking about barefoot. Discalced monks and nuns would be a living accusation of the luxury of a Christian world gone bourgeois.

As might have been foreseen, the majority in Teresa's own convent opposed these burdensome affectations of a "hundred- per- center." Being a Christian was fine—but everything in moderation, please. So Teresa had no other option but to prepare the foundation of a new settlement—as that seventeen-year-old fellow nun had proposed in her naive enthusiasm. Yet why *not* be naive out of love for the Gospel?

Teresa found a rich benefactress who acquired a house in the name of Teresa's brother-in-law. Only four daring comrades-in-arms in the Encarnación convent knew that she had secretly set up a tiny church there, that at night she sewed coarse habits and was preparing a scandal that would make church history.

On August 24, 1562 ,the elegant nun Doña Teresa de Ahumada took off her shoes, picked the simple name *Teresa de Jesús*, and clothed her four fellow sisters with the rough habit reminiscent of hermits' cowls. Then she waited in her new little convent, San José, on the outskirts of Ávila to see how the Incarnation convent and the leadership of the Order would react to the unexpected competition. Her benefactress had, it is true, gotten a papal letter of protection, which put the the new foundation under the authority of the Bishop of Ávila. But from the standpoint of canon law, the nuns themselves belonged to the convent of the Incarnation as much as ever. They had not a penny at their disposal, and still didn't know how they would live.

Teresa was by no means looking at her successful work with pride and confidence of victory. She racked her brains, troubled by remorse and fears for the future. "With so strict a rule of cloister the nuns would likely not hold out in this house. And so it had been folly to enter a new convent, since I already was in one . . . I thought I had taken too much upon myself, and would certainly break down. . . . A sadness, a gloom wrapped me round, such as I could never describe."

In the middle of these dismal thoughts the sound of powerful blows was heard thundering on the doors of the little convent. A raging mob was threatening to break down the gate. The rumor had gone around that this was a convent for the poor, without the usual guarantees of support by fathers or other relatives of the sisters. So they were pious starvelings, simply out to beg away the last possessions from charitable folk who themselves scarcely had anything they could sink their teeth into. Who knew what immoral ideas this strange women's commune would think of next to ensure their keep? (These people were later embarrassed to see at the gate of San José the nicely finished weavings and needlework with which, in accordance with Teresa's rules, the sisters earned their meager bread.)

Mayors and policemen tried in vain to clear the house. No doubt they were driven away less by the intrepid reistance of the nuns than by the discreet hint that, "You wouldn't want to make the bishop and pope your enemies, would you?" But the convent of the Incarnation fetched back the five escapees; and a distinguished ad hoc committee made up of city councilmen, canons, jurists, and monks debated for days about the unheard-of event of a revolt in a religious Order. The upright mayor argued that, after all, innovations always caused unrest and tumult in the state. They damaged good habits and seduced people into disobeying the laws and . . .

The complacent fear of any disturbing of the peace would likely have triumphed over Teresa's protest-convent, had it not been for the unconquerable radiance that at the crucial moment turned her mistrustful enemies into true friends. For example, there was Bishop Don Álvaro de Mendoza, who at first thought, despite the letter of papal approval, that there already were enough unprovided-for convents in Ávila. But after meeting with the foundress, he became a vigorous supporter of her work. Then there was the Dominican, Pedro Ibañez, who in the previously mentioned tribunal vehemently took Teresa's side, and reminded those present that *all* Orders had arisen out of the idea of reform.

And again there was another gentle but irresistible voice, that at the height of her despair told Teresa: "Don't you know then I am strong? Why are you afraid?"

Nine months after her move under cover of night the provincial of the Order offically granted permission for the five sisters to transfer to San José.

Charactcristic of life in the reformed Carmelites was, first of all, an unheard-of seriousness in striving to come close to God. "No, my sisters," Teresa states, "this is no time to negotiate with God over trivial things." Love costs something. God's friendship doesn't fall into your lap without your taking a hand in it.

The second peculiarity of Teresa's sketch is the thought of representation: Prayers, vigils, penitential practices, and fasts weren't to be an end in themselves, but had to serve the Church and the world. Otherwise they were useless. Nowadays we are witnessing the rediscovery of contemplative life along these same lines: Silent men and women, entirely concentrated on the essentials, make God present in a cold, hectic, aggressive environment. A credible community sets an example of the transforming nearness of God.

For Teresa, contemplatives were "standard bearers." Though they do not fight in the battles themselves, they march forward banner in hand and are just as much in danger as the others. Of course, the only way to understand what forces such representation liberates is by accepting that all men and women are wrapped round by a single great love, and that prayers are a power: "Naturally it helps to pray and to know that we are one with the force that helps the blade of grass pierce the asphalt. Naturally it helps to wish, to dream, to talk about it, to have a vision and to communicate it in action" (Dorothee Sölle).

Finally, the third distinguishing mark of the reformed religious life that Teresa was aspiring to was the combination of discipline and humanity. "God preserve me from saints with peevish faces!"

she cried out. She felt that a discontented nun was more to be feared than a whole horde of evil spirits. The poor "barefoot nuns" lived according to a strict Rule, but all hardness only makes sense if it makes the heart free for God. Teresa, on the other hand, considered it absolutely unchristian to sour one's life artificially.

She was mad about pink bonbons and freely admitted it. She feared "melancholy nuns" like the plague and laughed at a pious woman to her face when she got indignant over Teresa's appetite: "Instead you should praise the kindliness of your Lord and note: When eating partridge, eat partridge; when doing penance, do penance." Admittedly, on the way to God you shouldn't creep along "like a toad," but neither should you force yourself to do something you can't handle. To a depressed correspondent, she recommended neither devotions nor penances but walks in the fresh air. And the incapacity to pray could also stem from a sudden change in the weather or from circulatory disturbances: "So you should realize that you are sick, and put off the hour of prayer to another time."

When she learned that some priest friends of hers were whipping themselves till the blood flowed, she wrote to them in dismay to tell them simply to stop. In the end, she said, the "evil spirit" was seducing them to such mortifications so as to finish them off before they had done enough work for God. Granted, one should fight against weaknesses, but in such a way that human nature doesn't succumb to them: "We have to guide our soul gently."

FOUNDING CONVENTS IN A BOLD STROKE

YET A WOMAN like Madre Teresa was by no means about to be satisfied with the successful project of San José. In the following years she founded more than thirty convents all over Spain. She covered the country with a net of reform centers, systematically building up the alternative Order of the "Discalced Carmelites." How adventurous things often were has already been described at the outset. Often enough the nuns took possession of their future convent building in something like a *coup de main*.

All you who fight beneath this banner,
don't sleep, don't sleep,
for there is no peace on earth!

Like a brave general,
our God plunged into death;
because we gave him up to death,
let us follow him decisively.
O what a splendid lot he won
as booty from this battle—
don't sleep, don't sleep,
earth lacks God!

No one must prove a coward,
let us stake our lives,
for nobody will guard it better
than he who gave it up for lost.
Jesus is our leader
and the battle prize after the victory—
Don't sleep, don't sleep.
for there is no peace on earth!

Let us offer ourselves, every one,
in all seriousness to die for Christ,
and in heaven we shall celebrate
a blissful wedding.
Let us follow this banner,
for Christ leads us in the chaos of battle—
don't fear, don't sleep,
for there is no peace on earth!

—COMPOSED FOR THE CEREMONY OF TAKING VOWS

Julian de Ávila reports with dry humor about one such lightning action that he was on hand for: "The foundation in Medina del Campo, that was something! We had to get out at the entrance to the city, because the one wagon we had left made such a hellish ruckus in the silence of night that it would have waked all the inhabitants. . . ." The monks and nuns crept through the streets with their church gear "like gypsies and robbers," barely escaping six bulls that were being driven to the bull ring.

"Soon it began to dawn," Julian continues in his report. "You should have seen the mother prioress, the nuns, all of us, some with brooms in hand, others standing on ladders, so as to fasten the wall-hangings or a clock. We had no nails, nor was it the time to buy any. Mother Teresa re-used the old ones that she found in the walls. . . . The altar was adorned, the chapel was beautifully done up, but we had only one meager candle to give us light, and in the darkness we wondered whether we had really settled inside a house. Maybe we were in the middle of the street." As a matter of fact, in the light of dawn, the discalced Carmelites determined that their house consisted only of some dilapidated walls, minus a roof.

Teresa herself was amazed how these "dovecotes"—as she called her foundations—survived so many difficulties. When she occupied a house, all the convent's worldly goods consisted of a pair of straw mats and borrowed blankets. "That way we were never lacking a bed." Once she decided to have a church enlarged, and asked her financial administrator about the current state of their cash flow. "We still have a penny," he answered with a sigh. Teresa was blissfully happy, and began at once with her building projects.

Incidentally the *Madre Fundadora*, as everyone had come to call her admiringly, was not just in command. She drew up building plans, sewed habits, scrubbed and hammered, wrote countless begging letters, negotiated with authorities and benefactors, pacified the other Orders, drew up estimates, chose candidates and confessors.

"She noted with some surprise that she had become "quite business-minded" and played down the the real dangers and constant discomforts of her travels across the length and breadth of Spain. She spent days and weeks at a time on the back of restive mules or in a bumpy covered wagon. Frozen blue and trembling in biting frost, parched and fighting for air in the scorching heat of a Spanish summer, this strange caravan of disguised, veiled figures headed off through villages and mountain plains, spending the night in abandoned, ruined barns or in dreadful dives with thieves and whores. "God supplied us with a good many opportunities to suffer for him," was Teresa's comment on these uncomfortable business trips, "even if only because of fleas, goblins, and the hardships of travel."

Once the muleteers lost their way (the path was buried under debris) in the endless serpentine twists of the mountains of Castile and just missed plunging into the abyss. Another time, as they were crossing the Guadalquivir River, a ferry with two oxcarts was swept away by the current and landed somewhere on a sandbank in the middle of the wilderness. As night fell, there was no rescuer in sight. But Teresa serenely rang the little bells she had mounted on her oxcart, sang the evening prayer, and prepared the straw mats for the nuns.

All this with her chronic sickliness from headaches, fevers, and shivering fits to rheumatism, kidney troubles, gall bladder problems, and a weak heart. She went through practically every conceivable kind of suffering, and often several at a time. "The Lord continually gives me bad health," she noted sarcastically, "and when despite everything that I can do, sometimes I have to laugh about it." Others would have spent their life in a sickbed. But the Lord preferred that "no limits be set to his works."

In any event the face Madre Teresa showed her nuns wasn't that of an ailing bundle of nerves or of a hypersensitive churchmouse. Despite the Spartan lifestyle, they had a great time, for she thought that nothing was worse than a "grumpy superior." When she was in the mood, she would pick up a tambourine, dance, and sing, composing impromptu, silly songs.

No wonder that this boisterous temperament was contagious. One time after early mass, Teresa saw ten nuns walking behind a crucifix in a solemn procession, carrying candles, as they entered the chapel. She listened in astonishment to their weird refrain: "You have given us a new garment, heavenly king; free this wool from the nasty little breed!"

Solution to the puzzle: the sisters had decided to wear the habit on their bare skin, but they were afraid that fleas might have nested in the coarse material. Teresa grasped the situation at once and made up a pedagogical antistrophe: "This creature bothers souls at prayer that are shaky in their devotion. You who have come here to die, do not vacillate. Be not afraid of the filthy little tribe."

And when her fellow nun Sister Petronia died, Teresa forbade the usual hymns of grief, and composed instead lively songs of joy, with which the nuns danced around the coffin. Isn't it inhuman to forbid mourning? "I don't understand," Teresa argued, "how we can weep over those who will have eternal rest."

Her style of leadership must have been understanding and sensitive, paired with tact and respect for the individuality of each one of the sisters. "As there are many mansions in heaven," Madre Teresa adapted the New Testament saying, "so there are also many ways to get there." She had the capacity, seldom found in spiritual leaders, to let go. And she warned against measuring one's fellow men and women by one's own standard: "Let us not force those whom God lets fly like eagles to trip forward like tied-down chickens . . . Why not leave them to Himself?"

"The holy mother wanted the prioresses to treat the sisters like daughters of God," a certain Francisca de Jesús would put on the record at the canonization trial. To be sure, la Madre also showed signs of authoritarian strictness; and she once said a superior has to be feared. She refused to accept a candidate with a deformed face, brusquely remarking that she wanted no one-eyed nuns. But in the testimony that has come down to us, the prevalent impression is one of a genuinely sisterly way of dealing with her nuns. She asked their opinions and often enough followed their advice.

The airs of a princess-abbess were foreign to this poor barefooted woman. She cooked, cleaned, spun, and busied herself with sewing, even while she was dealing with visitors through the parlor grille. She warned her nuns against dreaming only of spiritual experiences and looking down on kitchen work: "The Lord awaits you amid the pots and pans."

Nuns from a Franciscan reformed convent in Madrid wanted to meet the famous Carmelite sister and afterwards remarked with bubbling enthusiasm: "Praised be God, who let us see a saint whom we can all imitate. She speaks, sleeps, and eats as we do, and is not ponderous in company, nor does her mind flow like honey."

Evidently, Christians didn't begin wishing for "normal" saints only yesterday.

In reading her writings one likewise gets the impression of an extremely natural, sincere woman, far from the cliché of a hysterically devout "expiatory soul." The manuscripts of her work that has survived fill nine thick volumes: reports on the foundation of convents, advice for prioresses and "visitors," a substantial autobiography, above all, manuals on spiritual life with titles like *Camino de perfección* ("Way of Perfection") or *El Castillo Interior* ("The Inner Castle"), plus 450 letters.

Almost all these manuscripts were written at the request of her confessors, hastily and during pauses from work, without real enthusiasm, "because writing disturbs me when I am spinning." But they became religious bestsellers, and have thus far reached 1400 editions in every conceivable language. They strike the reader as genuine and rousing because instead of endless theories about the life of pious souls, they communicate all sorts of personal experiences. They seem at pains to be authentic ("Never assert something that you don't know"). They unaffectedly reveal emotions ("Never before would I have been so glad to tear a letter out of your hand as this one"); and they are relieved by a healthy dose of jokes and sarcasm. One sample of her epistolary style: "This letter is full of advice that resembles an old, not very humble person. God grant that I have more or less hit the nail on the head. If not, at least let's remain good friends."

Teresa's poems are no hackneyed idylls from a soul's flower-bed of anemic, affected piety. They are powerful, emotionally charged, indeed, pugnacious songs in the thudding rhythm of medieval battle songs—like her heavy "Don't sleep, for there is no peace on earth," or the lively challenge *Caminemos para el cielo, monjas de Carmelo*: "Let us make our way to heaven, nuns of Carmel!"

The Order's Foundress under House Arrest

Some people were now calling this most popular nun in Spain *Santa Madre*, Holy Mother. But, along with the number of her foundations,

Nada te turbe,
nada te espante . . .
Let nothing frighten you,
let nothing perplex you,
everything passes away.
God remains the same.
Patience achieves everything,
Whoever clings to God
will lack nothing.
Sólo Dios basta.
God alone is enough.

—After her death a note with this text
was found in Teresa's breviary.

there was also a larger crowd of envious people who observed her unconventional methods with mistrust. They feared the worst for the Church if Teresa were allowed such freedom of movement. She was, after all, a woman untrained in theology, who couldn't be controlled by the authorities. Didn't the learned General of the Dominicans, Tomás Cayetano de Vio, declare that monastic reforms were a matter for superiors, "not for women, whose head was a man"? Didn't the no-less-learned Melchior Cano propose that for safety's sake women should be prohibited from reading Sacred Scripture?

But when this go-getting woman with her reformist zeal decided to go after men's monasteries (she needed confessors and spiritual teachers for her convents), that was the limit. Besides, the general of her Order was out of sorts because the papal nuncio, like the king of Spain, evidently sympathized only with the barefooted religious and, bypassing the leadership of the Order, appointed a friend of Teresa's as *visitator*. The Father General struck back: He refused to acknowledge the papal overseer, dissolved all the convents set up without his approval, and forbade Madre Teresa to found any new ones. She was to be placed under house arrest in Castile.

And ever more frequently the rebellious nun was denounced to the Inquisition. At that time it was very easy to be suspected of heresy in Spain. The official Church felt just as threatened by the numerous groups that were looking for an emotionally accentuated, personal religious experience as by the nascent school of humanism, with its respect for personal self-determination. In both cases weren't subjectivity and dubious emotions replacing the reliable message of Christ, preserved by the Church's magisterium?

Teresa promoted silent prayer without the use of texts blessed by the Church—that in itself was suspicious. Indeed, the Inquisition's tribunal in Toledo had just taken drastic action against the *Alumbrados* ("enlightened") movement. Its justification was that these people met "in dark corners" for group Bible-readings. In 1559 the Grand Inquisitor, Fernando de Valdés, forbade all spiritual literature in the vernacular.

And those dubious relationships of *la Madre* with sixty (at least) all too young and enthusiastic monks. John of the Cross, for example, was a poet and mystic like her, though unworldly and shy. Along with him, she was reforming the male Carmelites, constantly encouraging him like a motherly friend.

On the other hand, she seems to have downright fallen in love with Fr. Jerónimo Gracián—quite platonically, of course. Until well into our century, most biographers have passed this episode over in embarrassed silence because they found it just as disquieting as the guardians of orthodoxy did back then. So they erased Gracián from Teresa's life—though naturally that could be done only by censoring her letters. This ruthless attitude looks at enthusiasm for another person and can see nothing but weakness, obviously taking God to be a very jealous lover.

Was it so bad, then, that there should be human warmth between the two reformist warriors? (Gracián became the first Provincial of the Discalced Carmelites). Was it so bad that the *Santa Madre*, who was forever leading, making decisions, pressing forward, radiating power and optimism, now wanted to collapse for a change, and longed for security? Are the little exaggerations of her happy letters really so shocking? So what if she compares Gracián to an "angel," gratefully calls Christ her *casamentero* (matchmaker), and the days with Gracián "the most beautiful of my life"?

O Lord, the thought of your greatness and majesty amazes me. But it is still more astonishing that you favor with your love the sort of person that I am. Yes, one can converse with you about everything, one can talk with you as one wishes . . .

My love and my trust in the Lord began to grow strong, when he showed me he was someone I could talk to at any time. I saw that for all his divinity he was also truly human and was not outraged by the weaknesses of human beings . . . Though he remains the Lord, I can deal with him as with a friend.

I notice that he is not like the lords of this world, who base their standing on borrowed splendor. One can speak to them only at certain times, and only prominent people are admitted into their presence. If a poor, ordinary person has a concern, he must do all sorts of things and clear all sorts of hurdles until he can address such a Lord.

O Lord of all kings! Your kingdom is not so wretchedly constructed. With you we don't need a mediator before we can get started.

What sort of hard-hearted Christianity would get all disturbed over the innocent tenderness of a nun for a dazzling priest? Gracián must in fact have been a highly cultivated, cheerful, intelligent charismatic man, at once a lively comic and a strict reformer. Besides, Teresa by no means stumbled open-eyed into a scandal. She started using code names in her correspondence with Fr. Gracián—for seven years she wrote him almost every day—and she carefully warned him: "I would like to avoid any occasion for getting you talked about. For various reasons I can afford to do it, to show a great deal of love in my dealings with you; but not all nuns are allowed to. Nor would all their superiors be like you, my father, with your openness."

"I can afford to do it"—even in this admonition to be careful we can hear the sort of emancipated consciousness that the representatives of the male Church could no more endure than they could her emotionally charged piety and her solo efforts at reform. One has to be familiar with the uniquely misogynistic tradition of sixteenth-century Spain to categorize Teresa's bold protest correctly.

"Legs crossed and at home" is how a popular proverb of that time characterized the decent woman. Unmarried women were controlled by their fathers or brothers. When they got married, the rights of possession and claims to power were transferred to their lord husbands, who, in contemporary letters, are often addressed as "Lord and Good of my life" (signed, "Your wife and slave, who loves you very much"). Their realm was the kitchen and children's room. Archbishop Hernando de Talavera, Queen Isabella's confessor, advised women to stay within the four walls of their house and to renounce unnecessary intellectual education.

One widely read spiritual author, Francisco de Osuna, made the following recommendation, without batting an eyelash, to husbands concerned with their households: "The moment you see your wife running back and forth on pilgrimages and devoting herself to sanctimoniousness, imagining that she is a saint, close the door of your house. And if that should fail, then break her leg, if she's still young. That way she can limp from her house to paradise, without chasing after suspicious pious exercises. For a woman it is enough to hear a sermon. If she wishes more, she can have a book read to her while she is spinning, and subordinate herself to her husband's hand."

True, there was a trend in the Renaissance toward increasing respect for the intrinsic value of human beings, and thus logically toward a higher estimation for women. Alcalá was the site of the first girls' school in Europe, and it had a woman professor of rhetoric. In Salamanca there was a woman teaching Latin and Greek. But they remained lonely exceptions.

Teresa—how could it have been otherwise—naturally did not remain untouched by the prejudices of men. Half ironically, half seriously she would engage in constant complaints over the weaknesses of women. But in a way that was absolutely revolutionary for Spain and the world of medieval monasticism, she refused to be restricted to a woman's role—which simply meant exclusion from the exercise of power and from every activity that changed the world.

She suffered from being "a weak little woman," whose development was blocked by "natural cirucmstances": "Ah, poor butterfly, how many chains hold you down and stop you from flying as you would like!" But she found herself in conflict with almost all her contemporaries, women included. She chided men for their injustice to women and lack of respect for them; she criticized women for their fearfulness and indecisiveness.

She said it was "far more often the women than the men to whom the Lord grants his grace," because women made more progress on the "inner path" than men. Teresa deliberately opposed the Inquisitors' fear of this inner way. And she knew: "Lord of my soul! When you still walked in this world, you always showed your special affection for women. You found no less love and faith in them than among the men."

It was rather nervy of her, in the heyday of the persecution of heretics, to write such earth-shaking sentences as these: "The world is wrong when it demands that we not be allowed to work for you. Nor would it have us speak out truths for whose sake we weep in secret, nor have you lend an ear to our just requests. For you are no judge like the judges of this world, the sons of Adam, in short, nothing but men who think they have to cast suspicion on every good capacity in women. . . . But I reproach our time for rejecting minds that are strong and gifted for all that is good only because they happen to be women."

In the second edition of Teresa's *Way of Perfection* the reader will search in vain for that confession. It was struck by the censor. But in spite of the Inquisitors, Teresa stubbornly clung to her convictions and maintained: "There is something great about the certainty of conscience and the freedom of the mind." When well-meaning friends told her to watch out for the all-powerful religious authorities, she found such warnings "amusing. I had to laugh, because, as far as I am concerned, I was never frightened." She was, after all, ready to "die a thousand times" for the truth of Scripture and the most insignificant church ceremony. She encouraged her fellow sisters to hold onto contemplative prayer (outlawed by the

Inquisition), and openly declared that she would be only too glad to hold discussions with the people in charge of such things.

Such a debate, of course, would have been beneath the dignity of the Lord Inquisitors. Instead of that they simply excised her friendly invitation.

Such petty measures couldn't rob Teresa of her sense of self because it was based on God's friendship, not on recognition from church authorities. *La Madre* knew the value of the clever head that God had given her: "It is no little cross when one has to subordinate one's understanding to somebody who has none," she confessed. "I have never known how to do that, nor do I believe that it would be right."

And she didn't shy away from questioning the supposedly godly presuppositions of the Church's power politics and even from opposing St. Paul by pleading for an order of creation in which women would in no wa be, treated as inferior. Fine, so Paul thinks that women should keep silent, and, in a vision, she quite despondently made that objection to God: "But then the Lord spoke to me: 'Tell them that they shouldn't just invoke *one* passage of Scripture, but consider the others as well, and they shouldn't think that they can tie my hands!"

"A DISOBEDIENT VAGABOND"

THERE WERE DIFFERENCES of opinion among the censors about the dangers posed by this scribbler, and, as a precautionary measure, her books disappeared into the archives of the Inquisition. Meantime the conflict between the two factions in the Carmelites was escalating. Spain got a new papal nuncio who ruthlessly persecuted the Discalced and called Madre Teresa a "restless female," a "vagabond, disobedient and obstinate." "She thinks up false doctrines under the appearance of piety." He took control of all the reform convents, excommunicated the reluctant members by the dozen, and subordinated the barefooted Carmelites to the calced leadership of the Order.

"I am old and tired," confessed the sixty-three-year-old woman, "but that doesn't apply to my wishes!" She fought for her work, negotiated, wrote letters, stormed heaven, and tried in vain to prevent some of the discalced from declaring themselves an autonomous province of the Order: that was playing into the hands of the opponents of reform. Finally, Teresa's closest collaborator, Fray Juan de la Cruz, was imprisoned for months in the monastery of the calced Carmelites in Toledo, and beaten every day till he bled. Finally, he managed to knot a rope out of the blanket on his plank bed and strips of his shirt, lower himself from his jail window, and flee to Teresa. She found him "emaciated and disfigured like a corpse." That was probably the only time in her life she quarreled with God: "I always have to think of what they did with Father, and I don't understand how God could let something like that happen."

In the meantime, however, some influential aristocrats switched over to the side of reform. The nuncio, a strict but self-critical man, began, to his consternation, to revise his opinion, when the noblemen made him see the dispute in a totally different light. And Teresa de Jesús wrote in desperation a sharp letter to the king of Spain, Philip II, in which she complained about the chicanery of a prior of the calced in Toledo.

She argued that he was making life miserable for the Discalced nuns, and keeping their confessors imprisoned. "I mean, this man has become Vicar General; and he must have really been cut out for this work, because he knows how to make martyrs like nobody else. The whole city is up in arms. . . . It deeply pains me to know that both our brothers are in their hands. It would have been better for them to have fallen among the Moors, who might at least have taken pity on them . . . If Your Majesty doesn't intervene, I don't know how far things will go. No one else on earth can help us."

As a matter of fact, King Philip—otherwise a conservative person, who took a skeptical view of Church reforms—read the riot act to the nuncio: "These attacks on people who have always demonstrated strict morals and other merits, strike me as highly suspicious.

I hear that you have given no support to the Discalced. From now on show yourself favorable to virtue!"

In 1580, after five years of bitter disputes, two years before Teresa's death, Pope Gregory XIII finally approved the reformed rule of the Order, and raised the discalced Carmelites to the level of an autonomous province. "Now we are all in good peace, calced and discalced," *la Madre* rejoiced, "and nothing disturbs us in God's service anymore."

God—that was the key word in her life. *Friendship* with him was her strongest longing. To be sure, such friendship presupposes respect. God's greatness is incompatible with crude familiarity. She adresses God as "Majesty," like the king in Madrid, and she admonishes her sisters, "If you wish to speak with God, then you must do so as befits so great a Lord. And since it is good that you consider whom you are speaking with, and who you are, so that you may at least speak with decency." God was no doubt for her a Spaniard, a Spanish grandee, all majestic distance—but all fire, too.

Indeed, her God was a fiery lover, much more passionate even than she. Teresa had no anxieties about what to call God, of the kind we have with our cerebral religion. "Chosen lover" she calls him, "good friend." And for her the right way to pray was nothing but "a conversation with a friend, with whom we get together often and gladly, so as to talk with him, because we are sure that he loves us."

This God "can be spoken to at all times," one can converse with him "as with a friend." No need to fear that this sun might set. "God doesn't leave us in darkness. Only if we leave him, do we go under."

This personal bond of friendship with God is perhaps Teresa's most important message for us today. Broken and sick as we are, alienated from God and our fellow men and women, she encourages us to speak again with him and with one another, to overcome our barriers. God hasn't bidden us farewell. God is no mere principle, no abstract figure, designed to fill up the last empty places in our sober world-picture. He is no blurry cypher for humanity.

If we leap over the walls, God can be our friend, our brother, and Lord. Just leap, Teresa says, and you will finally manage to live in identity with yourselves and in friendship with the Other. For friendship with heaven changes the earth.

Teresa's love for people was realistic. She resisted religiously packaged attempts to violate human nature. "We are no angels," she said, "We have a body. It would be foolish to want to turn ourselves into angels on this earth." No, "God keep us from people whose minds are so highfalutin that they want to make each and every thing into an object of perfect contemplation."

Teresa's faith was a modest, everyday affair. Now and then she loved God, as it were, with clenched teeth. One needs no wings, she thought, to seek God. The "hidden treasure" lies within ourselves. "Soul, seek thyself in me, and seek me in yourself." These words spoken by God in one of her most profound poems is, upon closer inspection, not quite so mystical at all; it is the sober renunication of fruitless stratospheric flights. A person need only head off on the path to his or her own interior world to find something there that can't come from himself or herself. "Wholly within himself this person becomes aware, as in a deep abyss, of the presence of God."

"Accustom yourselves always to have Jesus with you," she told her sisters. That's enough. It is unnecessary to reflect a great deal about Jesus or to engage in penetrating theological reasoning. From time to time look up briefly from the things of daily life and gaze upon him—that in itself will transform the daily routine.

This is a very modern way to friendship with God, a way that factors in our divided and distracted hearts and minds. The only thing that matters is spending a while with God, even if we are "full of a thousand disturbing cares and worldly thoughts" (Teresa). As opposed to the reeling off of prayers, a widespread pious practice then and now ("bad music" she called it), she wants us to reflect on this: "It is enough for God if we pray just one Our Father in an hour. The important thing is to think that he is near us." Indeed there's no need whatsoever to speak out loud with him. "God, who dwells in us will make himself understood to us."

And what if he doesn't? Like us, Teresa was familiar with the experience of emptiness. However, she didn't use it as an excuse for ceasing to believe in God's nearness. "We have to do our work. People treat us unjustly; we keep struggling with pain and ill-feeling—all sorts of circumstances in which we can't feel enraptured and elevated. *At such times Christ is an especially good friend for us.* We see him as a person, we see him in weakness and suffering, we have him for a companion."

"God Preserve Us from Foolish Devotions"

IF WE MAY BELIEVE the witnesses, *la Madre* was one of the greatest mystics and visionaries in church history. Summing up, she said that she had seen a light, by comparison with which the clarity of the sun seemed unsightly. "I go around, almost as if intoxicated," is how she describes the "glorious madness" of her ecstasies.

But at first she mistrusted herself so thoroughly in this regard, she sought so earnestly for objective standards in the spiritual life, that the defamation campaigns by the people around her really weren't necessary. And second, as she constantly stresses, a decent life and well-done daily work are much more important than any states of rapture. The highest degree of perfection, she argued, consists not in elevated transports and prophetic gifts but in conforming our will to the will of the Lord. "Let us do what is right. But God preserve us from foolish devotions!"

No, her mysticism wasn't the pastime of a escapist or the egocentric pleasure of a woman who had fallen in love with the landscape of her own soul, but a source of strength for an improbable activity. "This is the purpose of prayer," she made it clear, "to produce action, nothing but action." Or, still more succinctly; "Acting means praying." For if a person has familiar dealings with God, that must also bring salvation to others. Ultimately love for one's fellows is the touchstone that tells whether the love we evince for God is genuine, for, "We can't tell whether we love God . . . but people can see whether we love our neighbor."

Both belong together: the solid anchoring in the eternal and the keen eye, the open heart, and the decisive, vigorous hand attending to the needs of our fellows. Teresa knew that hectic activism is an "enemy of the soul," but it would be just as bad to deny a concrete call from God under the pretext of piety. It's obvious that more than four hundred years ago this great nun had her problems with the rather unappealing kind of person we sometimes call a holy Joe.

As she writes in her typical sacrcastic style: "When I see people who are so crazy about their method of prayer that they lock themselves up stiffly and rigidly in themselves—as if they didn't dare budge for fear of losing a single crumb of their devotion. In this way they reveal how little they know about the path that leads to union with God. They think everything depends upon the pleasures of devotion. No, my sisters, the Lord wants works! If you know that you could obtain relief for a sick person, then drop your devotions at once and do it."

"The Lord wants works!" Although Teresa's health was hopelessly wrecked after surviving one more severe epidemic of grippe at the age of sixty-five, in the two years she still had left she founded another six convents. She had to grapple with an unruly prioress and a testy cardinal. She was irritated with her own body, which no longer obeyed her. Walking and talking were hard now, her head shook with nervous twitches. She was in great pain, but she awaited death without fear.

On the contrary, when she sensed the end was near, her face began to shine and she cried out: "Now it's come, the hour I yearned for so often and so ardently, my Lord and bridegroom. It's time that we see each other, my beloved, my Lord. It's time that I start off on the way. Let's be off, the hour is at hand."

She begged her weeping sisters to forgive the "bad example" she had set for them, and not to imitate her in any of that. "For I was the greatest sinner in the world, and I kept my Rule and constitutions the least of anyone."

Then her face became cheerful again, and she peacefully fell asleep—on October 4, 1582, in her convent of Alba de Tormes near Salamanca, at the age of sixty-seven.

Just forty years later Teresa de Jesús was canonized. With founders of Orders the process goes rather quickly because an effective "lobby" is available, and there's no need to do the tedious business of starting a sponsoring organization. Today her writings are still read by Christians of every persuasion. Seventeen thousand women and men live according to her Rule in twelve hundred monasteries and convents.

On September 27, 1970, Pope Paul IV raised Teresa of Ávila and Catherine of Siena as the first women in history to "doctors of the Church." In addition, 230 scholars from eighteen countries recently granted Teresa the triple doctorate.

It has been said that with the title of honor conferred on her by Rome, the possibility of conversing with God and having him for a friend, as Teresa did, should be elevated into the consciousness of contemporaries, and that her inseparable linkage of love for God and service to the world should be stressed. The pope himself gave still another emancipatory accent to the solemn act when he said, "The time has come when the vocation of woman is being realized to its full extent. Women filled with the spirit of the Gospel can help the human race not to be inhuman" (Paul VI).

But back then the great theologian Karl Rahner—perhaps some pope will declare *him* a Doctor of the Church in the distant future—voiced cautious skepticism. One may be allowed to ask, he said, whether this honor might not be "just a pretty gesture," ultimately designed to get the hierarchy off the hook: now they wouldn't have to give living women in today's Church the rights and responsibilities that belong to them and that they have long not possessed to the extent they obviously should.

However, Rahner added a second reflection: "One may also wonder whether even today women in the Church are ready to take on their position and function that they can have if they want it."

Martyr of Conscience

Thomas More,
British Lord Chancellor
(1478–1535)

How a Person Lives and Dies with Dignity

> A man can lose his head
> without damaging his soul in the process.

*A*fter fifteen months of imprisonment in a narrow, unlit cell, too cramped to move around in and with no fresh air, the fifty-seven year-old candidate for death was unsteady on his legs; and the hastily built stairs to the scaffold seemed rather rickety. And so he turned in his polite, faintly ironic way to the commandant of the Tower and said: "I pray you, master Lieutenant, see me safe up, and as for my coming down, let me shift for myself."

And after laying his head on the block, he carefully pushed aside the long beard he had grown in prison, and explained with a smile: "This hath not offended the king."

The stories of More's death are immortal. Everyone knows the anecdotes about the indestructible humor of the lord chancellor who fell into disfavor and who still had time for an enigmatic joke when the executioner stood nearby with his axe raised and ready. Here we have Thomas More as a prime example of a stable character. He is a man whom nothing can shake, who goes calmly and even smilingly to his death, as though he were merely accepting an invitation to an elegant party. This is Thomas More, the classic conscientious objector, who would rather die than say anything he can't take responsibility for.

That is the halo history has decorated him with; and God knows that with his sincerity and readiness to die, Sir Thomas More earned it. But readers who see only the halo are a long way from knowing Thomas More the man.

The prisoner, who was afraid of torture, who admitted to being hypersensitive to pain, who certainly never pressed for martyrdom, explained to his judges that he hadn't led such a saintly life "that I could boldly deliver myself up to death." He was a careful man. As long as he could, he stayed out of the controversy over his king's divorce. And he maintained an iron silence over the reasons for his refusal to swear the oath. But then suddenly after the death sentence was pronounced, he broke out with a passionate prosecutorial speech that squandered any chance he might have had of being pardoned.

He was incorruptible. As a twenty-six year-old M.P., he brought down an extravagant demand for money by the king, thereby causing serious difficulties for his father, a respected judge.

He was a brilliant humanist who fought against some narrow-minded super-pious types, and at the same time revealed a terrifyingly aggressive intolerance toward the Lutherans ("One should not just preach to such dogs," he said, "but thoroughly beat them with whips and clubs").

He was an intellectual who exchanged flawless Latin and Greek epigrams with his friend Erasmus. And he was also a person of childlike piety, who Sunday after Sunday served as a precentor in the little church near his home, wearing a simple choir robe, even after he had become lord chancellor.

He was a joker, who, even in his death cell, showed himself to be a born clown. Yet often enough he displayed features of contempt for the world. "God grant," he said, "that we use it (the world) like people who are tired of it."

Saints never quite fit into a pigeonhole. And whoever wants to straighten them into harmless ideal images without corners or edges, without breaks and contradictions, is taking away the color that differentiates a living person from a plaster statue.

THE CARDINAL'S THEATRICAL STAGE

IN THE YEAR Thomas More was born, 1478, the first printed book appeared in England. In Italy, Sandro Botticelli was painting, for the first time a completely new type of Madonna, full of tender beauty. In Germany, the humanist chancellor of Württemberg, Niklas von Wylle, was translating short stories and ethical essays from the Italian. Everywhere in Europe there was a new intellectual departure.

Thomas' father, Sir John More, judge at the royal court in London and himself the son of a jurist, seems not to have unconditionally shared the premiere-like mood of his time. He tried to dampen, in whatever way he could, his offspring's enthusiasm for philosophy and ancient languages. A solid legal education for Thomas was his goal, because he realized very clearly that the jurists and administrators had long been in the process of taking over from the exhausted clergy as the power elite in European cities. He sent Thomas to St. Anthony's School in London, where he was to learn "to read and write (and dispute in) Latin." The thirteen-year-old boy must have gotten used to good manners as a page at the house of the cardinal and lord chancellor, John Morton, in

Canterbury. The political and intellectual greats of the country consorted here, and Thomas got his first insight into the mechanisms of power.

At the cardinal's insistance, Thomas More transferred, at the age of fourteen or fifteen, to the Canterbury College of the Benedictines at Oxford. Nevertheless, he didn't limit himself to law but developed a real passion for French and history. He learned to play the flute and violin, wrote mini-comedies and sharp-tongued epigrams (even back in Canterbury he had amazed audiences with his improvised appearances on the cardinal's private stage). For this reason his father kept him on a short leash and took him to Lincoln's Inn, the school for lawyers in London.

At the age of twenty-one, Thomas More was a lawyer himself. He was already a living legend in those years thanks to his pronounced feeling for justice. He is supposed to have said once to his son-in-law, Roper: "If my father was on one side and the devil on the other, and if the devil's cause were just, then the devil would get his due."

At the law school of Furnivall's Inn, the newly minted jurist was already allowed to give lectures. At twenty-six he succeeded effortlessly in making the leap into the House of Commons. England listened when this greenhorn in Parliament smashed the king's demand for ninety thousand pounds dowry for his daughter. As a result of More's solid arguments and the general distaste for permanent tax increases, he was willing to accept less than half of that. Henry VII took out his rage on Thomas' father (he is even supposed to have have him locked up in the tower), and the rebellious newcomer to Parliament went abroad for a while.

Yet as early as the next year after this, the barrister again did successful work as a legal advisor to the Mercer's Company, the highest ranking city guild in London, which included cloth and silk dealers. In 1510 he became undersheriff of the city of London, that is, legal advisor to the mayor and at the same time a judge in civil cases. In complicated conflicts between guilds and corporations he was a sought-for mediator. More was active as a justice of the peace in Hampshire, as a member of the Doctor's Commons, a scholars' club, as speaker for the lay assessors and artisans corporations. And of course, in his laboriously-won leisure hours, he was a humanistic writer.

The humanists, the prototypical thinkers of the early Renaissance, were aesthetes, admirers of beauty, in love with antiquity, classical literature and art. With their quest for a rational explanation of the puzzles of the world and natural processes, with their discovery of the self-determined individual, they upset centuries-old dependencies. They dethroned a world-image people had unquestioningly believed, thereby helping pleasure and enjoyment to get their rights.

But this early humanism in England was a Christian humanism, which based the dignity of humans precisely on their relationship to God, and strove for a better understanding of the Bible through recourse to its original languages. This was a humanism that for all its love for beauty and life didn't bracket out death, but faced it with faith in the risen Christ. Among More's very last publications was his translation of a biography of Pico della Mirandola (d. 1494), who wanted to fuse faith and knowledge, religion and philosophy, Christian and Jewish tradition, in one universal Church.

"To be sure we are sinners, insofar as you look upon our guilt," says a prayer that goes back to Pico, which More translated very freely and completed with some of his own verses:

Yet, when you once again look at your gifts,
your noble, wonderful, kindly gifts,
so will you find in us men and women
who by nature are your servants, but through your grace
are at the same time your children and have long been such.

This sort of conversation with God already differs enormously from the bashful, guilty consciousness of medieval man.

More wrote English and Latin poems in those years, some of which are still known as folksongs. In his deadly accurate, often quite malicious epigrams (e.g., "If your foot were as light as your mind, you could catch a hare in the middle of the field") he took aim at feminine weaknesses and masculine vanity. He mocked incompetent lawyers and dilettante painters, but he also engaged in profound meditations on human life.

With biting irony, Thomas Morus defended (the Latin form of his name, generally used among humanists, means "fool"), the forward-looking renewal of the sciences and the importance of classical education. He fought against small minds, who smelled danger and disintegration everywhere: for example, someone in Oxford got up in the pulpit and thundered against Greek literature and Latin culture.

More responded by asking: "Doesn't he have more fertile material in the seven deadly sins? There, at least, he has a topic that he handles better . . . Are we to say that he merely wanted to condemn an exaggerated love of literature? That sort of crime is certainly not too widespread. No sermons are needed to stop you from drowning in study. But no, without more ado the holy man openly declares that all those who study the Greeks are heretics, the professors are devils, and their students little demons."

By contrast, More considered it indispensable to know Greek well in order to be able to understand the New Testament sources of faith, and the Church fathers, so as not to have to rely on the interpretations of scholastic theology. His friends had exactly the same idea. They included the comprehensively educated theologian John Colet, the chancellor of Cambridge University, John Fisher (who later died, like More, as a nonjuror), Konrad Peutinger and Willibald Pirckheimer, Hans Holbein, his portraitist, and above all the renowned Erasmus of Rotterdam. Both were very close. "This man could get me to dance on a tightrope," Erasmus confessed. More prompted him to write his *Praise of Folly*, a satirical critique of state, church, and society. Erasmus' bottom line was: "Human life is a fool's play."

"NO SCENES, NO BEATINGS"

FOR A LONG TIME, Thomas didn't know where he belonged. For four years he had lived in the guesthouse of the London Carthusians and taken part in the spiritual life of this serious community that followed strict rules. He prayed, fasted, got used to four hours sleep a night, and to wearing a penitential shirt of goat hair (as lord chancellor he wore it under his gorgeous official robes). For a while he toyed with the idea of entering the Franciscans. "And there would have been no objection to devoting himself to this way of life, if he could have shaken off his longing for a woman," Erasmus states with fine candor.

So instead, Thomas married Jane Colt, the seventeen-year-old daughter of a country squire—and the lay world got one of its few saints. Their relationship must have been very tender. He called his spouse "my dear little wife," but as Erasmus explained, he had sought out a very young girl, "so as to be able to form her entirely according to his taste."

We get a more sympathetic impression from his report on family life in the More house: "No scenes, no beatings." In those years the rod was an inevitable part of all education, but at the Mores it consisted of two bundles of soft peacock feathers.

More provided his three daughters with an education that by the standards of the time was unusually emancipated. They were taught Latin, Greek, philosphy, logic, mathematics, and astronomy—because "women can be just as successful in the sciences as men," as he wrote to his tutor. "They both speak the language of humanity. Nature gave them both understanding, which differentiates them from the beasts. Thus man and woman have an equal right to study . . ."

In all this he remained realistic, and bitterly confessed to his favorite daughter Margaret ("Meg"), who had scholarly ambitions: "Fate deals badly with you, for you will never be able to enjoy your hard-earned success. Never will people really look upon your writings as your own work. Everyone will assume some sort of help behind them. Perhaps they will even believe that you copied it all from somewhere . . ." Simply because she was a woman, no woman could ever become as famous as she deserved to be. But, thank God, Meg sought to compensate for this lack through special zeal in her studies and in the "virtues of a good mother." "Of course," More said, "I prefer such a girl to three boys."

No wonder that this family stuck fiercely together and maintained its loyalty to their imprisoned father. Thomas' love for his wife and children, Erasmus tells us, never gave way to a morose fulfillment of duty. They made music together, had serious conversations—and foolish ones as well. In the evening the whole household gathered for prayer, and before meals one of the daughters regularly read an excerpt from the Bible, as was the custom in monasteries.

For even as a husband and father of a family, Thomas More stuck to his almost monkish habits: daily mass and a kind of breviary prayer, a Spartan bed, pilgrimages on foot, of the kind now beginning to be frowned upon among the better class of people. More often walked incognito through the poor neighborhoods of London, to find people suffering from misery and ashamed to admit it. He founded and financed a hospital, and sometimes he abruptly brought hungry people to sleep over at his house. The Mores kept an open house and especially liked to invite the peasants from the neighborhood to dinner.

After six years his beloved Jane died and left him a widower with four little children. A few weeks later Thomas remarried a merchant's widow named Alice Middleton, six years older than he, a not especially prepossessing woman, but very resolute. According to Erasmus it was a marriage "more in the interests of the family than of pleasure." But she loved her stepchildren, and learned to play the harp and flute as a favor to her husband. And Thomas dedicated to his two wives a grave inscription as tender as it is astonishing: "Here lies Jane, the beloved little wife of Thomas More, who is holding this grave for Alice and me. . . . It is hard to say whether I loved more the one or the other. Ah, how happily we three would have lived together, if fate and morals had allowed us to! I pray that this grave may join us together, as heaven will. Thus will death give us what life could not."

Thomas More had long been the most renowned barrister of London, beloved for his sense of justice and humor. Now he could afford a house in the exclusive London suburb of Chelsea, with exotic birds, a poodle, a weasel, a beaver, foxes, some monkeys, even his own house fool. When careless neighbors caused a fire, and all More's grain barns burned down, he wrote calmly to his wife: "I beg you, try to find out what our neighbors have lost. Tell them not to worry, for I will call no spoon my own so long as one of them is suffering need."

By no means did he fleece his clients. It is reported that often enough he convinced them to bury their conflicts or at least showed them a way to go to law less expensively. For many he waived his legal fees.

This was the man Thomas More, whom Eramsus may have most accurately characterized in the one short sentence: "He let no one go away sad." And Thomas himself accounted for his hearty manner, unburdened with affectations and patrician condescension, with this piece of advice: "Let a man reflect in his heart that every poor devil is just like him."

Independence and incorruptibility were his defining character traits. Judge More once decided against his own wife a case involving a little dog. As undersheriff of London he turned down a lucrative yearly pension because the citizens, whom he was serving, would then no longer be able to trust him. Just as decisively, after retiring from the chancellor's office, he rejected the five thousand pounds with which the English bishops wished to reward him for his Catholic polemical writings. Actually this "honorarium" was meant as discreet help for a man who had fallen into bitter poverty, and the Mores had to heat their house with brackens, since they had no more fuel. But he turned it down.

He must have had extremely varied interests; he was all eyes and ears for the world around him, a collector of curiosities and a lover of rare animals, as we have already seen. Meanwhile he was lovable, tranquil, with a pleasant appearance and a winning nature. His son-in-law, Roper, never saw him "in a fume for sixteen years."

He was full of respect and tact. In a manuscript written in his death cell, he suggested that one must always seek an "inner contact" with the other person. You had to think your way into him, for in an "untender way" you couldn't advise or help anyone. He was tolerant (even toward his Protestant son-in-law!), accepting of others, discreet, and reserved. In letters to their governments about the close-lipped diplomat, foreign ambassadors complained, "There is no way to elicit even the slightest indiscretion from him."

Averse to all fanaticism, he combined a sort of Prussian awareness of duty and a legendary work pace with the capacity for true leisure. He was a true friend, not at all fastidious, and free from arrogant hypocrisy. "Let us not cherish hatred against anyone," More said, "for either the person is good, or he is evil. If he is good, then we make ourselves guilty, because we hate a person who is virtuous and blessed by God. But if he is evil, we would be behaving like barbarians if we hated a person who must suffer in the other life. . . . But we poor sinners want to stand up for our our guilty brothers, because at every moment our conscience tells us that we are in just as much need of indulgence and forgiveness."

Anyone who thinks this way will never take a grim view of things, will never take human relations with deadly seriousness. To be sure, More was no mere onlooker, no cynic raised up above people's troubles. He committed himself. Still he knew, as Erasmus explains, how to see the pleasant side of everything human and how to enjoy learning as much as foolishness. His humor wasn't cynical, but compassionate. It enabled him to remain cheerful and faithful to God in situations where others became desperate. "To tell the truth, I am by nature half a joker and more than half." He wrote that in his death cell—and added with a sigh: "I wish I could improve my disposition as easily as I can understand it. Yet I can scarcely bridle it, old fool that I am."

Of course he also had his weaknesses. Sometimes he seems too soft, too adaptable, because he tried to please too many people. He flattered his predecessor as chancellor, Cardinal Wolsey, and the king—naturally using the sympathetic justification that praise encourages people to do still better. And his irony could also cause pain, when he now and then mocked uncultivated, intellectually inferior persons. When a young Carthusian monk dared to criticize Erasmus' translation of the Bible, More hurled at him the Pope's grateful acknowledgment of Erasmus: "Here is something that the supreme head of the Christian world honors with his support; and you, a wretched little monk, unlearned and unknown, from the hole of your little cell, you wish to cancel it with your abusive tongue?"

That is how insulting this model of Stoic calm could be. But Thomas More never claimed to be a saint. Only a few of his prayers and meditations that have been preserved (some of the texts ascribed to More such as the well-known "Prayer for Good Digestion" do indeed breathe his spirit, but surely do not come from his pen). In these texts he again saw himself as a little person entirely dependent on God, weak and in need of help amid all sorts of temptations. Then he could pray like a child.

"And give me, good Lord, an humble, lowly, quiet, peaceable, patient, charitable, kind, tender and filial mind in all my works, words, and thoughts, that I may have a foretaste of your holy, blessed spirit!"

More, the candidate for death, was no masochist (he stressed that God orders man to do his utmost in the strugggle against his own and others' suffering). And he never concealed his fear. Ultimately he said it was no shame to be afraid of death and torments, because Christ himself had felt and borne this fear.

But he got over the fear, because he was a realist (death was, after all, a part of life, and "you are a fool if you hope for a long stay"), because he was a believer and in death heard a call of love. This was reason enough for boundless trust. "I have never begged God to take me away from here or to preserve me from death," he confessed to his daughter Margaret in prison. "But I left everything to his pleasure, for he knows better than I what is the best for me." God would take "under his wings" the person who came to him full of trust. "If we wish to stay there, we are safe. No power can drive us from there against our will."

A KING'S PIOUS EXHIBITIONISM

THOMAS MORE'S POLITICAL career is inseparably linked with the reign of Henry VIII, commonly known only as the irritable, bloodthirsty, bloated monster that he was by the end of his career. From

Reputation, honor, fame, what is all that but a breath of air from another person's mouth, no sooner spoken but gone? Thus whoever finds his delight in them is feeding on wind.

He can be sure that they do not spend the whole day speaking of him. And those who praise him the most will nonetheless doze off for a while every twenty-four hours and forget him. Besides, while someone speaks well of him somewhere, somewhere else another man sits maligning him. And finally some of those who praise him to the skies in his presence, mock him behind his back.

And yet there are fools so mad for fame that they constantly feast on the notion that they are incessantly praised. As if day and night people did nothing but sit there singing their praises and incensing them.

—Comments by More from his death cell

this perspective we can easily lose sight of the hopes everyone had at the beginning of his rule, when he was a lovable, cultivated, artistic young man. "This day is the end of slavery and the birth of freedom," More had written effusively at the time. The new ruler understood a great deal about theology, had composed two masses, and behaved like someone true to Rome and the pope. By writing a polemical piece against Luther, he earned the honorary title *Defensor Fidei*, defender of the faith, which British monarchs bear to this day.

Of course, More soon sobered up as he realized that behind such activities of the king lay not so much genuine faith as a great deal of exhibitionism. More, the honest skeptic, can't have been pleased by the way Henry invoked Christ and theology in order to justify his bloody campaigns of conquest. In vain he sought to get the king to tone down his undiplomatic hymns to the successors of St. Peter as the rulers of the world.

Martin Luther reacted with an extremely hostile reply to "Henry, by God's disgrace king," accused him of having soiled the crown of Christ with "his filth." So, like it or not, Thomas More had to write a piece in defense of his monarch. That was, however, good practice, because over the next ten years More's literary production was to consist almost exclusively of such controversial pieces against the reformers.

More's relationship to Lutherans and "heretics" is not easy to understand. He got worked up over abuses in the monasteries and preachers who reduced their moral appeals to absurdity by the way they lived their own lives. Nonetheless, he seems never to have gotten a good grasp of Luther's motives. He compared the Reformation to a cancerous ulcer; he openly rejoiced over Zwingli's death, and he could write in a style just as offensive as that of the people he attacked: "Who in truth would be more of a filthy swine than those heretics who yelp at the holy sacraments?"

In the interest of pure doctrine he could be very hard. Measured against the levels of fanaticism and bloodlust customary in that epoch, however, he behaved rather fairly. When he presided as lord chancellor (it was one of his duties) over the hearings of heretics, he exhausted every possibility to preserve the religious deviants from death. He himself never sent a single heretic to the stake. Some would charge him with the three or four executions that occurred at the end of his term in office, but these would seem to be, at most, a question of putting his signature to judgments passed by others and no longer reversible.

The key to understanding More, the "intolerant" Catholic, is his fear of the consequences of a half-understood subversive doctrine spread in a coarsened form. In the end, the whole substance of the faith might be thrown overboard along with the undesirable developments in need of reform. Sometime or other, someone would reject Christ along with the old Church, "And if such an unfeeling buffoon stands up, he will not lack for fellow travelers, given the present insane situation of the masses. . . ."

In 1518 Henry VIII hired the forty-year-old More, who had been proved in embassies and export businesses. He was put to work as a privy counsellor, as a secretary and master of requests, which means a judge in a court that was supposed to furnish legal protection for ordinary people. Just three years later, he was ennobled, which entitled him to call himself Sir More or even Knight.

As sub-treasurer he advanced to the important post of liaison man between the king and the lord chancellor.

His brilliant intellectual gifts, his discretion, and his capacity for standing inconspicuously in the background while holding all the threads in his hand made him indispensable at court.

More the statesman took part in several important peace negotiations. He had a crucial role in the Peace of Cambrai (1529), which ended the decades-long war between France and the Habsburgs. England had come to play an important part in this quarrel through a policy of alliances as flexible as it was lucrative.

And yet he wasn't at all enthusiastic about this activity. The secret republican in him resisted the gradually emerging tyrannical ambitions of the king. He longed for the secluded life of the literary scholar and aesthete. Only with great aversion did he accept the post, he wrote to Bishop Fisher, and he felt uncertain, "like someone sitting on a horse for the first time."

This overt dissatisfaction with his own career surely also contains a little coquetry, of the sort common to all celebrities. But characteristically it was during those years that he wrote his most deeply pessimistic book, *The Four Last Things*, an exhortation to the proud, lazy, miserly, sybaritic person to remember death and judgment, heaven and hell.

Thomas had always been skeptical about power and the powerful. "The prince's disfavor means death," the Duke of Norfolk had warned him, when the consequences of his refusal to swear the oath were at issue. "Is that all, my lord?" the prisoner gaily replied. "Really, then there is no other difference between your grace and me, than that I shall die today and you tomorrow."

And with his unique, dry humor he sadistically quoted a high dignitary at the royal court: The man had once stood too long before the monarch with his hat deferentially doffed—and caught a cold for his trouble. Since then he placed considerably less value on marks of respect than on his warm cap, if only they let him keep it on.

If princes wouldn't take on too much, More felt quite certain, there wouldn't be so many wars and so much suffering for countless people—for a king who could barely handle one realm often wanted to rule over five. With his criticism of the nobility, More found himself in agreement with all other English humanists. In his *Utopia* the aristocracy appears as simply superfluous and harmful. Nobility, he argued, was based not on virtuous behavior, but on extraction from a rich family.

This *Utopia*, the philosophical fairytale about a country called "Nowhere," the dream of an ideal state founded on reason, has entered our vocabulary—and in the process has been as misunderstood as scarcely any other book in world literature. Enlightened philosophers of state and imperialistic colonial politicians, both liberals and communists, have made the work their handbook. Yet according to all indications, More had no intention of composing a confessional piece. Rather, with an intellectual playfulness, both serious and ironic, he wanted to discuss the social prerequisites for the realization of human hopes.

For this reason, we are given a satirical description of a fictional ideal people, who share all their property, consider war barbaric, despise gold and silver (the moral: some pagans live in a more Christian manner than the Christians!). Along with this we get a very concrete critique of the social reality of sixteenth-century England. More relentlessly unmasks the connections between the accumulation of possessions by a small class of rich people and the material and moral wretchedness of the lower classes.

Why, then, are there so many thieves that the gallows scarcely suffice to handle them? Because countless unemployed mercenary soldiers wander around England. Because nobles and abbots expropriate farmland and buy it up with nasty tricks. They drive off the tenants to acquire pasture for sheep, and they do good business with the wool. But, then, where were the people driven off supposed to find work? How many noblemen, "idle as drones," lived off the work of others and surrounded themselves with an enormous entourage of loafers? Then when their lord died, they would be thrown out, leaving them with only two choices, to rob or go hungry. Thus, instead of hanging them, it would be better to provide the thieves with a livelihood.

Thomas More was, in practice, unconditionally loyal to the king, still these modern states were "nothing but a kind of conspiracy of the rich, who seek their own advantage in the name, and under the legal title, of the state." The new society of his Utopia was altogether different. In it private property was done away with, and farmland was fairly distributed to the individual households. Everyone had a job, and work time could be shortened for the sake of education and personality development. It was a society, finally, in which the heads were elected and all important matters were decided by a senate or popular assembly.

But to More, structural reforms alone are not enough: "For nothing will be good, nothing perfect, until people themselves have become good, and it will be some time before that happens." The original sin was not the unjust distribution of goods, but *superbia*, pride or arrogance. And so he was not quite happy with the idea of a community of goods: "For how shall the quantity of goods suffice when everyone ducks work, when there is no sort of compulsion for people to make their own living, and trust in other people's diligence makes them lazy?"

In any case there are good reasons why *Utopia* was first published in Antwerp, Paris, and Basel in Latin, and didn't come out in England until sixteen years after More's death. The author had spoken too disrespectfully about the clergy—a community of "lazybones," he called them. He had been too reckless in his description of religious tolerance in his ideal state, quite apart from his unsparing caricature of the sacred cows of the British nobility. For example, in the land of Nowhere, hunting was assigned to the butchers, as a "business unfit for free men." A true landlord could only take More's naiveté for shameless sacrilege. "Why is it more fun when the hound chases the hare than when one hound runs after another hound? Yet it's the same thing in both cases: there is running. . . . ."

THE COMEDY OF THE REPENTANT SINNER

OF COURSE WITH every passing year of Henry VIII's reign, More's British homeland drifted farther away from such paradisiacal dreams. The monarch turned into an English Nero, despotic, whimsical, bloodthirsty, excessive in every way. (It mustn't be forgotten that at the beginning of the Tudor Dynasty in 1485, England was by no means an absolutist state. Parliament, the landed gentry, and justices of the peace had a certain very real autonomy vis-à-vis the king.)

One chapter in this evil trend toward tyranny was the well-known story of the court lady, Anne Boleyn, who began to spread confusion through English politics. "Myne awne Sweetheart," Henry wrote to the coy beauty, "I wish (especially in the evening) I were in the arms of my beloved, whose lovely breasts I hoped to kiss." But Anne made considerably more difficulties than her mother and sister, who had already been his mistresses. She demanded a legal union and a place on his throne.

But stupidly enough, that place had already been occupied for thirteen years by the Spanish princess, Catherine of Aragon. Long before Anne's arrival, Henry and half of England had been dissatisfied with this queen. After a long series of stillbirths, she had managed to give the country only one princess, but not the longed-for male heir. Memories were still fresh of the weak Queen Margaret of Anjou (d. 1482), whom the nation had to thank for a quarter century of civil war.

Henry thought of annulling his marriage. He suddenly developed violent pangs of conscience: Catherine was the widow of his brother Arthur, who had died young. He had married her with a papal dispensation, and now God was obviously punishing him for this incestuous relationship by denying him an heir. So the king began to play a rather unseemly comedy as a repentant sinner. He conducted embarrassing investigations, citing dozens of witnesses in order to prove that although the marriage with his brother had lasted only five months, Catherine had in fact consummated it (which she denied). But Henry ran into a brick wall with the pope. For Catherine's nephew was no less a man than Emperor Charles V, and not even the pope could afford a quarrel with the emperor.

Thus the only solution was for the king to go his own way—and to break with Rome. Thomas More, of all people, was supposed to

help the monarch make this rupture acceptable to the English public. In 1529 the king named him lord chancellor (the first layman to
hold the post) and keeper of the Great Seal. This, despite the fact that
More had left no doubt that he wasn't on the king's side on the question of his marriage. The chancellor shared the general concern over
the lack of a male heir, but he found no sufficient legal or theological grounds for annulling the marriage. In response the king, though
saddened, assured him that, of course, he would respect his opinion and never force him to do anything.

And he really did give his favor to Sir Thomas, that lonely "Mr.
Clean" and walking advertisement for his court. He showed up
unannounced for lunch in Chelsea, and he went for a walk in the
garden with his chancellor, his arm amicably flung over More's
shoulder. Needless to say, the skeptical More didn't let himself be
especially impressed by these grand gestures. "I don't have any
illusions about that," he told his son-in-law. "For if my head would
win him a castle in France, it should not fail to go."

For months and years he kept out of the unproductive dispute
until he ultimately saw that in his exposed position even silence
had to be considered consent. More tendered his resignation—in
vain. The king feared, quite rightly, the snubbing effect of that
sort of step.

Then events took off in rapid succession: Henry's spokesmen
sent reports from universities to Rome—not least of all thanks to
generous contributions—for the anullment of the marriage. No
luck. The crown confiscated the incomes from the first year in office
of every newly named bishop, which had hitherto been sent off to
Rome. No luck. In 1531 the church assemblies at Canterbury and
York had to recognize Henry as their "sole and highest lord." Brave
Bishop Fisher just managed to pass the limiting clause, "so far as
Christ's law allows."

On May 15, 1532, the bishops of England were pressured into
renouncing their ancestral right to enact church laws even without
the consent of the king and Parliament. That marked the last step
toward an established church, and there was no longer any mention

Little as I meddle in the conscience of others, I am certain that my conscience belongs to me alone. It is the last thing that a man can do for his salvation: to be at one with himself.

As I have often told you, Margaret, I do not make bold to decide or discuss the matter. Nor do I reproach or blame other people's way of acting. Nor did I write or speak to anyone any word of reproach for anything that Parliament has decreed. Nor have I interfered in the conscience of others who either think differently from me or merely say they think differently. But as for me, I will say to your comfort, daughter, that on this matter my own conscience—I condemn no other person—is on good terms with my salvation. Of this I am as sure, Meg, as I am of the fact that God is in heaven.

And so, concerning everything else, goods, lands, and body (if it should come to that), I trust, since my conscience is at peace, in God. He will rather strengthen me to bear the loss than that I should swear against my conscience and bring my soul into danger. For all the reasons which induce other people to the opposite side are not convincing to me, that I should change my conscience because of them.

—MORE TO HIS DAUGHTER MARGARET

of Rome. The next day, Lord Chancellor More turned in his resignation for a second time, for reasons of health (he actually was suffering from a sort of cardiac asthma), and this time he was successful.

Sir Thomas withdrew to his country house, tried to find new jobs for all his servants, came to terms as cheerfully and serenely as ever with his sudden poverty—"Then may we yet, with bags and wallets, go a-begging together, and hoping that for pity some good folk will give us their charity, at every man's door to sing *Salve Regina*, and so still keep company and be merry together"— and clearsightedly prepared for death. Although he took great pains to avoid dangerous statements, and didn't even allow writings in his house about the hotly- discussed marriage, he had no illusions that his discreet departure from office was the end of the matter. At some point or other the deeply offended king—whom

I will not mistrust the Lord, Meg, although I feel myself to be fearful. Indeed, and even if my fear becomes so vehement that it threatens to throw me down, then I will think how St. Peter began to sink at a gust of wind because of his weak faith, and like him I shall call on Christ and beg him to help me. And I trust that he will then stretch out his holy hand to me and save me from drowning in the stormy sea. Yes, and if he lets me go on playing the part of Peter, lets me fall completely and swear false-ly . . .—even then I trust that in his kindness he will look ten-derly and compassionately on me, as he did on Peter and . . . will let me arise again and once more confess the truth of my con-science.

But I know that he will not let me be lost without my fault. Therefore I wish to entrust myself to him full of hope . . . Truly, Meg, I trust that his tender mercy will keep my poor soul safe and will let me rejoice in his compassion. And thus, my good daughter, trouble yourself over nothing that could befall me in this world.

I will pray for us all with my whole heart, that we may meet one day in heaven, where we shall forever be gay and have no more pains.

—Thomas More in conversation
with his daughter Margaret in the Tower of London

he stuck to, just as before—would demand an unambivalent confession.

Till then he devoted himself to his long-neglected writing and got accustomed to see death, which in the *Four Last Things* he had still painted in the most dismal colors as a "cruel hangman," as a friend who opens the door to God. More wrote: "Give me the live-ly desire to be with you; not to be freed from the misfortunes of this sad world . . . indeed, not even in order to obtain and enjoy the joys of heaven, but solely out of love for you!"

One whole year later the ex-chancellor stumbled definitively over his uprightness when he stayed away from the coronation of the heavily-pregnant Queen Anne Boleyn, despite an express invitation. From now on he had to confront the most senseless reproaches, out of which the furious Henry VIII would have been glad to forge a charge of high treason. But first of all, More, the brilliant jurist, was too clever to leave himself wide open, and secondly, he had an absolutely clean slate.

But ultimately the day of decision did come, and more quickly than he had thought. Henry (who had meanwhile been excommunicated by the pope) proposed a law of successsion that declared his first marriage invalid and sanctioned the claim of the childen he would beget with Anne Boleyn. Everyone had to swear the so-called oath of supremacy, or else risk prison and expropriation. From the bishops down to the little country pastors, the majority swore fidelity to the new absolute ruler of the English Church, at most quieting their conscience with the softly murmured addition " . . . so far as I do not thereby break God's commandment" (the limiting clause in the old formula of the oath had been dropped).

Sir Thomas thought this sort of thing shabby. He could accept the regulation of succession to the throne, but not the rejection of papal authority expressed in the preamble to the oath. Admittedly, all Englishmen owed obedience to the king appointed by Parliament. But no power in the world could declare him the head of the English Church, for that was a matter of faith.

THE CONDEMNED MAN IN THE TOWER

ON APRIL 13, 1534, the former chancellor was invited to swear the oath before the king's commisioners in Lambeth Palace. The Lords built golden bridges for the man who was still beloved and secretly admired as well: if he would not condemn the others who took the oath—so argued Thomas Cranmer, the Archbishop of Canterbury, a marionette of the king—and merely held it doubtful whether he himself was allowed to swear, then he should rather stand by his sure duty of obedience to the monarch and drop the uncertain conscientious doubt.

As More later noted, this line of argument had at the time actually seemed "penetrating and weighty," but he very quickly recovered himself and answered, "However other people understood the matter, the truth seemed to me in my conscience to lie on the other side."

In the face of so much courage, the Lords doubtlessly stirred self-consciously in their seats. The abbot of Westminster tried once again to appeal to More: Did he claim to be wiser than the Great Council of the Kingdom? Whereupon More, untouched, said: "He had a much greater Council on his side, the conviction of all of Christendom."

Incidentally, Sir Thomas was stubborn in rejecting any justification for his refusal to take the oath, so as not to provide his opponents with extra ammunition. After this hearing he no longer returned to Chelsea but landed without delay in the Tower.

He left his good suit of clothing to the master jailer—who had a claim to it—with the smiling observation that he would hardly have any further need of it for affairs of state. And should he complain about the food and lodging, "Don't hesitate to throw me out!" There was no bitterness, blustering rage, or trembling fear. "Thanks be to our Lord," he wrote to Meg in his first letter from his prison cell: "I am in good bodily health and in good peace of mind, and I desire no more of worldly goods than I have."

The illusion-free candidate for death, who knew the vengefulness of the king, who was racked by cares about his family back home, nevertheless managed to look upon his damp dungeon as the cloister cell he had once longed for, and emprisonment as an opportunity for reflection. "I believe, Meg, that they that have put me here think they have done me a high displeasure. But I assure thee, on my faith, my own good daughter, if it had not been for my wife and you that be my children, . . . I would not have failed long ere this to have closed myself in as strait a room and straiter too. . . . For me thinks God sets me on his lap and dangles me."

The man who said that was a prisoner tormented by cold and darkness, frightened by rats, and tortured by all sorts of pains. Naturally he couldn't simply fall back upon his cheerful serenity. That was the fruit of constant hard battles with his own fear. What the freezing, humiliated ex-chancellor smuggled out of his prison hole

reveals not just an admirable faith, but also a quite ordinary crea-
turely fear: "Believe me, Meg, you could not have a more despondent
heart than your father," he confided to his daughter. He said he was
"by nature so whining that I shrink back from a bump in the nose."
Long before he was consigned to the tower he had endured deathly
fears, "and they were not small, and my heart was heavy with fear;
and I imagined all threatening forms of death, and lay a long time
restless and awake, while my wife thought I was asleep."

"I am already on the point of dying," he confessed another time,
"and since I came here, I have already several times been in the condition that I thought I had to die within an hour . . ." Not to mention the fearful thoughts about his wife and children in Chelsea,
who had to endure house searches, suffer material want, and were
just as defenselessly exposed to the revenge of the king as their husband and father was.

And yet during 445 days in prison, he was stubborn as a mule
in turning down all the ruses by which both the impatient ambassadors of the king and his own concerned friends tried to make
swearing the oath palatable to him. Even his cautiously arguing
daughter Meg and his resolutely chattering wife Alice failed to
break down the prisoner's obstinate resistance.

"Ah, for goodness' sake, Master More," begins one of Alice's
tongue-lashings, "I marvel that you, who have always hitherto been
taken for so wise a man, will now so play the fool to lie here in this
close, filthy prison, and be content thus to be shut up among mice
and rats, when you might be abroad at your liberty, and with the
favor and good will both of the king and his Council." And then
came an alluring reminder of study rooms and books and orchards
in Chelsea and the gay companionship of his family.

"I pray you, good mistress Alice," Thomas finally interrupted
her after her verbal torrent, "Tell me just one thing: Is not this
house as nigh heaven as mine own?"

"Good God, will this business never have an end?" Alice groaned,
and wrung her hands at so much philosophically-trimmed nonsense.
What was she supposed to be able to do with the crazy arithmetic,

which her husband, now threatened with execution, presented with a smiling face. "My good woman, you are no good at doing business. Do you really want me to exchange eternity for twenty years?"

Alice's commentary on such arguments: "Tilly vally, tilly vally. Stuff and nonsense!"

To say no was the only freedom still left to prisoner More, and he didn't want anyone to take it away from him. But where did he get the strength for that?

The manuscripts More wrote in the tower give a clear answer to that. The *Treatise on the Suffering of Christ*, which was left a fragment, the harmony of the Gospels *On the Sadness, Affliction, Fear of Death and Christ's Prayer Before His Arrest*, and finally the famous *Dialogue of Comfort against Tribulation* all revolve around one subject: human suffering and the liberating death of Christ. His servants could claim no greater privilege than their Lord, we read in the *Dialogue*: "Would we wish to enter his kingdom comfortably, when he went into his own only through suffering?"

More recognized ever more clearly with what love Christ delivered himself to an agonized criminal's death. And he found it embarrassing that many lovers would risk their lives for their beloved, but that out of fear of bodily death so many Christians would abandon their redeemer, "who was willing to endure such a painful death rather than leave us in the lurch."

No, Thomas would let himself be frightened neither by man nor the devil. "For surely if we are so loving as our Lord was, and do not hate those who kill us, but have compassion on them and pray for them, if we worry about the danger they bring upon themselves, then the fire of love that we fling in the devil's face will blind him at one stroke so that he can no longer see where he might play another trick on us."

ALL ENGLAND HEARS THE SILENCE

THE KING AND his officials, for whom prisoner More prayed every day, gave him small thanks for this attitude. When in his harmony of the

Gospels, he came to the scene on Mount Olivet, where it says in Luke and John, "and they laid hands on him," exactly at this passage the prison guards took away all his manuscripts and writing materials. From then on Thomas More could only occasionally communicate with the outside world by writing with pieces of coal on smuggled-in scraps of paper. Of these precious last letters his daughter Margaret said, "Although they were written only with coal, in my opinion they are worthy of being set down in letters of gold."

More had no need to send out to the world, say, great polemical pieces or justifications of his behavior. The mere fact that the beloved erstwhile lord chancellor had been imprisoned so long, and that no reconciliation with the monarch was taking place, created a widespread impact that was not to be underestimated, and gave many people in England food for thought. The king's negotiators chided that his attitude was a "cause of a great deal of murmuring and unrest in the kingdom." This laconic prisoner's silence was better understood all over England than any speech of protest could have been. This prisoner was giving the crown's jurists sleepless nights. For he couldn't be sent to the scaffold solely for refusing to take the oath. They had to tease some sort of statement out of him that could later be interpreted as high treason. Naturally Thomas knew this too—and kept silent.

More or less under pressure, the Parliament passed a whole bundle of laws, some of which were directed solely at the former lord chancellor. The king was officially declared supreme head of the English Church. More and Fisher were proscribed for refusing to take the oath. A law on high treason threatened every "malicious" statement (as though any judge could define that) against the king's authority to rule over the Church with the fantastic penalty of having one's stomach slit open and being disemboweled.

Sir Thomas saw the fearful effects of this arbitrary law with his own eyes. Like him, the London Carthusians had refused to swear the oath and were condemned to death, because their non-recognition of the king's supremacy over the Church had occurred in a manner that was in principle "malicious." (The jury agreed with this remarkable interpretation only after massive threats.) The Emperor's ambassador sent home a report on the sadistic manner of their execution. He said they had been hanged one by one, and immediately taken down from the rope, "their genitals were cut off and thrown into the fire. Then they were cut open and their entrails ripped out. Finally they were beheaded. But their bodies were quartered, and before this their hearts had been ripped out and rubbed into their mouth and faces."

More was there with his daughter when the monks were led out to execution, and he managed to say: "Look, don't you see, Meg, that these blessed fathers are now going as cheerfully to their deaths as bridegrooms to their marriage . . . whereas . . . God still leaves your silly father here in the world, further to be plunged and turmoiled with misery." Only someone who knows what Thomas More had experienced in the tower will be able to appreciate correctly his readiness for death—but also to understand that he wasn't pressing unconditionally for martyrdom.

No one, he once wrote, should be a daredevil and expose himself to such a hazard, unless he was sure he could stride forward with serenity and dignity. If he couldn't bring off the climb to the peak, he risked plunging into the abyss. And he openly confessed to his judges that he hadn't led such a holy life that he could boldly deliver himself up to death.

All in vain. By now the king and his creatures had had enough of this seemingly, unassailable prisoner, who, with his sovereign silence, drove them to white-hot rage. On July 1, 1535, they subjected him to a show trial in Westminster Hall, a macabre farce with corrupt judges and an intimidated jury. A witness had to be suborned to foist off on More the desired statement against the king's supremacy over the Church. "If you have not committed perjury, sir," the accused responded indignantly, "may I never see the face of God"—and withdrew into silence again. "No law in the world can punish a man simply because he refuses to speak."

But the false witness was enough for the jurors. After a few minutes they were ready with their sentence: "Sir Thomas More shall . . . be hanged until he is half dead, then while still alive be taken down and violated, his belly shall be ripped open, and the four parts of his body set out on the four gates of the city, but his head on London Bridge."

And now, in the middle of the proclamation of the sentence, Sir Thomas broke his silence for the first and only time.

Rising to his full height, with a few terse sentences he swept away this wretched court's arguments. "This condemnation is based on an act of Parliament that immediately contradicts the laws of God and his holy Church, whose highest direction no worldly prince may arrogate to himself on the basis of any law. . . . Hence this is no law on the strength of which Christians may accuse a Christian." For every English bishop who had sworn the oath he could cite a hundred holy bishops of Christendom who had thought as he did . . .

A few days before, his friend Bishop Fisher was beheaded. With his brave protest speech, More had apparently squandered any chance of being "pardoned," i.e., of being executed in this relatively humane fashion. On his way back to the tower he embraced his children in tears. With a piece of coal he wrote a calm letter of farewell on a scrap of paper, without any pathos, not saying a word about his terrible fate: a few heartfelt greetings and blessings for everyone and the hope of seeing them again happily in heaven.

"Grant me the grace," it says in his last prayer from his death cell that has come down to us, "to better my life and to direct my eye to my end." In the face of dying he indulged in one more precious jest. He called for the court ambassadors, claiming that he had changed his mind. And when the envoys rushed into his cell, believing that England's last rebel would now finally swear the oath, he informed them with a solemn expression on his face: "I really have changed my mind, my lords. For at first I wished to have my beard shaved before the execution, but since then I have decided to let it share the fate of my head." (In the meantime, Henry VIII, in a burst of humane feeling, had changed the sentence to beheading.)

On July 6, 1535, at nine o'clock in the morning, under heavy guard (evidently there were fears that the people might set him free), the ex-chancellor made his way to the scaffold. Weakened by fifteen months of imprisonment, he laboriously stumbled forward. As in the long weeks before, he thought of the Passion of Christ. He turned down the glass of wine proferred by a kind-hearted woman with the explanation that during his suffering Christ had drunk only vinegar.

The executioner, in accordance with English custom, knelt down before him and begged his forgiveness. He embraced the man with the kiss of peace. His last words from the scaffold went into history, while everything that Henry VIII ever uttered has been forgotten: "I die in and for the faith of the holy Catholic Church. Pray for me in this world, and I shall pray for you in that world. Pray for the king that it please God to send him good counsellors. I die as the king's true servant, but above all God's true servant."

He is supposed further to have given the hangman the discreet advice: "Pluck up thy spirits, man, and be not afraid to do thine office; my neck is very short; take heed therefore thou strike not awry, for saving of thine honesty." Then he laid his head calmly and decisively in the groove of the chopping block.

What did Thomas More die for? Most certainly not for the primacy of the pope, as Catholic historians used to like to claim. He was indeed personally convinced of the supremacy of the the pope over the Church. But he didn't consider it a dogma, and also insisted that the pope in no way stood over a general council. He was concerned with church unity, for which the office of Peter, despite the unworthy caricatures who served as pope in that era, certainly remained the guarantor. "Your law has broken up and destroyed the unity, the peace, and the cohesion of the Church," he chided the Lords after his sentencing. "But the Church, as everyone knows, is a body that is one the world over, whole and indivisible. And so in religious matters nothing can and may be decided without the approval of the entire Church."

So the martyr for papal primacy unexpectedly turns into the martyr for ecumenical longing, and it suits this Thomas More that in the Anglican church of St. Dunstan's in Canterbury, where his severed head is buried, an ecumenical worship service is celebrated every year on the day he died.

More didn't die for the letter of a dogma, but for his unconditional conviction: He could say nothing but what his conscience commanded him to. He reproached nobody for swearing the oath, but left everyone to his own conscience—"And I would find it only reasonable to be left to my own." More certainly didn't go to his death for some private quirk or obsession, but for conscience, which guarantees human dignity and freedom, and makes the individual a person, a subject.

This right to free, conscientious decsions, which More defended against all intimidation and cowardly conformity, is clearly different from mere individual whim, from a position based on whatever one's mood or fancy is. For More, conscience is the next to last authority, over which God still stands, as ever. It's a question of an *informed* conscience (". . . and I have not formed my conscience hastily, but studied for many years and thoroughly reflected.") And finally More in no way invoked only his subjective ego, but the *whole Church*. He never thought of orienting his conscience to the extreme legislation "against the general counsel of Christendom."

No one has to obey unjust laws, he insisted to his daughter. But when does resistance become a duty? When is civil disobedience against seemingly-legal developments necessary? Anyone who keeps raising such questions has a good adviser in Thomas More. It was no accident that Pius XI canonized him in 1935, even as in Europe a gigantic attempt was being made to eliminate conscience and force it to conform.

In those years the martyr for conscience in the Tower acquired followers and comrades, and they wrote in their death cells quite similar letters and meditations. The Protestant Dietrich Bonhoeffer announced that he could feel the closeness of God's hand ("Come now, death, highest feast on the way to freedom"). "I try hard not to crash, even though I should end up on the gallows," joked Alfred Delp, a Catholic priest, four months before his execution, "God's help go with us on all paths." And Alexander Schmorel, a member of the circle around the Scholl family, who had to die at twenty-six, noted reflectively: "What did I know before about faith, about the true, deep faith, the final and unique truth, about God?"

Doesn't that have a striking resemblance to the prison letter from Thomas More, who at the end of his life was hoping for a God who was not a mighty ruler, but a "very tenderly loving father," and who sought to reassure his daughter Meg that that he was "in good bodily health and in good peace of mind"?

"I beg our Lord," the prisoner went on scribbling on his bits of paper, "that he may make you all merry in the hope of heaven. And that of which I so often would have liked to speak with you, namely of the world to come, may he now inspire you with that, and I trust that he will do so, and better than I, through his Holy Spirit—may he bless and keep you all. Written with a coal by your tender loving father, who in his poor prayers forgets none of you, neither your little children nor your nurses, nor your good husbands and clever wives, nor your father's clever spouse, nor our other friends. And so for lack of paper, farewell—Thomas More, knight."